Governance by green taxes

Fiscal measures are being used increasingly by governments to secure environmental policy objectives. This is the first book to examine how 'green taxes' have worked in practice.

The author uses twenty years of environmental policy experiences to test the effectiveness of economic instruments. Through a pioneering comparative study of the water policies of Denmark, France, Germany and the Netherlands, he shows how, in contrast to administrative regulation, green taxes have made pollution prevention pay and promoted the 'ecological modernisation' of industry.

He goes on, however, to challenge the prevailing orthodoxy on green taxes, arguing that environmental problems are caused by a delicate interplay of 'market failures and state failures', and that there are significant constraints on the market mechanism. Andersen returns to the work of Pigou and Coase, the originators of economic instruments, and shows how the partial equilibrium theory of contemporary economists has missed essential points of their reasoning. Earmarked taxes present a sophisticated and cost-effective policy instrument, virtually unexplored by economics.

Issues in Environmental Politics
Series editors Tim O'Riordan *and* Albert Weale

already published in the series

Governance by green taxes

Making pollution prevention pay

Mikael Skou Andersen

Manchester University Press

Manchester and New York

Distributed exclusively in the USA and Canada By St. Martin's Press

Copyright © Mikael Skou Andersen 1994

Published by Manchester University Press
Oxford Road, Manchester M13 9NR, UK
and Room 400, 175 Fifth Avenue, New York, NY 10010, USA

Distributed exclusively in the USA and Canada
by St. Martin's Press, Inc., 175 Fifth Avenue, New York,
NY 10010, USA

British Library Cataloguing-in-Publication Data
A catalogue record for this book is available from the British Library

Library of Congress Cataloging-in-Publication Data
Andersen, Mikael Skou.
 Governance by green taxes : making pollution prevention pay /
Mikael Skou Andersen.
  p. cm. — (Issues in environmental politics)
 Includes bibliographical references.
 ISBN 0–7190–4231–3. — ISBN 0–7190–4232–1 (pbk.)
 1. Environmental policy—Economic aspects—Europe.
 2. Environmental protection—Taxation—Europe. I. Title.
 II. Series.
 GE190.E85A53   1994
 363.7'0094—dc20   93–44232

ISBN 0 7190 4231 3 *hardback*
    0 7190 4232 1 *paperback*

Typeset in Hong Kong
by Graphicraft

Printed in Great Britain
by Bell & Bain Ltd, Glasgow

When a man sets out upon any course of inquiry, the object of his search may be either light or fruit – either knowledge for its own sake or knowledge for the sake of good things to which it leads . . . One who desired knowledge of man apart from the fruits of knowledge would seek it in the history of religious enthusiasm, of martyrdom, or of love; he would not seek it in the market-place. When we elect to watch the play of human motives that are ordinary – that are sometimes mean and dismal and ignoble – our impulse is not the philosopher's impulse, knowledge for the sake of knowledge, but rather the physiologist's, knowledge for the healing that knowledge may help to bring. Wonder, Carlyle declared, is the beginning of philosophy. It is not wonder, but rather the social enthusiasm which revolts from the sordidness of mean streets and the joylessness of withered lives, that is the beginning of economic science.

(A. C. Pigou, 1920)

Contents

List of figures

Preface

Planning for this book began several years ago, during my stay at the Free University in West Berlin in 1988, where I had the chance to become acquainted with the exceptionally strong research community on environmental policy, which had thrived in West Berlin since the early 1980s, both at the Free University's Forschungsstelle für Umweltpolitik and at the Wissenschaftszentrum. The ecological modernisation debate had been especially intense in Germany in the wake of the death of forests, and the German environmental policy literature was exceptionally rich. I was impressed with how many resources German research institutions had already then devoted to environmental studies within both economics and political science.

A small article by Jan Bongaerts and Andreas Kraemer on effluent charge systems in Europe stimulated my interest in comparing the Danish experience with the – even then – much heralded green taxation policies. In spite of its claims to possess 'the world's best environmental legislation', the Danish environmental record was none too convincing and our knowledge of environmental policies even in our neighbour countries was very sparse. Furthermore, the advent of the internal market made apparent the clear differences in environmental regulations within the European Community, and there was much scepticism, and only little concrete knowledge, about the possible common denominator that Denmark would have to accept during the integration process.

The project eventually took me on another interrail excursion, to a Europe in profound transformation. It took me through the corridors of ministries, universities and water authorities and through numerous Dutch, French, German and Danish archives and documentation centres. The project led me from the lectures in the very same university building in Berlin where Joseph Mengele had planned his eugenic experiments during the national socialist regime to a curious houseboat on an Amsterdam canal, the home of a Dutch political scientist; and on to the impressive headquarters of the French river basin agency at Rue Salvador Allende, just behind the Grand Arch in Paris. In a period of integration my fieldwork sensitised me not only to the similarities of public regulation, but also to the basic historical and cultural differences among the Western European countries.

I returned to Berlin in the autumn of 1990, this time working at the Wissenschaftszentrum (WZB). Located near to Potsdamer Platz, in the course of the reunification this now found itself in the maelstrom of history. The hexagonal library tower of the WZB, with its exceptional collection of literature on environmental policy, was now shaken by the dense traffic of mostly East German trucks and 'Trabis'. Back in Århus, there was more tranquillity to work, or so I thought until I was persuaded to contribute to the elaboration of the Danish government's Strategic Environmental Research Programme, and was soon entangled in the controversies of our national research community, which caused a considerable delay in the preparation of this work.

There are many persons who have offered help, comments and advice on my work, and it is impossible to mention them all. Jørgen Grønnegård Christensen recommended the Carlsberg Foundation to support my first stay in Berlin, without which I would probably never have become a university researcher, and has continuously followed and commented on critical points of my work. Martin Jänicke's encouraging and thoughtful lectures at the Free University provided the impetus for this work, and, although I did not always agree fully with his conclusions, he and his colleagues at the Forschungsstelle für Umweltpolitik provided important inspiration, not least Jochen Lamm and Markus Schneller, who taught me how to spot environmental data in unlikely places.

At the WZB, Udo Simonis generously made his office available to me during my second stay in Berlin and directed my attention to novel elements of environmental economics. Hans Vos, an experienced OECD consultant, shared my interest in the practical aspects of environmental taxes and was an occasional but important source of inspiration too. In Århus my supervisors, Erik Albæk, Peter Nannestad and Peter Munk Christiansen, followed the tedious clarification of the case studies, and read with patience (and sometimes puzzlement) most of the voluminous papers that preceded the chapters in this book. My assistant, Henrik Ebbesen, helped me to sort out the vast amount of environmental statistics with meticulous care. Steven Sampson decisively improved my written English, and Anette Riber worked with her exceptional energy to transform a sloppy manuscript into a proper book. Finally my father, Kjeld Skou Andersen, who is also an experienced journal editor, reviewed the manuscript carefully to spot typing errors and urged me to present the figures more consistently. It is perhaps needless to add that, in spite of all this help, I alone remain responsible for any errors or omissions. In a comparative perspective, the economic working conditions for this project have been quite favourable, and for that I would like to express my indebtedness to the Danish Social Science Research Council as well as to the Board of the 'Regulation and Governance' programme and its chairperson, Ellen Margrethe Basse. Without the confidence and the generous economic support of the Council, the research project would probably never have seen the light of day.

Also invaluable was the diversion, patience and support of Lasse and Rikke.

Mikael Skou Andersen
Århus
March 1993

Introduction

In the last few years pollution taxes have moved from being the subject of footnotes in economic textbooks to being matters of high-level politics. National policy-makers are considering how to apply economic instruments for environmental politics, and international policy-makers now consider green taxes and levies a salient issue. This prominent placing in the debate has been due, in some measure, to a public more concerned about environmental deterioration and the urgent search for more effective ways of controlling pollution. Some countries have already introduced 'green' tax reforms with an increased reliance on pollution and energy taxes, but the motivations appear to have been fiscal more than environmental. The most significant appreciation to date of economic policy instruments, as a remedy to control pollution was expressed in the directive proposal of the Commission of the European Communities to curb greenhouse gas emissions by introducing a Community-wide tax on carbon dioxide. Although the proposal is encumbered with a much disputed conditionality clause relating the introduction of such taxation to a similar move in the United States, the appearance of the Clinton administration has made the simultaneous introduction of such a tax in the most important industrialised countries move considerably closer.

This prominent role of economic policy instruments in discussions on pollution control is in a way surprising. It is perhaps not so surprising that the public has changed its opinion about pollution taxes so significantly. It appears that a general market orientation and the rise of neo-liberalism have contributed to the popularity of market-based policy instruments. It is more surprising that the importance attributed to this policy instrument is based on an economic theory, which itself is based on strict assumptions that are unlikely to apply in practice, and that the absence of convincing empirical evidence of its effectiveness till now has been disregarded.

The merit of environmental economics is clearly that it has shown us the principal differences between traditional administrative regulations and economic incentive regulations. Still, every time I have attended the lectures of environmental economists in an audience of practitioners (administrators, politicians, business managers, environmentalists) I have noticed how the message has been received with a shaking of heads. Practitioners know that economic instruments will not be able to replace all administrative regulations, that there are substantial problems in monitoring pollution and that the number of pollutants is so immense that a comprehensive charging scheme could become amazingly complex. Nevertheless, neo-classical economics continues to treat the issue in a world of partial equilibrium analysis, and the discipline fails to provide even an appropriate theoretical understanding of the complex process of regulation under which economic policy instruments would have to be applied. Political scientists have often pointed out that economic instruments are unlikely to be applied in practice under the strict conditions prevailing in economic textbooks, and that they would be distorted in the same way as regulations.

The approach as well as the conclusions in this book are quite different from what one would find in an economics textbook on the use of economic instruments for environmental policy. Rather than the partial equilibrium analysis of policy instruments, which dominates neo-classical economics, this book explores the use of green levies in the institutional and political context in which such policy instruments have been implemented in practice. Through an analysis of the role played by economic instruments in the water pollution control policies of four countries, this book seeks to gain a new insight in the principles and dynamics of green levies. Such insight ought to be of interest to theoretical economists as much as to students of public administration and policy-makers. Although the analysis confirms the basic power of economic instruments, it questions conventional views among economists of how such economic policy instruments should be designed.

The significance of state failure

The basic starting point in economics for the prescription of pollution taxation is the concept of 'market failure'. Thus, the market fails to include the costs of pollution, which are simply 'externalised', and the allocation of resources does not take place according to Pareto optimal criteria. However, a tax may serve to correct the imperfection. This book questions whether such a starting point really presents an appropriate description of the basis for applying economic instruments. It is no longer the free market per se that can explain the accumulation of pollution problems, but rather the complicated interplay between the market and the state as well as the deficiencies of this interplay.

To a political scientist it is evident that 'state failures' at present are just as significant in generating pollution as are 'market failures'. I refer here not to the broad literature of public choice on 'government failure' but to the more specific concept of state failure developed in the German environmental literature. State failure refers to the absence of integrated, preventive pollution control strategies, and to the subsequent disparity between the costs of intervention and the output of environmental regulation. Governments have in fact sought to control pollution since the end of the last century, but often by means that have proved to be inappropriate. A first move by most governments was to require official permits for industrial discharges, but the permit procedures were often lax and provided little more than an official sanctioning of pollution. Consequently, measures at the source of pollution were avoided, and regulation moved along in stages, first of dilution, then of end-of-pipe solutions. The common interest of the public bureaucracy and industries, e.g. in the application of standardised routine solutions to pollution control, created a paradox of catastrophe; only after years of problem-shifting did the effects of misregulation occur and cause a change in strategy. I argue, using Martin Jänicke's theory on state failure, that eco-industrial complexes have evolved in the course of this failure, and that they tend to help maintain rather than prevent pollution.

Thus, we are not introducing economic instruments to correct a malfunctioning market. As a matter of fact, in most of the areas in which it would be interesting to introduce economic instruments we are dealing with complex cases of market failure *and* state

failure. With this background one could wonder whether economics is the appropriate starting point for an understanding of economic policy instruments. However, as this book reveals, both
Pigou, the originator of externality taxation, and Coase, the originator of the more laissez-faire property rights approach, have indeed
more to contribute than has been exploited by economics so far.

Rediscovering Pigou

In neo-classical economics the arguments of the founding fathers
of environmental economics, Coase and Pigou, have been transformed into neat geometrical presentations and formulas that nicely
disregard the complexitites of modern regulation. What I attempt
to show in Chapter 2 on the Coase–Pigou controversy is that economics hereby also has disregarded and misinterpreted essential
arguments of Coase (who complained to this effect in his seminal
work 'Notes on "The Problem of Social Cost"' of 1988) as well
as of Pigou.

Neo-classical economics regards the externality tax as a price,
which should be equal to the 'damage' caused by pollution. This
is the reason that a growing number of economists are putting an
effort into refining methods for valuing the environment. If one
can estimate the damage caused by pollution, it is also possible to
estimate the break-even point for the optimal level of pollution
and to determine the appropriate level of green taxes to reach this
break-even point.

Pigou's argument appears to be different. Although one could
interpret Pigou as recommending a tax sufficiently high as to match
the costs of pollution, it appears that what he actually prescribed
was a more pragmatic earmarked tax, that is a tax on pollution
where the revenue is earmarked for pollution control purposes.
This becomes especially clear in his later work *A Study in Public
Finance* (1928). The difference from the neo-classical tax is striking; there is no need to undertake the dubious exercise of valuing
environmental damage. Instead the pollution tax simply works as
an 'extraordinary restraint', while the earmarking of the revenue
for pollution control purposes works as an 'extraordinary encouragement'. Contrary to the prudish attitude to subsidies inherent in
modern environmental economics, Pigou's approach implies the
establishment of a government-controlled fund based on pollution

taxation, and with government priorities for the use of these funds for pollution abatement purposes.

Furthermore, Pigou is much more cautious about his pollution taxation scheme than certain of his followers. Contrary to modern environmental economics, Pigou is conscious about transaction costs as well as the deficiencies of public intervention. Much of the Coasian critique therefore applies better to the so-called Pigouvian tradition than to Pigou himself. I argue that it is not so much Coase's plea for well-defined property rights to internalise pollution costs on the market, as his basic idea of examining the institutions that govern the markets, that is his true merit. In his essay on 'The Lighthouse in Economics' (1974), Coase brilliantly demonstrated how economists have disregarded institutional factors in their theories, and he eloquently showed what can be achieved through empirical studies of such institutional constraints. Using Majone's concept of institutions, the argument is essentially that, to refine the understanding of economic instruments for environmental policy, we must now turn to empirical studies of their application. Neither Coase nor economic theory offers much guidance to such policy studies, which allows political science to contribute to this important field. Political science is, if anything, the science of institutions.

How to approach the study of environmental policy

However, political science has tended to disregard the significance of particular policy instruments, and has traditionally focused more on the impact of particular policy styles. This applies also to Martin Jänicke's theory on ecological modernisation, which is the first attempt yet to build a theoretical framework for comparative environmental policy studies. In this book, Jänicke's theory is used as a point of departure for creating an analytical framework for case studies of pollution control policies relying on economic instruments. Contrary to Jänicke, it is argued that policy styles (whether 'consensus-seeking' or not) are not decisive for the relative success of environmental policies, but that they rather tend to shape institutions and function as a background filter for the implementation of particular policy instruments.

Since it is difficult to separate the effects of particular policy instruments in single case studies, a multiple case study design is attempted to investigate whether the use of green levies makes a difference in practice. In France and the Netherlands, economic instruments have been applied for water pollution control since 1970, and in 1976 the Federal Republic of Germany decided to introduce such instruments from 1981, but in Denmark such instruments have not yet been applied. The similarities and differences that may be detected between the experiences in the last twenty years in these four countries are significant for the evaluation of economic policy instruments. The insight to be gained from a study of these in a way trivial and inferior levies offers a unique opportunity for improving our understanding of the employment of economic instruments for pollution control.

Only by keeping constant as many variables as possible, is it possible to say whether or not the application of economic instruments made a difference in practice. An answer in the affirmative may be seen as an encouragement to the present widespread application of such instruments. In evaluating the clean water policies of four countries, we will see how Denmark, not utilising green taxes, fell behind those countries that did apply them – environmentally, economically and technologically. It is rare for political science to create front-page headlines in the newspapers, but this was in fact the result when the first findings of this study were published at a governmental research conference on the aquatic environment in Denmark in 1991. Apparently, the dynamics of green levies came as quite a surprise to the press, although the huge overcapacity in Denmark's public sewage treatment plants, created as a result of the lack of economic instruments to curb industrial emissions, also fulfilled the newspapers' demand for 'bad news'.

The failure to use economic instruments in Denmark created significant state failures in environmental policy. An exaggerated desire to take public responsibility for the control of pollution led Denmark to invest billions of crowns in public sewage works, and Denmark failed to make its industry control pollution at the source. Essentially the outcome of the Danish water pollution control efforts has been the transformation of waste water into sludge. Now, as industries are introducing clean technology, local municipalities responsible for sewage treatment works offer new discounts on sewage to maintain the pollution level in order to avoid the embarrassment of half-empty sewage plants.

The lenient treatment of Danish industry was caused by an institutional set-up that delegated the implementation of pollution control policies to local authorities, and which was based on consensus-seeking with industry. It appears that the use of hydrologically based water authorities in the Netherlands and France assured a more succesful outcome, not only environmentally but also economically. Such authorities were not open to political pressure to the same extent as local municipalities, and were more successful in safeguarding economic incentives.

A case for earmarking

The success of particularly the Dutch water pollution control programme, but also the French and partly the German, as compared with the Danish, should not deceive the reader into believing that economic instruments can always replace administrative policy instruments. What I argue is that comprehensive policy designs that include economic instruments may turn out to be more effective than those that do not, and that the challenge is to design effective, yet simple, schemes of pollution control that combine economic and administrative instruments. Still, the insight from the case studies provides justification for the revision of theories on ecological modernisation in general and on economic instruments in particular, although it is important to keep the restrictions of the case studies in mind with regard to representativeness.

What the present case studies suggest are, first of all, that the choice of policy instruments can make a difference in practice. A theory about the conditions for ecological modernisation should thus focus more specifically on the significance of particular strategies and policy choices than Jänicke does. It does make a difference whether governments choose to introduce economic policy instruments or not. I argue, therefore, that we should distinguish among four basic environmental strategies and test these through further case studies. In fact, studies of sectoral pollution control programmes offer a more fruitful basis for testing hypotheses on policy instruments. Whereas there are only thirty to thirty-five industrialized countries to investigate, the number of programmes in these countries exceed several hundred.

Secondly, the case studies suggest that earmarked taxes are a much more attractive choice than is usually assumed by economists. Experiences in the Netherlands and France with earmarked taxes suggest that this policy instrument is much underestimated – in practice as well as in neo-classical economics. While these taxes are usually regarded as being too small to induce any change in behaviour, and the earmarking is expected to distort priority setting in public finances, these objections are refuted by the case studies.

The reason earmarking may be quite a feasible choice has to do with the combination of market and state failures. The state failures inherent in the modern welfare state tend to distort or bias the price signals that emanate from green taxes. The fact that most of the environmentally sensitive markets, whether in agriculture, transport or waste, are distorted quite often renders the effects of taxation uncertain. These 'markets' are shaped by decades of public intervention, and the way the actors will respond to green taxes will frequently depend on a number of other regulations rather than on free market forces. Earmarked green levies may be used to create funds that can be spent by the environmental authorities to ensure the most favourable responses, by offering subsidies to those polluters who are prepared to take the most efficient measures. Even if the levies provide an insignificant price signal, the earmarking of revenue may ensure a favourable outcome. This is, in a nutshell, the Dutch and the French experience. A further asset of earmarked taxes is that, given the significant political resistance against 'true' green taxes (which tend to be very high in order to reflect 'true' environmental costs), they are more acceptable to polluters, because the revenue does not fill an empty treasury but is returned to polluters taking control measures.

My argument should not be misinterpreted; I do not imply that one should abstain from ecological tax reforms, or that economists should neglect the development of methods to estimate the costs of pollution or the value ascribed to the environment, just to apply arbitrary taxation on pollution. The implication is instead that one need not necessarily await the development of such techniques before one begins to integrate economy and ecology. In practice, a combination of fiscal taxes and earmarked taxes may prove to be most advantageous; for instance, by taxing energy resources with fiscal taxes and using earmarked taxes on the more complex pollution sources, from fertilisers to PVC. Energy use is, after all, the most significant factor in generating environmental problems, primarily through its contribution to the greenhouse effect. It would be quite inappropriate to earmark the revenue from energy taxes for environmental purposes; in Denmark these taxes generate more than DKr 20 billion annually and make a significant contribution to the state budget. But, when it comes to the more diverse spectrum of environmental taxes, whether on water, manure, plastics or waste, full or partial earmarking is a sensible choice.

Economy and ecology

The integration of economy and ecology will be a major challenge in the rest of the 1990s. While economy and ecology were previously regarded as being in conflict, there is a growing understanding of both the necessity of and the options for this integration. In fact both economy and ecology derive from the same ancient Greek word: *oikos*. *Oikos* means household, and the ecological modernisation that the industrialised countries are facing is essentially a question of a better household: avoiding the waste of energy and resources and preserving the environmental heritage for future generations. Obviously, the integration of economy and ecology cannot be entrusted to the free play of economic self-interest among the members of the present generation, nor can it be assured by indigenous government bureaucracies. It requires a meticulous balancing of incentives with clear policy goals, of economics with institutions. The purpose of this book is to increase our understanding of this process.

1

Environmental policy between market failure and state failure

Introduction

It is now more than twenty-five years since the ecologist Garrett Hardin published his influential article 'The Tragedy of the Commons', in which he summarised the fundamentals of the environmental problem.[1] One major reason why this article has been so frequently quoted since then is that it represents a basic plea for government intervention to protect the environment. 'Freedom in a commons brings ruin to all', asserted Hardin, referring to the outcome of the rational pursuit of self-interest among individual citizens. As long as there exist no restrictions on the access of the commons, the utility for each individual of cleaning up their share of the waste discharged is bound to be less than the costs of purifying it. Hardin's plea was one for government coercion, and twenty-five years ago there was confidence in the ability of governments to control pollution.

The strength of the faith in government is well illustrated by the way in which many environmentalists regarded the capabilities of the so-called planned economies. In 1978, two US political scientists reviewed the Soviet environmental experience and concluded that, despite certain deficiencies, a planned economy would have a systemic advantage over a market economy in controlling pollution. They did not claim that the Soviet planned economy was performing better than the USA in pollution control, but they stipulated that a planned economy had an *a priori* systemic advantage over a market economy, especially in generating the necessary information for intervention. Their findings, published in a scientific journal, were indeed challenged, but the pronounced faith in government intervention did not remain a peculiar academic standpoint.[2]

The last two decades have witnessed comprehensive efforts by governments to control pollution. Remaining faith in the potential of planned economies has vanished, and the strong belief in the unequivocal benefits of government intervention in the market economies has also begun to crumble. A number of studies have demonstrated that government intervention has often failed to address pollution problems at their source, and the most visible result of environmental policies appears to have been problem displacement – the dilution of pollutants or the transformation of air and water pollution into waste problems.[3]

How short-sighted government intervention may be is well illustrated in the acid rain that fell over Europe in the 1980s. Acid rain was a result not so much of 'market failure' as of 'government failure'; the high-stack policy was deliberately pursued to dilute airborne pollutants instead of preventing them. The blue sky achieved over industrial centres was an optical illusion in the sense that environmental policies had only diluted pollution over larger areas. Governments had failed to attack the problems at their source by reducing energy demand and facilitating cleaner energy sources. Instead, considerable resources had been wasted on an expensive, problem-displacing high-stack policy.

This and several other examples indicate that government failures are as significant in generating pollution as the traditional market failures. This is quite a different point of departure from that suggested by Hardin, and contrasts with the approach usually taken for granted in environmental economics. This chapter introduces the theory of state failure with regard to environmental policy, and discusses the historical significance of state failures in environmental policies. The question raised is whether economic instruments, usually perceived as a means to correct market failures, can also be adequate policy instruments with regard to state failures.

Government failure

Within neo-classical economics, the mounting problems of pollution are seen as a typical example of *market failure*.[4] Economic theory treats several examples of market failures, where the market fails to allocate resources efficiently, monopolies being another classic case. In cases of market failure the market fails to ensure an optimal allocation of resources, but for different reasons. In the case of pollution, the problem is that the environment is a public good to which there is free access. In a market economy, where people or institutions pursue their own economic self-interest, this leads to the over-exploitation of natural resources and subjects the environment to excessive external effects of market transactions in terms of pollution.

The theory of *government failure* is less developed than the economic theory of market failure. Recent years have seen the growth of the 'Public Choice school', which has explored the implications of the assumption that all actors seek to pursue their own self-interest, including within government institutions.[5] The government failure concept developed by Public Choice is very broad, as is the market failure concept in economics, but it lacks specificity with regard to the pollution problem.

Public Choice has difficulty explaining the emergence of environmental regulation, since no individuals appear to have a strong personal interest in the promotion of such regulations. On the contrary, those subject to regulation have strong interests in action not being taken, and have the advantage of possessing more detailed information about the nature of the pollution problem. Wilson explains the emergence of environmental regulations in an area where costs are concentrated and benefits are spread with the existence of 'watch-dogs', entrepreneurial organisations that push for anti-pollution measures in the general interest.[6] However, it is questionable whether this altruistic explanation falls within the stricter conditions of Public Choice theory. In fact, Public Choice is stronger at explaining why environmental regulations are so often distorted and biased to the benefit of the polluters. Following Niskanen, this tendency may be regarded as a result of the interest asymmetry between polluters and environmentalists.[7] While the latter have only a rather general interest in action being taken, polluters will have very strong interests in influencing the exact design of environmental regulations, and in avoiding or ameliorating specific demands.

In the following, the concept of state failure as elaborated by Martin Jänicke is explored, because this theory offers a more precise and sophisticated understanding of government failures with regard to environmental policies than does the mainstream Public Choice school.[8] Jänicke's theory also differs from Public Choice in viewing state failure as resulting from the unfavourable interaction between the market and the state, rather than as the result of the Parkinsonian pathologies inherent in public bureaucracies as such.

The theory of state failure

According to Jänicke's state failure theory, most of the environmental problems that we would traditionally view as resulting from market failures are really failures of public intervention. The basic definition of state failure is the disparity between the quantity and quality of government intervention, i.e. the disproportionate relationship between the output of public intervention and the costs imposed on society. The modern welfare state is seen as misregulated rather than over-regulated.

However, the lack of effective public intervention is explained as resulting from the relationship *between* the state and the market. It is not government failure per se, in terms of bureaucratic behaviour or inefficiency of administrative regulations, but an unfavourable interaction between the market and the state that is the core of the state failure. In spite of this somewhat different starting point from mainstream Public Choice, Jänicke's basic premise is that both government bureaucrats and industries tend to pursue their self-interests, and it is exactly the role of these two groups in policy-making that state failure theory attempts to elucidate.

When public goods tend to be overpriced or of substandard quality it is explained as a result of the failure to take preventive action. Two groups play a key role in this process: the bureaucracy and the sector of industry that is among the clientele of the welfare state.

Bureaucracy–industry complexes

The 'state' and the 'market' are no longer two separate worlds, if they ever were. Many important tasks that concern the delivery of public goods are not executed independently by the public sector. Rather, the state contracts with private companies to deliver certain goods or services. This contracting out of services not only takes place in fields where it is possible to tender out entire sectors, such as road-building or bus services. Contracting out is an integrated part of almost every government service, whether it concerns the protection of the environment, health care or even day nurseries. Private companies act as suppliers of commodities to the production of public goods. While the supply of nappies to day nurseries is quite uncontroversial, the suppliers of certain public goods acquire a substantial definition power with regard to the general strategies of public intervention. This is notably the case in complex fields of regulation, such as health care or pollution control, where technical and scientific complexities prevail.

Although the public bureaucracy and the contracting industry also have conflicting interests, there is a basic commonality of interests among them with regard to the choice of strategies for the production of the public goods in question. Furthermore, because they operate in fields of complex regulation, where politicians lack specific knowledge, they have obtained considerable powers in defining the strategies of public intervention adopted by the state.

Both bureaucracy and industry are structurally more similar than one would normally think. According to Jänicke, they both tend to favour strategies entailing central control, routine solutions and mass production, and that result in predictable and stable outcomes. Furthermore, both bureaucracy and industry have a common interest in expanding the costs of intervention, since they tend to measure their success in terms of increased budget shares (bureaucracy) or extension of markets (industry). They prefer strategies of intervention that rely on standardised measures and, because of this technocratic approach, the complexity and variety of the problems are often disregarded. If bureaucracies can prescribe well-defined standard solutions and industries can produce their goods and deliver them on a regular, stable basis, it serves their standard operating procedures best.

The results of this commonality of interests are that more complex solutions tend to be ignored, and that preventive policies are replaced by expensive solutions that at times combat symptoms rather than causes. This produces a disparity between quality and quantity in which qualitative problem-solving is replaced by costly quantitative measures. Taxpayers receive an output of public intervention but, compared with the costs, performance is poor.

The symbiosis between private industry and the public

bureaucracy enables both parties to benefit from the activities of the state, while increasing the costs of public intervention. In several sectors of the welfare state, bureaucracy and industry form complexes, which are . . . 'in some sense the civilian counterpart of the military–industrial complex . . . They both produce public goods for the state, military and civil. Thus, both depend on government orders for their livelihood . . . These modern "court-suppliers" of the parliamentary system have opened up the civil objectives of the state as an enormous "market".'[9] The contractor to the welfare state can be regarded as the modern counterpart to the Royal Purveyor to the Court. It has always been a privilege to be a Court purveyor, since the Court traditionally demands commodities in large quantities and is able to pay well. To be purveyor to the Court is a sign of the respectability of the supplier, and the title serves to indicate their creditworthiness. Today, the welfare state has replaced the Court as the most wealthy customer on the market, but it is perhaps even safer to contract with the officials and experts who have replaced former courtiers.

The health industrial complex is a classic example of these bureaucracy–industry cartels. Health policies have been decisively influenced by the common interests of the medical industry, the medical experts and their interest organisations. Preventive policies are replaced by costly and standardised routine solutions and the industry that provides drugs and advanced medical equipment has become a major recipient of public tax revenue. The health industry's investments in the development of products far exceed its attempts to pursue preventive health policies. The medical profession is biased towards products that can provide public officials in this field access to new advanced methods of treatment associated with prestige, rather than to ensuring a proportional relationship between costs and the resulting public good: health care.

Within the domain of environmental policy, a similar eco-industrial complex has evolved, as society has increased its willingness to spend money on pollution control.[10] While the public bureaucracy was searching for technical solutions to pollution control that did not call into question existing patterns of production and consumption, the eco-industry had developed standardised end-of-pipe solutions that one could prescribe on a mass basis. A general feature of these 'solutions' has been problem displacement – the transformation of air and water pollution into waste problems, or the diffusion of regional and national pollutants to the international level.

Technocratic iatrogenesis

Iatrogenesis refers to the phenomenon of disease induced by the doctor, and according to Jänicke the modern welfare state suffers from a technocratic iatrogenesis. Paradoxically it is government intervention, rather than its absence, that has produced so many of the world's environmental problems.

This paradox of iatrogenesis, explains Jänicke, develops in several stages. The failures of the state are partly rooted in the failures of the market. The state seeks to correct the market failures by channelling resources to problem areas of the industrial community. However, the more money the state spends on these problem areas, the less the interest in taking preventive action. If there exist major subsidies for end-of-pipe pollution control, industries will also direct their resources to these solutions, rather than seeking to prevent pollution.

State failure thus has a strong self-reinforcing effect: the less preventive action and the more repairing action needed, the more the state depends on the tax dividends of the growth economy. Since repairing actions tend to be more expensive than preventive policies, the lack of ecological restructuring will lead the state to rely on continued industrial expansion. By taking a technocratic approach to pollution control, and by failing to take preventive measures, the costs may strain the economy as a whole to the level where it will require increased economic growth, and at least partly offset the gains from pollution control. As such, the growth in public expenses reflects not the powers of the welfare state but, rather, its impotence and powerlessness vis-à-vis the industry–bureaucracy complexes.

In the following sections it will be shown how environmental policies have developed along the lines of state failure, and how bureaucracy–industry complexes have emerged during the most recent decades of environmental policy. The central position of economic instruments in the present debate on environmental policy will be explained, and the question will be raised whether economic instruments are at all appropriate to deal with government or state failures.

Strategies of government intervention

Technological remedies

Although failures of environmental policy have perhaps become more visible in most recent years, government failures in fact have a record that is almost as long as that of market failures. Understanding past government failures is important in accounting for the dynamics of environmental policies. As Prittwitz has observed, the development of environmental policy has been characterised by a paradox of catastrophe.[11] Changes in strategies for government intervention only seldom follow from a rational process in which scientific findings provide the justification for new means of pollution control. Rather, strategies of government intervention have been changed as a result of sudden catastrophes, when years of state failure have accumulated pollutants to the level where the balance of the environment has tipped. We have many examples of catastrophes or disasters that have triggered a new stage of environmental regulation, also of an older date than the hole in the ozone layer. Since the cholera epidemics of the nineteenth century, disasters have been one of the prime movers behind environmental policy. To understand the various stages of state failure, we need first to consider the various technological remedies for pollution control.

Figure 1.1 shows the four basic typologies of technological means that governments have had at their disposal. The figure differentiates basically between removal technologies and prevention technologies. Both dilution and end-of-pipe technologies fall within the category of 'removal'. Among the preventive strategies, one must differentiate between clean technology strategies, which aim at innovations in the production process itself, and more structural strategies. Clean technology typically aims at reducing emissions at the source by decreasing the amounts of raw materials used as inputs for the production process, or simply by recycling waste streams. Clean technology can thus be defined as 'a subsystem which integrates inputs and outputs, resources, product and wastes'.[12] Structural policies, on the other hand, aim at reducing the demand for pollution-intensive products, such as, for example, the reduction of traffic. Energy consumption is thus reduced through changed patterns of urbanisation.

	val	Prevention	
	End-of-pipe technologies	Cleaner technologies	Structural changes
	Sewage treatment	Water recycling	Dry processes
High-stack policy	Fluid-bed	Energy efficiency	Demand policy
Waste sites	Incinerator	Recycling	Packaging policy

Figure 1.1 Environmental management strategies – principal types and examples

Although these technological measures have been applied through a historical process of policy-making, all four stages are still practised (as also indicated by the examples given in the figure). While dilution technologies were common in the early days of environmental policy, end-of-pipe technologies have been more characteristic of modern environmental policy; i.e. the two decades between the UN Stockholm conference in 1972 and the UN Rio conference in 1992. The apparent failure of environmental policies to address pollution control at source have brought the need for more preventive management strategies on the agenda. The use of cleaner technologies is currently promoted by most governments. However, structural changes that could reduce the overall demand on resources have been long in arriving, although some examples can be found in transport policies.

In the following review of the experiences of pollution control, it is shown how changes in the technological approach to environmental policy have been triggered mainly when the failure of the previous stage has become evident. Although state failures are inherent in environmental policies, problem displacement does not grant them unlimited scope.

Classical pollution control
In the late nineteenth century the parliaments of the Netherlands, France, Sweden and Prussia were all considering pollution laws

and establishing study commissions to consider regulations. Indeed, the first pollution regulations in response to industrial pollution appeared in the late nineteenth century, but they were few and very limited.*[13]

Even though the technology of sewage treatment had been developed, it was generally regarded as too expensive to apply, and the experts claimed that pollution could be effectively diluted in water courses, or, if too severe, by pipes leading the effluents directly to the sea. The scientific basis for this approach was provided partly by von Pettenkofer's theory on the self-purifying effects of rivers. Furthermore, there existed considerable faith in technological development as a means of reducing pollution problems. Direct government intervention was not deemed necessary, since it was argued that the general technological development of industry would lead to reduced emissions. For example, in 1921 the Swedish government dropped its detailed proposal for an extensive water act with the following justification: 'As technical development, from which it is in industry's own interest to benefit, proceeds, the various nuisances being discussed here will, if not entirely disappear, then increasingly diminish.'[14] Nevertheless, systems of water supply and sewers were introduced in the course of industrialisation. As a direct response to the cholera epidemics, and championed by health experts, sanitary conditions were improved, primarily through improved water supply systems and newly constructed systems of underground sewers, where effluents and diseases could be flushed away. This saved the cities from experiencing further epidemics but created a new problem in terms of pollution of water resources. Nearby rivers and lakes were polluted by the essentially untreated refuse of households and factories. Time was gained, but in this way a human health problem was converted into an environmental problem. Outside the cities, people were still dependent on drinking water and fish from surface waters, and, as sewers were extended and sewage effluents increased, public reaction materialised gradually. It came, however, from people who were less articulate than the doctors and hygiene experts, who pushed for sewers and toilets at the expense of the environment.[15]

* The first pollution control authority was established in 1863 in Great Britain, but this was an exception.

The reason for the superficial management of pollution problems was not that pollution was still moderate, for there are many vivid reports of pollution around the turn of the century. Governments favoured the installation of sewer networks or of higher smokestacks, urged by hygiene experts. This standard was acceptable to industry, in that it did not question the production as such. However, in the 1960s, as industrialisation again gained momentum, the limitations of the dilution policy became evident; detergents filled streams, lakes and rivers, and the effects of air pollution were more visible than ever in the metropolitan areas. The industrialised countries began to take more serious measures to control pollution. The failure of the early laissez-faire policy was most evident in Japan, where more than 100,000 persons were registered as official pollution victims.

Modern environmental policy

The United Nations Stockholm conference in 1972 is usually regarded as the starting point for the period of modern environmental policy. Japan had been the first country to introduce modern, comprehensive pollution laws, and by the year of the UN conference in Stockholm more than sixteen advanced industrial nations had taken the first steps to institutionalise a modern environmental policy, while a similar number of countries were preparing to do so.[16] The Stockholm conference was a demonstration of the ambitions to ensure a more protective and effective environmental policy. Rather than relying on dilution, new technologies were to be employed for treating and preventing pollution. The 1960s had witnessed a period of rapid growth and technological innovation, and there existed widespread optimism concerning the technical capabilities of society to overcome the imperfections of the market economy. The new strategy for government intervention required more from industries and polluters, and policy instruments became a separate issue of concern.

The term 'command-and-control' is often used to characterise the standard approach to environmental policy developed in the 1970s.* In spite of the absence of an authoritative definition, the

---

* 'Command-and-control' covers in fact a broad range of situations, and its accuracy is questionable. Borrowed from military vocabulary, it first appears in the literature on American environmental policy. Royston (1979) distinguishes between American and European versions of 'command-and-control', but environmental

general understanding of the term is that command-and-control regulations tend to force all businesses to adopt the same measures and practices of pollution control and thus accept identical shares of the pollution control burden regardless of their relative impacts.[17] One can differentiate between the use of performance-based and technology-based standards. The latter approach tends to define more narrowly the methods and equipment necessary to be in compliance, for instance in terms of a 'best-available-technology' standard. Performance standards set a uniform control target, but leave some room to manoeuvre as to how to meet the target, although its basis will often be a specific technology.

Command-and-control policies tend to support the application of standardised pollution control technologies that are applied at 'end-of-pipe'. For the newly established environmental bureaucracies, this was also the most feasible strategy. Knowledge and scientific research on the nature of pollution problems were poorly developed, and standardised routine solutions, such as sewage treatment plants or scrubbers, were well-known technologies. Furthermore, the usual suppliers of such technologies were offering their know-how in the new market that developed. The emergence of state failure in environmental policies was far from a 'conspiracy' of bureacracy and industry, but rather the eventual outcome of an incremental regulatory process.

The 'polluter pays' principle

Criticism was indeed voiced against the one-sided use of administrative policy instruments. In several countries the use of economic instruments was advocated by professional economists in order to achieve a better balance between the costs of intervention and the environmental benefits. However, economic instruments were not very popular, either with industrialists or with environmentalists. While industry perceived command-and-control policies to be less expensive, environmentalists feared that 'pollution-pricing' would allow firms to pay for the right to pollute, rather than persuade them to clean up.

policy literature has continued to use the term as a catch-all classification for policies relying on traditional administrative policy instruments. While the US policy has been more 'structured', several European countries have favoured a more 'adaptive' policy.

Using the rhetoric of the early seventies, it was not difficult to reject proposals to rely more on economic instruments. For instance, the Danish Minister of the Environment then in office, Jens Kampmann, argued that the outcome of using economic instruments would be 'that those who can afford it will be allowed to pollute, and those who cannot afford it will not be allowed, and we don't want to bring class policy into environmental policy'.[18]

Although the economic incentive approach to environmental policy was generally rejected in the early 1970s, the recommendations of the economists were partially taken into account by the OECD, which shortly before the Stockholm conference agreed on the influential 'polluter pays' principle. The Stockholm conference also recommended this principle, giving it considerable publicity, but in fact it represents only a 'no-subsidy' principle. It merely states that, once desired environmental standards have been set, polluters will have to bear the costs of governmental requirements.[19] The principle was established primarily to avoid some countries opening up their treasuries to subsidise pollution abatement, which would distort the terms of competition in international trade.*

The second stage of failure

Compared with the optimism of the early 1970s, the results of environmental policy have been mediocre. Some environmental problems have been solved, but many new and more complex ones have appeared.

In the early 1970s, interest had focused on the most visible sources of pollution – the point sources of effluents from industry. It was here that results could be achieved quickly, and where well-known technologies could be applied. However, the advanced sewage plants and fluid-bed devices quickly accumulated sludge and clinker, for which disposal problems mounted. Furthermore, more attention began to be devoted to the more serious non-point, plural sources of pollution. This was owing partly to the now visible effects of the dilution policy, and partly because new pollution problems,

---

* The principle was not without exceptions, and the OECD did not rule out the possibility of subsidies for pollution control. In fact, the guidelines on the 'polluter pays' principle allowed for certain provisional subsidies. The 'polluter pays' principle tended to be applied carefully, and most countries provided considerable subsidies to compensate their industries for the more rigorous environmental regulation. The 'polluter pays' principle accorded well with the prevailing command-and-control philosophy, although it contained the seeds for a more radical policy alternative.

such as leakage of nitrate into the groundwater, had to be acknowledged. Whereas the point sources could be managed through
end-of-pipe measures (even though these could be rather costly),
plural pollution was much more complicated to control by such
means. This was a challenge to the standard procedures favoured
by industry and regulators, since, while it was fairly easy to impose
well-defined end-of-pipe measures on industries and communities,
there were only seldom standardised solutions in the case of plural
pollution.

In some manufacturing industries, costly treatment techniques
were replaced by new production processes, which both saved
money and improved the environment.[20] Although a certain awareness was expressed of the necessity for preventive, cleaner technologies in the environmental programmes of the early 1970s, the
eco-industry mainly refined its existing knowledge of end-of-pipe
treatment.[21] Preventive innovation was generally undertaken by
outsiders, often in response to demands for energy efficiency or
other non-environmental factors.[22]

The technological challenge varies, however, from one pollution
sector to another. Whereas acid rain and the plural air pollution
from cars and industry can be managed by traditional add-on
technologies, the leakage of nutrients and pesticides from farming
is more intricate to control. The appearance of global environmental problems, such as the destruction of the ozone layer and the
greenhouse effect, has added new items to the list of problems that
traditional technologies cannot manage. The need to avoid irreversible impacts on the local and global environment has caused an
increased demand for preventive action, and thus new forms of
production – less energy intensive and relying on different raw
materials.

Whereas traditional removal policies, whether of the dilution or
the end-of-pipe types, could be prescribed on the basis of administrative policy instruments, preventive policies are difficult to
standardise. To prevent pollution requires detailed insight into the
technologies of the various sectors of industries. Such insight has
only rarely been available in the environmental administration,
and it has been absent as well in considerable sectors of industry,
especially smaller and middle-sized firms. Only in larger firms
making intensive use of research and development has the employment of clean technologies been a feasible solution.

Promoting clean technology through economic instruments

It was the *Our Common Future* report, published in 1987 by the
UN World Commission for Environment and Development, headed
by the Norwegian Prime Minister Gro Harlem Brundtland, that,
with its plea for sustainable development, succeeded in placing
the concept of cleaner technology in a key position. Although the
Brundtland Report, contrary to the Club of Rome, maintained the
necessity of economic growth, it asserted that continued growth
without irreversible damage to the environment would be possible
only if more energy-efficient and less raw-material-intensive processes were introduced. By emphasising the development of cleaner
technologies, the Brundtland Report provided the essential key
behind its concept of sustainable development. The report not
only called for research on cleaner technologies, but also recommended the use of economic instruments as a powerful public
incentive for developing such technologies.[23] This was an innovative combination, in the sense that it revitalised the idea of
employing economic instruments for pollution control.

The recommendations of the Brundtland Report reflected discussions that had been going on for some years. In the early
1980s, two books by the German economist Lutz Wicke, director
of the Umweltbundesamt, the German environmental protection
agency, had attracted attention, even outside Germany.[24] In *Der
Öko-plan – Durch Umweltschutz zum neuen Wirtschaftswunder*
(1984), Wicke predicted that the environmental challenge could
stimulate new economic growth, similar to the *Wirtschaftswunder*
that Germany had experienced in the 1950s and 1960s. Wicke
rejected the accepted wisdom that environmental protection would
close down industries and produce unemployment. Since Germany
was facing a recession, it would better serve the country to create
new jobs and spur technological development by promoting environmental protection. Wicke pointed out that economic instruments provided the most powerful means of regulating pollution
in a market economy, since such instruments, apart from ensuring
economic efficiency, would provoke the development of cleaner
technologies: 'Market conformist instruments, which give companies the possibility of finding the most efficient path to pollution
control, promote self-interest and competition in the search for
efficient solutions.'[25] In *Die ökologischen Milliarden* (1986) Wicke

estimated the annual economic damage caused by pollution and concluded that, with insufficient environmental regulation, Germany was creating a considerable ecological debt. As Wicke was a prominent member of Germany's Christian Democratic Party (CDU), his writings reflected a changed attitude among German policymakers resulting from the death of forests, although both the leftist Greens and conservative Christian Democrats maintained their scepticism towards market-based instruments.

The revitalisation of market-based instruments, conceived in Germany, spread quickly, stimulated by the Brundtland Report. The OECD contributed by publishing a study of actual experiences of economic instruments for environmental protection. By the end of the 1980s, economic instruments had become a basic element in the environmental programmes of most governments. A new regulatory concept had entered the minds and toolkits of policymakers.[28]

Economic instruments in principle and in practice

There exists a considerable body of economic theory concerning the use of economic instruments for pollution control purposes. The main problem with this literature, however, is that it regards economic instruments as a complete alternative to administrative regulations, and that its argument rests on the premise of market failure. Its argument is essentially one of efficiency: economic policy instruments ensure an optimal allocation of resources by internalising the external effects of pollution, while command-and-control policies fail to ensure such optimality.

This argument presupposes that administrative regulations are fully abandoned and that licences are replaced with a price per unit of pollution. In contrast to guidelines, which require all firms to treat their emissions so that they are brought down to identical levels, regardless of cost per unit, pricing allows the individual firm to treat pollution on the basis of its marginal cost curve, finding its equilibrium between treatment and pollution. At the socio-economic level, this ensures that treatment takes place where it is cheapest, thus perhaps making it profitable for Firm A to remove 90 percent of its pollutants and Firm B 25 percent, whereas a command-and-control policy would require both of them to remove 50 percent.[27]

However, this efficiency argument is quite narrow, and does not really address the technological nature of the pollution control problem. Furthermore it fails to treat pollution as a problem of state failure, seeing it simply as an instance of market failure. However, there are scholars, for example Mitnick, who have argued for the use of economic instruments from a government or state failure point of view.[28]

These scholars argue that administrative regulations are frequently distorted during implementation. It is often possible to negotiate the terms of implementation with the local bureaucracy, and once a licence has been issued there is no further incentive to reduce pollution. A pollution levy, on the other hand, is a continued incentive for polluters to consider ways of reducing emissions, and it is usually more complicated to negotiate with the tax authorities, who are insensitive to technical and political complaints, than with the environmental inspector.

Furthermore, there is the assumed technological impact of economic instruments. Administrative policies are designed for standardised routine solutions, whereas economic incentives are regarded as better means of stimulating research and development activities in the direction of more environmentally conducive technologies. Economic incentives ensure that environmental problems remain a continuing concern for any company when investing in new production facilities.

Finally, it is assumed that economic instruments will relieve the burden on public expenses by shifting the costs back to the market. Even without subsidies, pollution control has been a costly affair for the public treasury, in both the short as well as the long run. An additional public bureaucracy has been necessary to enforce command-and-control policies, thus in itself contributing to increased public expenditures, and imposing even greater costs on the public for the clean-up of failed anti-pollution 'measures' of the past. Presumably economic instruments would reduce both the need for a large bureaucracy and, by their preventive character, the high costs of clean-up. Economic incentives might also increase revenue. Rather than regulating by public expense, economic incentives represent regulation by public income.

A number of arguments are, however, voiced against the use of economic instruments, also of a more scientific character. One serious problem is valuing the environment. To set an optimal pollution tax in the economic sense, the government would have to know how strong the economic preferences are for the environment. There are several methods of estimating these preferences, but none of them is satisfactory. If one does not know the exact value that citizens would place on the environment, it is impossible to set the pollution tax at the correct level that assures Pareto optimality. The intertemporal character of pollution complicates the problem even further; while there may be methods for valuing, e.g. clean groundwater among members of the present generation, how are we to determine the value of clean groundwater to future generations? Because of the options of problem displacement inherent in pollution control, the intertemporal issue is crucial for correct assessment of the costs of pollution. One survey found that 65 percent of a sample of professional economists did not believe that the economic instruments recommended in textbooks would be superior to standards in practice.[29]

Political scientists have traditionally regarded economic instruments with scepticism.[30] Majone, for instance, has argued that decisions about the use of economic instruments have to be taken by the same political system that has voted for command-and-control policies, and that various interest groups will seek to influence the way in which economic instruments are utilised. To be effective, economic instruments would have to impose high costs on pollution, but, since polluters have very strong interests in avoiding such expenses, they would use their influence to achieve exceptions, or to diminish the rate of levies. The same forces that influence and distort the instruments of administrative regulation also attempt to bend other policy instruments.

Moreover, most political scientists have been uneasy with the way in which the issue of policy instruments has been treated in the economic literature. The general critique, also put forward by Majone, has been that policy instruments are not chosen and implemented in an ideal, institution-free world, but constitute but one element within a broader institutional context. Hence, the important choice is not among abstract pricing principles, but among specific institutional arrangements to implement them. The essential question, then, is not whether or not to employ economic instruments, but constructing the proper mixture of policy instruments.

Economic instruments – another technical fix?

Are economic instruments just another 'standard solution' for pollution control, with inherent deficiencies that may spur new state failures? It is tempting to interpret the application of environmental charges as a uniform regulatory procedure that disregards the complexities of the environmental problems. For the bureaucracy, the method appears to be straightforward, although it may reduce the need for staff, and there are few reasons why the eco-industry should oppose it.

In spite of the considerable literature praising the use of economic instruments, surprisingly few attempts have been made to evaluate the actual effects of such instruments. Perhaps this is because, at least until recently, they have been applied in so few instances. It is probably also related to the fact that it is complicated to carry out such evaluations. As stressed by Majone, economic instruments are applied not as prescribed in the economic textbooks, but as part of a more comprehensive mix of regulatory instruments and institutions.

The first empirical studies were not really evaluations, but rather descriptions of systems of economic incentives, often by authors quite keen to identify the existence of such instruments outside the textbooks at all. The application of these economic instruments was described in detail, but there were no attempts to evaluate their possible impact on pollution or the environment.[31]

The second generation of studies, dating from the 1980s, was more informative, with detailed research having been undertaken to estimate the effects of specific charge systems. The most renowned of the charge systems studied is the Japanese system of sulphur dioxide (SO_2) levies, imposed to raise pensions to pollution victims. The system was introduced in 1974, and in the following decade air pollution decreased dramatically. As a result, Japan became a leader in scrubber technology and led the industrialised countries in reducing SO_2 emissions. Today Japan emits only 7 kg/capita compared with 84 kg/capita in the United States.[32]

Several analyses have been carried out on the Japanese levy system.[33] The size of the levy varies between different zones, and one study shows that reductions in SO_2 emissions have been most significant in those areas where the levy was highest. These studies also raise several questions essential to an evaluation of the economic instrument. The levy furthered the application of scrubbers (a typical *end-of-pipe* technology) but apparently not *cleaner* technologies. Furthermore, the scrubbers were developed as the result of a research programme initiated in the 1960s, i.e. before the levy was introduced. Other instruments were also employed, most importantly voluntary agreements between companies and the authorities. The reductions were achieved partly through structural displacements of the most polluting industries to South Korea and Taiwan. What emerges is a complex regulatory situation where the effects need to be evaluated more carefully with regard to both the results achieved and the role of independent variables.

Several systems of water charges have also been analysed. A pioneer study of selected industrial sectors in six US cities was carried out in 1980, showing how charges entered into the day-to-day considerations of individual firms.[34] For some companies, the increased water charges were of no consequence, whereas other firms responded partly according to the economic theory. The second generation of studies have generally been case studies, one country and one charge, with little possibility of controlling the many variables in play.

While a few multiple-case studies have recently been carried out,[35] these can best be described as a registration of the application of economic instruments in various countries. The OECD study reported more than 150 economic instruments in current operation, although nearly 30 percent of these were subsidies. The OECD study concluded that strict application of the 'polluter pays' principle had not occurred. Greater concern was directed towards ensuring the political acceptability and the revenue fund-raising properties of economic instruments. The OECD study thus confirmed the objections raised, particularly from political scientists, that the chances of employing economic instruments as prescribed in the standard economic textbook were rather small. However, the study did not explore other policy instruments or the institutional context of the economic instruments.

What is needed most are empirical studies of the interplay between economic and other policy instruments, including the institutional setting for such regulation. Economic theory has touted *ad nauseam* the advantages of economic instruments, and political scientists have asserted repeatedly that such instruments are not

feasible in the 'real' political world. Yet Majone, in his most recent critique of economic instruments, is hardly very persuasive,
since he mainly repeats arguments from his article of thirteen
years earlier.[36] Although Majone cites some empirical evidence, his
argument could have benefited from current empirical research on
such economic instruments. If political science research is to contribute to the renewed public interest in environmental taxes, it
must develop or refine its arguments and theories on the basis of
the experiences of the last decades.

This book attempts to treat the issue of economic instruments
from a different approach from the partial equilibrium analysis of
economic theory. It seeks to compare pollution control experiences
from similar countries, making it possible to analyse whether
economic instruments actually make a difference in practice. The
question is not merely whether or not such policy instruments
fulfil their claims of effectiveness, but also whether or not they are
at all appropriate in a situation of state failure rooted in the
unsuccessful interaction of market and state.

Notes

1 Hardin (1968).
2 McIntyre and Thornton (1978); Ziegler (1980).
3 Mayntz et al. (1978); Jänicke (1978a); Downing (1979); Marcus
(1980); Mann (1982).
4 Samuelson (1983).
5 Le Grand (1991).
6 Wilson (1980).
7 Niskanen (1971).
8 Jänicke (1986).
9 Ibid., 36.
10 Gerau (1978).
11 Prittwitz (1990).
12 Royston (1979).
13 Hill (1983).
14 Lundgren (1992).
15 Wey (1982); Lundgren (1992).
16 Lamm and Schneller (1988).
17 Stavins and Whitehead (1992).
18 *Folketingets forhandlinger*, del F, spalte 3929, 1973.
19 OECD (1975), 6.

20 Royston (1979).
21 Gerau (1978); Drouet (1987).
22 Husingh et al. (1985).
23 Verdenskommissionen (1988), 214–15.
24 Brunowsky and Wicke (1984); Wicke (1986).
25 Brunowsky and Wicke (1984), my translation.
26 See, for instance, David Pearce et al. (1989).
27 For an introduction, see Baumol and Oates (1988).
28 Mitnick (1980).
29 Kelman (1981).
30 Marcus (1982); Majone (1989).
31 Honert (1973); Johnson and Brown (1976a); OECD (1977); Bower et al. (1981); Johnson and Brown (1984).
32 OECD (1991a).
33 Tsuru and Weidner (1985); Foljanty-Jost (1988); Weidner and Tsuru (1988); Hidefumi (1990).
34 Hudson, Lake and Grossman (1981).
35 Umweltbundesamt (1985b); Hahn (1989); OECD (1989a).
36 See Majone (1976); and Majone (1989), 116–44.

2

Turning the invisible hand green: The Coase–Pigou controversy revisited

Introduction

The idea of imposing a tax on pollution is far from new. It stems from the earliest period of environmental policy and was devised by the British economist Pigou against the background of severe air pollution, not least the lethal London smog, around the turn of the century. Externality taxation, as the principle was named, was an integrated part of early welfare economics, but remained somewhat academic in the minds of most policymakers until around 1970. In the economics literature, however, the principle was subject to considerable interest, first in the 1920s and again in the 1960s following the theoretical attack by Ronald Coase. In the 1970s a whole branch of microeconomics evolved around externality taxation.

The Coase–Pigou controversy is *the* theoretical dispute about externality taxation and has generated numerous contributions to economic journals. Yet, only few authors have apparently taken the trouble to study Pigou's orginal work, and to a contemporary reader of Pigou it is highly questionable whether the common interpretation of his work is fully justified. Pigou was not as naive a state interventionist as is often claimed, and much of the Coase critique is more applicable to the environmental economics that developed from externality taxation in the course of Pigou's work, than to Pigou.

In standard economics textbooks on the subject, state intervention is indeed assumed to take place in a frictionless world without political or institutional constraints. Environmental economics has generally been developed within the framework of micro-economics, without paying much attention to 'real-world' issues.[1] Paradoxically, a similar theoretical literature has evolved around the so-called 'Coase theorem'. This formal geometric demonstration has little in common with the point Coase wished to make, and, in his seminal work *The Firm, the Market and the Law*, Coase has in fact dissociated himself from the theorem.[2] Rather, Coase sought to show that the transaction costs that follow from diverse institutional arrangements of the market are essential to the choice of regulation, and unlike most economists, who do not pay much attention to institutions, Coase's claim is that institutions certainly do matter.

Coase's concept of institutions pertains primarily to property rights, but there are indeed many other political and administrative institutions that characterise and constrain the 'markets' on which environmental goods are to be priced. The main problem with the theory of externality taxation is that it focuses on the market mechanism without clearly specifying the markets on which it will have to operate. It is hardly possible to implement the market mechanism without defining the specific institutional structures that characterise each individual and particular 'market'. What one calls a market will always be a system of social interaction characterised by a specific institutional framework, e.g. a set of rules – formal or informal – that specify and limit the activities of the market actors. Property rights belong to the formal rules, but a number of informal rules and institutions are just as important if the 'market mechanism' is to function.

In spite of Coase's critique, externality taxation and property rights theory have remained within the sphere of partial equilibrium analysis. Environmental problems persist, however, in a world that is much more complex and fragmented, and it is necessary to leave the exercise of partial equilibrium analysis, however neat it may be, to the economist. This chapter not only discusses the fundamental theoretical positions on externality taxation, but attempts to expound Pigou's and Coase's contributions with regard to the institutional problems pertaining to the market internalisation of externalities. Both Pigou and Coase have a lot more to say than has been repeated by economic theory.

Pigou's externality taxation

Welfare economics

Professor Arthur Cecil Pigou (1877–1959) was one of the founding fathers of welfare economics, and his principal work, *The
Economics of Welfare* of 1920, contains an economic justification
for most of the welfare regulations that were implemented in the
inter-war period and later.[3] The predecessor to *Economics of Welfare*, *Wealth and Welfare* of 1912, has even been called a blueprint
for the welfare state.[4] Whereas the interest of Keynes, one of Pigou's
close colleagues, was macroeconomic theory, Pigou is regarded
as a pioneer of microeconomic theory. Although most of Pigou's
work has merged into and constitutes a cornerstone of general
welfare economic theory, his notoriety lies in his work on externality
taxation. Pigou's theoretical work was only to some extent
influenced by the experience of a closely regulated economy during
World War I, but it was not, as often claimed by modern regulation
theory, this experience on which his welfare economic theory was
modelled. On the contrary, Pigou presented a differentiated account
of that experience, arguing that the war regulations could not
serve as a general model for economic regulation.

The core of Pigou's welfare economy is the welfare loss that can
be identified as a result of the differences between the 'marginal
private net product' and the 'marginal social net product'. The
purpose of public regulation is then to correct such differences in
order to maximise the national dividend. Pigou stated that 'there
is ground to believe that even Adam Smith had not realised fully
to which extent the System of Natural Liberty needs to be qualified and guarded by special laws, before it will promote the most
productive employment of a country's resources'.[5] Pigou pointed
out that the social institutions that guarded the market at the time
of Adam Smith had been weakened in a way detrimental to the
national dividend. Although, in practice, public regulation has often
been justified by the dim concept of the 'general interest', Pigou
made it clear that public intervention was to be undertaken only
if it would be beneficial to the economic concept of the 'national
dividend'. The purpose of public regulation is to restrict or police
individuals to the advantage of the social net product only if the
private net product deviates from that.

The externality concept

Market failures play a key role in Pigou's economic theory and constitute a major reason for regulation. Pigou defines an externality in this way:

> the essence of the matter is that one person A, in the course of rendering some service, for which payment is made to a second person B, incidentally also renders services or disservices to other persons (not producers of like services) of such a form that payment cannot be exacted from the benefited parties or compensation enforced on behalf of the injured parties.[6]

According to this definition, three parties are in fact required before there is a situation with externalities: two parties (A and B) who perform a transaction, and a third party who suffers or benefits from this transaction without being part of it. The usual example quoted from Pigou regards the sparks from a railway steam engine that set fire to surrounding woods and thus cause economic damage, but Pigou also referred to pollution problems and to scientific evidence that 'in London, owing to the smoke, there is only 12 per cent as much sunlight as astronomically possible, and [that] one fog in five is directly caused by smoke alone, while all the fogs are befouled and prolonged by it'.*[7]

Included in Pigou's externality concept were also the so-called intertemporal externalities, i.e. externalities imposed by one generation on the following, and Pigou criticised the traditional utility concept for being biased towards present consumption as compared with savings for future consumption.[8] A traditional Pareto-optimal situation omits the utility function of future generations; thus a situation can be perfectly Pareto optimal at present without being so in the future:

> There is also waste, in the sense of injury to the sum of total economic satisfaction, when one generation, though not destroying more stuff than it itself obtains, uses up for trivial purposes a natural product which is abundant now but which is likely to become scarce and not readily available, even for very important purposes, to future generations.[9]

---

* Apart from establishing the evident loss to economic welfare from pollution, Pigou also quoted some of the first attempts to assess such damage. An inquiry in Manchester in 1918 proved an annual loss of £290,000 in terms of extra laundry costs, artificial light and damage to buildings as a result of heavy air pollution.

For the same reason Pigou expressed his concern about capital and inheritance taxation, because they tend to discriminate against future consumption to the benefit of present consumption.

Taxation of externalities

Pigou's simple yet far-sighted idea was to curb pollution by imposing a tax on it. In terms of his general welfare economic theory, the tax would ensure an equivalence between the private net product and the social net product. By imposing a sufficiently heavy tax on pollution, a restraint would be placed on private market actors. In the case of a positive externality, a bounty (subsidy) could assure the equivalence.

In modern externality theory the standard 'Pigouvian solution' calls for 'a tax (subsidy) per unit on the externality-generating activity equal to its marginal external damage (benefit)'.[10] Yet, in *Economics of Welfare* Pigou never really stated the principles used to calculate the externality tax, nor did he specify what to do with the revenue. As will be made clear later, the problems are related, but externality theory has never really been concerned with the revenue question. From *The Economics of Welfare*, at least two different revenue solutions can be deduced: on the one hand, Pigou seems to assume that externality taxes are fiscal taxes equivalent to the damage imposed; on the other hand, he indicates that they work as 'extraordinary restraints' and are to be earmarked for special purposes or funds.

Taxes on petroleum and liquor were given by Pigou as models, although incomplete, for externality taxation. Their use as models would indicate that the tax revenue was to be assigned to the general treasury.[11] On the other hand, Pigou criticised the British road tax for the fact that the revenue was spent not on the maintenance of the existing roads, but for the construction of new roads: 'Thus, in the main, the motorist does not pay for the damage he does to the ordinary roads, but obtains in return for his payment an additional service useful to him rather than to the general public.'[12] From this critique it follows that funds ought to have been earmarked for road repairs.

In his later work, *A Study in Public Finance*, Pigou clarifies this problem:

When maladjustments have come about ... it is always possible, on the assumption that no administrative costs are involved, to correct them by imposing appropriate rates of tax on resources employed in uses that tend to be pushed too far and employing the proceeds to provide bounties, at appropriate rates, on uses of the opposite class.[13]

The taxation of negative externalities will raise revenue to be spent on correction of positive externalities, and Pigou even refers to this principle as a closed 'tax–bounty system', not to be confused with other taxation issues.[14]

It is surprising that modern externality theory hardly deals with the question of what should happen to the revenue from externality taxes, and that Pigou's tax–bounty scheme has largely been neglected. Externality taxation is instead treated in terms of a partial equilibrium analysis, where its implications for marginal costs are analysed extensively, but without considering whether or not it makes a difference if the revenue is earmarked or not. In fact the possibility of earmarking has been subject to much criticism.

Intervention by public authorities

Pigou shared the general optimism of welfare economics regarding public regulation's ability to serve the 'general interest', but he never succumbed to some of the more naive assumptions found in later works on the subject. Concerning externality taxation, Pigou displayed noteworthy caution, and stated that: 'In real life considerable administrative costs would be incurred in operating schemes of this kind. These might prove so large as to outweigh the benefit even of the optimum scheme, and, *a fortiori*, of the others.'[15]

Pigou did not present a partial equilibrium analysis of the kind that we find in externality theory, and, although a contemporary of Keynes, Pigou was in fact a pre-Keynesian economist, belonging to the old generation of national economists, whose mathematical methodology was limited. Pigou was reproached by Keynes and Hicks because of his 'unscientific' methodology, and with a defect in his unemployment theory this led to a declining interest in his work from the early 1930s.[16]

To a contemporary reader of Pigou, however, it is striking that, even though his welfare economic theory defines the need for regulation on the basis of market failures, Pigou does not assume that such regulation is simple to undertake. On the contrary, Pigou's reflections concerning the intervention abilities of the state call into question the novelty of theories of bureaucracy and public regulation that appeared during the 1960s and 1970s. Pigou writes:

The case [for regulation], however, cannot become more than a *prima facie* one, until we have considered the qualifications which governmental agencies may be expected to possess for intervening advantageously. It is not sufficient to contrast the imperfect adjustments of unfettered private enterprise with the best adjustments that economists in their studies can imagine. For we cannot expect that any public authority will attain, or will even whole-heartedly seek, that ideal. Such authorities are liable alike to ignorance, to sectional pressure and to personal corruption by private interest. A loud-voiced part of their constituents, if organised for votes, may easily outweigh the whole ... Every public official is a potential opportunity for some form of self-interest arrayed against the common interest.[17]

For a welfare economist, Pigou was remarkably critical of the bureaucracy, and was openly sceptical of the abilities of local authorities to undertake effective market intervention. He pointed out how politicians lacked professional competence, that their perspectives were shortsighted and dominated by the next elections, and that they were vulnerable to pressure groups. Furthermore, Pigou found a disparity between municipal districts and the optimum operational base of public utilities, which tended to change as technical developments proceeded.

Still, Pigou was so much a welfare economist that he thought such obstacles could be managed through a series of new organisational principles for the public sector. First, he recommended a degree of professionalism among politicians similar to the (past) German system of municipal government, with full-time mayors. Secondly, Pigou recommended the use of ad hoc commissions or boards; 'that is to say bodies of men appointed for the express purpose of industrial operation or control'.[18] Such boards were to be under some political control, but were primarily conceived as consisting of independent experts, with permanent tenure and thus free from electoral pressure. As examples of such commissions, Pigou mentioned the London Port Authorities and the American Interstate Railway Commission. Both were public, but operated independently from the government. Pigou mentioned a number of reasons why such boards would be better suited to undertake the production of public goods, but his general optimism about market intervention did not lead him to examine more closely the principles of such a regulatory state. The frequent use of boards and commissions since the 1930s has made clear that such regulatory commissions are not neutral bodies but create their own bias.

Generally, however, it is interesting to see that Pigou, as the originator of externality taxation, expressed much more caution about his scheme than did most of his successors. Furthermore, it is noteworthy how clearly Pigou recognised the intertemporal character of environmental problems. Because present generations tend to impose external effects on future generations in terms of pollution, there are clear limits to what can be efficiently communicated through the market mechanisms of the present. Pollution represents an evident case for state intervention on behalf of the general interest, and only public authorities are able to take care of the interests of future generations, although Pigou did acknowledge the major problems in operating schemes of pollution control.

Coase and property rights theory

Pigou lost his leading role among the welfare economists in the early 1930s, and, after a short debate in the 1920s, externality taxation was neglected for a long period. Coase's classic article, 'The Problem of Social Cost', served to revive the theoretical debate, although it presented an alternative approach to the pricing of pollution.[19]

Property rights
Coase questioned the externality concept as such, objecting that if only property rights are well-defined, the polluters as well as those suffering damage will be able to treat the problem through voluntary transactions. In general, Coase rejected the tax-bounty scheme and the implication that polluters shall by definition compensate those suffering damage. According to Coase, the question of compensation is fundamentally one of liability and thus of assignment of property rights.*

* The property right concept implies not a physical property right but a set of legal rights, and concerns (1) a set of rights to use property in certain ways, (2) a right to prevent others from exercising those rights, and (3) a right to sell one's property rights.

Coase's principal example was that of straying cattle that de-
stroy crops growing on neighbouring land. According to Coase,
the Pigouvian externality taxation principle implies that cattle-
owners should by definition pay compensation to the farmers.
Coase understood the problem differently as one of insufficiently
defined property rights. Coase's proposal implies that only when
property rights have been defined will the parties be able to enter
into an economically efficient transaction. If, for instance, the cattle-
raisers have the right to raise cattle, then the cattle-raisers are not
liable for damage, and the farmers would have to bear the costs,
including the costs of sufficient fencing to keep out the cattle.

Another option would be for the farmers to bribe the cattle-
raisers to raise fewer cattle, if this is feasible at smaller costs than
the price for fencing. Such a bribe would, under certain assumptions concerning the prices of cattle, crops and fencing, lead to a
more efficient allocation of resources than either taxation or fencing
and could be established merely on the basis of the interests of the
individual market actors, provided that property rights are well
defined.

In a situation where cattle-raisers are liable, they have an alternative of paying the 'Pigouvian' compensation. The cattle-raisers
could instead pay the farmers not to grow crops or to cultivate a
lesser amount. Since the cattle-raisers would have to pay farmers
only for the profits lost by not growing crops and not for the value
of the total crops, this would be a cheaper solution and would
lead to a more efficient use of resources. Coase proved that, regardless of whether property rights belonged to the farmers or to
the cattle-raisers, a transaction between them would lead to exactly the same resources allocation, provided that transaction costs
are zero. Whether it is the 'polluter pays' principle or the so-called
'victim pays' principle that is implemented is not important for an
efficient allocation of the resources, provided that the transaction
costs are zero.

Transaction costs
Coase's argument, resting on the premise that transaction costs
are zero, is also the basic premise of the more formalised 'Coase
theorem'. However, the Coase theorem was not invented by Coase,
and, in a curious preface to his last book, *The Firm, the Market
and the Law* (1988), Coase dissociated himself from the Coase

theorem. Coase stated that a situation with 'zero' transaction costs is artificial and inconceivable, and that it is precisely transaction costs that are decisive for the choice of regulation or not:

What I showed in 'The Problem of Social Cost' was that, in the absence of transaction costs, it does not matter what the law is, since people can always negotiate without cost to acquire, subdivide and combine rights whenever this would increase the value of production. In such a world, the institutions which make up the economic system have neither substance nor purpose.[20]

Coase found that economists had neglected the importance of transaction costs and that, when such costs were taken into consideration, then, even in the case of well-defined property rights, many actions performed by different actors would never become subject to market transactions. The transaction costs would simply offset the possible gains.

Since any state regulation of externalities is associated with considerable transaction costs, this results, according to Coase, in a risk of an even larger economic loss in the event of regulation. To achieve the most efficient employment of resources, Coase proposed to ignore most 'externalities', since the gain from regulation would not exceed the damage it creates:

The ubiquitous nature of 'externalities' suggests to me that there is a *prima facie* case against intervention, and the studies on the effects of regulation which have been made in recent years in the United States, ranging from agriculture to zoning, which indicate that regulation has commonly made matters worse, lend support to this view.[21]

Coase assumed that externality taxation would transfer a compensation payment from the polluter to the damaged party. But if a polluting factory is taxed, and compensation payments are offered to its neighbours, it is most likely to attract more neighbours, because it is possible to obtain a share of compensation payments. According to Coase, one would then have to impose a complementary tax on the neighbours of the factory to avoid rent-seeking behaviour, and he questioned the wisdom of such a scheme. He also questioned the methods by which one could calculate the actual damage caused by the factory.[22] Generally, Coase assumed that the transaction costs of such an externality taxation scheme were far too high to be justified. Such taxes were merely 'the stuff that dreams are made of'.

Institutional analysis

Coase's interest clearly centred upon the concept of transaction costs – a rather broad concept embracing the institutional factors that cause friction in market exchanges. Coase's basic idea, which he never fully developed, however, was to replace partial equilibrium economic analysis with a broader and more comprehensive involvement of institutional problems. Coase became an important source of inspiration for the new economic institutionalism. He was critical of what he called 'blackboard economics' – economic theory that failed to treat the institutional problems of the market. Coase identified serious flaws in the ideal economic world of economic theory – flaws that also resulted in false assumptions about the regulatory capacity of the state. On the blackboard, the economist and teacher might be able to comprehend and solve all problems, but in the real world there is no such collective authority.*

This critique of blackboard economics was primarily aimed at welfare economics in the Pigouvian tradition and, in 'The Lighthouse in Economics', Coase castigated the Pigouvians' neglect of institutional relations. Coase pointed out that the lighthouse had been the example par excellence of public goods in welfare economics. All great economists in Britain since John Stuart Mill had mentioned it as an example of an indivisible public good that the state must organise and finance because it is impossible to collect payments for its services.

However, in a study of the history of British lighthouses, Coase found that this service had never been owned or operated by the state. It appears that the lighthouses were originally privately initiated and owned, and later taken over by the users, the shipping companies, which organised themselves into special guilds for the purpose. Contrary to the theory that a lighthouse must be organised by the public because it is difficult to ensure payment

*'All the information needed is assumed to be available and the teacher plays all the parts. He fixes prices, imposes taxes, and distributes subsidies (on the blackboard) to promote the general welfare. But there is no counterpart to the teacher within the real economic system. There is no one who is entrusted with the task that is performed on the blackboard. In the back of the teacher's mind (and sometimes in front of it) there is, no doubt, the thought that in the real world the government would fill the role he plays. But there is no single entity within the government which regulates economic activity in detail, carefully adjusting what is done in one place to accord with what is done elsewhere. In real life we have many different firms and government agencies, each with its own interests, policies, and powers' (Coase, 1988, p. 19).

for its use, the actual method of payment was very simple: a levy charged on all ships that called at British ports. There were different reasons why lighthouses were transferred from private to user ownership, but it appears to have helped keep costs reasonable. Although the service of the lighthouse was indivisible, it appears that it had been organised by means other than public ownership. Coase thus had good reason to make sarcastic remarks about the inability of welfare economics to deal with the institutional aspects of economic problems:

> The explanation is that these references by economists to lighthouses are not the result of their having made a study of lighthouses or having read a detailed study by some other economist. Despite the extensive use of the lighthouse example in the literature, no economist, to my knowledge, has ever made a comprehensive study of lighthouse finance and administration. The lighthouse is simply plucked out of the air to serve as an illustration.[23]

In a review of some of Pigou's main cases of externalities, Coase also criticised the empirical foundations of Pigou's externality theory. Concerning the case of sparks from railway engines causing damage to surrounding woods, Coase found that the externality problem was caused not by lack of public regulation, but because of it: under British law, there was no right to compensation when a railway had been authorised by the government and was operated on the conditions set, except for compensation that under certain rather strict conditions could be granted to small landholders. Coase argued that this was a case of regulation failure rather than market failure.

Coase wanted to derive conclusions on the basis of studies of how such activities were carried out within different institutional frameworks in the real world. Such institutional studies would not only provide a firmer basis for conclusions, but also serve to add a wealth of social alternatives.

Implications
The general implication of Coase's position is that the question of externalities is primarily a problem of property rights. Once property rights are assigned, it should be possible for the different interests to engage in contractual compensation payments. If, for instance, the property rights for a water course were well defined, it would not be possible to discharge pollutants without the consent

of the owner. Such consent could be aquired by compensating the owner for the damage he or she would suffer. In general, such a fuller-scale privatization of the environment would, according to Coase, lead to more efficient solutions, since the actors would be engaging in contractual compensation payments in all those cases where transaction costs were not too excessive. Where transaction costs are prohibitive, they would simply abstain from it.*[24]

The limits of Coase

Coase's laissez-faire approach presents a comprehensive critique of Pigou's theory as well as of his methodology. However, it is questionable whether Coase has much to contribute to the formation of environmental policy. First, Coase has endeavoured to depict the Pigouvian approach as more naive and self-contradictory than is actually the case. Second, Coase's concepts of property rights are inaccurate descriptions of the present distribution and variance in property rights. Finally, his property rights theory fails to take into consideration intertemporal externality issues.

The compensation problem
One of the central issues in the controversy between Pigou and Coase is the question whether or not the Pigouvian externality

* Coase's position has been developed in the essay *Pollution, Property and Prices* by J. H. Dales (1968). Dales acknowledged that it would be complicated to ensure that transactions between polluters and victims were in fact carried out on the market, and outlined a system through which the state could establish a market for tradable pollution rights. The principal task for the state would be to define the environment's assimilative capability, and then, on a national exchange, auction off a number of pollution rights equivalent to this capacity. Supply and demand would then decide the prices for the rights, and companies that could reduce pollution more cheaply than the price for rights would choose to do so. Environmental pressure groups, perhaps dissatisfied with lax state standards, might likewise buy pollution rights, but abstain from using them. Hence, 'at least part of the guerilla warfare between conservationists and polluters could be transferred into a civilized "war with dollars"' (p. 96). An important implication of the Dales' solution is that the state retains ownership of nature and natural resources – it merely sells the rights to pollution, and only for a certain time span. The rights may run for a number of years, and before a new auction the state may even decide to reduce the pollution quota, if this should be necessary. Dales' model is a more limited model for deregulation and is certainly much more suited to practical management. It is difficult to see how problems of air pollution could be solved on the basis of Coase, but an adjusted version of Dales' proposal has been practised under the United States air pollution control programme.

taxation does in fact generate compensation payments to the victims. Coase assumed that the tax–bounty system is operated in a way that literally corrects the maladjustments of the market by transferring compensation from polluters to pollution victims. The very purpose of externality taxation is not, however, to compensate those who are damaged, but merely to impose restraints on polluters. Even if the revenue is spent in a closed tax–bounty scheme, it is certainly not for the purpose of compensation but to take measures to prevent or control pollution. Consequently, the whole issue of rent-seeking raised by Coase is quite artificial. If, as stated by Coase, the social gains accomplished with pollution from a factory's chimney are greater than the social damage to the neighbours, then an appropriate Pigouvian tax simply has to be set at zero. If revenue from environmental taxes were transferred as compensation payments, this would cause misallocations. In electing to perceive state intervention as a way to establish compensation payments, Coase imposes a problem on the Pigouvian externality taxation that, although logical, is quite false (as also pointed out by Baumol[25]).

The Pigouvian externality taxation is quite different from the idea of compensation, and Pigou made it clear that it was to be institutionalised only in cases where contractual agreements proved incapable of solving the problem:

It is plain that divergences between private and social net products of the kinds we have so far been considering cannot, like divergences due to tenancy law, be mitigated by a modification of the contractual relation between any two contracting parties, because the divergence arises out of a service or disservice rendered to persons other than the contracting parties.[26]

This seems especially evident in the case of diffuse pollution (air pollution was Pigou's favourite example) with many dispersed victims.

Variations in property rights
For Coase, property rights are conceptualised within the dichotomy of common property versus private property rights, with common property covering the cases of environmental goods for which no property rights have been assigned. But it is indeed questionable whether the problems of pollution merely pertain to unspecified

property rights, as claimed by Coase. In many cases, the state has assumed the rights to the natural resources, and allows pollution only after a permit procedure. The authorities may not possess the physical property rights, but they definitely control the legal property rights, in that they control access to the resource.

Bromley has suggested differentiating between four basic categories of property rights: private property rights, state property rights, common property rights and open access.[27] Since the state has assumed rights to most natural resources within its boundaries, and controls access to the waters and the air, for example, we should properly refer to state property rights. Bromley argues that this situation is in principle different from the situation of no property rights – the open access regime to which no property rights have been assigned. 'Open access' exists only seldom in the legal sense. Most industrialised countries have laws that prohibit discharges, and it is, rather, at the international level that we find situations of true 'open access'. Most of these situations are gradually becoming subject to control through the establishment of common resource management regimes. Bromley's fourth category is thus named 'common property rights', which differ from what is traditionally understood by 'common property'. Bromley argues that Hardin's classic article 'The Tragedy of the Commons' caused a false perception of this term, since what Hardin really referred to were situations of open access.[28] According to Bromley, common property rights are exercised by collective bodies, e.g. groups of individuals, such as the traditional pasture rights exercised by villages.

The laissez-faire solution implicit in Coase's approach fails to take into account the fact that environmental goods are no longer the open access resources they used to be, and that the usual market failure concept no longer applies. Environmental policies have gradually limited legal access to many resources, and the assignment of private property rights is not a simple alternative to open access regimes. Rather, it raises a number of distributional problems.

The intertemporal externality problem
The problem of intertemporal externalities renders the laissez-faire solution problematic. If present market actors engage in contractual relations concerning the trade-off between pollution and certain

economic activities, they will most likely not take into account the costs imposed on future generations when the prices are set. Even if somebody had been assigned the property rights to a river, or to a section of it, the price they would require to accept pollution damages would most likely not reflect the costs imposed on future generations, e.g. in terms of toxins accumulated in the food chain or in terms of heavy metals settled in river sediment. One could hope that the price set would be sufficiently high to prevent such damage, but it would be impossible to be certain, partly because future costs are uncertain. This is not to say that state management would *a priori* ensure that the interests of future generations would be taken into account; where there are no regulations that safeguard the interests of future generations, to trust the shortsightedness of present market actors seems, however, quite irresponsible.

The intertemporal problem may be interpreted as a case of considerable transaction costs, in terms of the asymmetry between present and future generations, but one would have to think of other institutional constraints than the assignment of private property rights to deal with this problem. Although Coase's critique of the partial equilibrium analysis of externality theory is very much to the point, his perspective on the institutional aspects of the market are too narrow fully to grasp its complexity. Hence, it is not surprising that it is in the Pigouvian tradition that the search for economic instruments to control pollution takes place, but it is Coase's merit that we should accept the idea of examining the institutions that govern the 'markets' being regulated, although in a broader context than property rights.

The institutional problem re-examined

Recent years have seen an increasing interest in institutional issues. Two questions can be posed: Can we understand economic instruments as isolated incentives in the way in which externality theory usually treats the problem? Are there specific institutional characteristics that constrain, limit or perhaps even further markets where such incentives are set to operate? Generally, it must be ascertained that the markets to be subjected to Pigouvian-style economic instruments are already highly regulated. Whether it is being considered to impose a levy on carbon dioxide (CO_2)

emissions or to tax fertilisers, one is dealing not with free markets but with markets penetrated by public regulation.

The previous chapter noted that policy failures in such markets constitute a major reason for turning to economic instruments. However, economic instruments will not be able to eliminate the established structures of such markets. Rather they will have to be applied incrementally and operate as a supplement to such institutionalised structures, whether they be political, administrative or historical. In practice, then, the situation is fundamentally different from the conditions of partial equilibrium analysis, where it is assumed that the externality tax is a pure alternative to regulation by norms and guidelines.

The economies of Western Europe are not 'free enterprise' economies, but mixed economies with a high degree of public intervention. Most of the environmentally relevant markets are well regulated. Agriculture is ruled by a system of subsidies and production quotas that would have to be analysed thoroughly before implementing taxes on pesticides and fertilisers. Energy supply is dominated by public utilities and subject to extensive planning, and so is a large share of the traffic sector. Waste management also takes place within a well-institutionalised market, and it is quite difficult to identify environmental problems that are *not* integrated in major sectors of complex regulation.

Obviously, economic instruments may be constrained by the institutional characteristics of the markets. Following Majone, we can understand such institutional constraints very broadly as 'laws, regulations, norms, organisations and decision-making procedures'.[29] It is in fact the entire machinery of government, including its more informal standard operating procedures and policy styles, which, when viewed from this perspective, may limit the effect of economic policy instruments.

Externality theory has always ignored such constraints, and has never ventured into the derived problems, although Baumol and Oates, by introducing the standard-pricing approach, admitted the importance of other policy instruments.[30] The standard-pricing procedure proposed using the Pigouvian tax merely as an incentive to reach an environmental standard set by the authorities in advance, and was designed to avoid the problem of having to assess the exact economic damage to the environment. Only Allan Kneese has dealt with the institutional issue; he advocated regional resource management regimes in combination with economic incentives.[31] Such regional resource management regimes, e.g. river basin agencies, represent a specific-purpose authority quite different from the usual administrative framework employed for pollution control, and Kneese assumed that such specific-purpose agencies would be better suited to undertake integrated pollution control. By employing the proceeds from effluent charges for pollution control, such agencies would possess both a stick and a carrot, and Kneese implied that they would be able to manage natural resources more effectively than local authorities, such as municipalities or counties.

The problem of earmarking

In general, however, economists have looked askance at the idea of earmarking revenue from environmental taxes, nor has this question been treated by externality theory, except in terms of the general arguments against providing subsidies. This is a paradox, since the OECD survey of economic instruments showed that earmarking revenue is the most common way of constructing such taxes. Baumol and Oates, for example, mention this question only in a footnote, stating:

In Europe, the level of fees has typically been set neither on the basis of damages nor targets of environmental quality. Rather, the authorities have employed schedules of fees that generate revenues sufficient to cover the costs of public pollution-abatement programs. This is surely a most unsatisfactory method for the determination of fee schedules, for it is not based on any goal for the changes in behavior that the fees are presumably designed to induce.[32]

The German economist Ernst Ulrich von Weizsäcker argues that both tax–bounty and ordinary user fees provide insufficient price signals compared with the damage caused by national and global externalities (see Figure 2.1). According to Weizsäcker, only proper green taxes, at a substantial level, will reflect the true ecological costs (intertemporal and at the global level) and thus induce the required changes.

If the total damage caused to future generations were also included, even more staggering figures on the costs of pollution would be reached than those Lutz Wicke calculated in his *Die ökologischen Milliarden*. Weizsäcker's solution seems straightforward: to apply fiscal green taxes that are high enough to curb

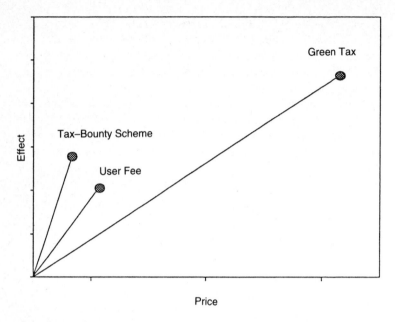

Figure 2.1   The ecological effectiveness of three different charge systems according to Weizsäcker. The steering effect is symbolised by the height above the horizontal line

pollution, preferably through an ecological tax reform that shifts taxation from income to pollution. According to Weizsäcker, it makes no sense to earmark possible revenues from the heavy green taxes necessary to internalise these costs in the economy, since the revenues would far exceed what one would sensibly invest in pollution control equipment for the present.[33]

Conclusions

From the review of the Coase-Pigou controversy, it follows that the idea of taxing pollution is not as 'market conformist' as sometimes claimed, but presents a hitherto neglected element of classic welfare economics. The more laissez-faire solution presented by Coase's property rights theory has basic fallacies that render it less promising than the pollution tax, except perhaps from the vantage point of transferable pollution rights.

There are basic ambiguities in Pigou's work, however, and it appears that modern externality theory has evolved along the lines of the pure externality tax, whereas the tax–bounty scheme has been neglected. Because most economic analyses of environmental taxes have been partial, we need to be cautious about even the most simple conclusions when it comes to their implications for practical environmental policy. Coase's principal account of the lighthouse in economics is highly relevant, and studies of actual experiences of externality taxes will most likely be able to enrich the theory conclusively. Partial equilibrium analysis needs to be complemented by a broader contextual analysis of environmental policies and their performance. In such contextual analyses, institutional constraints play a key role.

Notes

1 Baumol and Oates (1988); Crandall (1983); Helm and Pearce (1990).
2 Coase (1988).
3 The following references are all based on the fourth edition: Pigou (1932).
4 Collard (1981).
5 Pigou (1932), 128.
6 Ibid., 183.
7 Ibid., 84.
8 Pigou (1947), 96–9.
9 Pigou (1932), 28.
10 Baumol and Oates (1988), 55.
11 Pigou (1932), 192.
12 Ibid., 193, note 2.
13 Pigou (1947), 99.
14 Ibid., 101.
15 Ibid., 99–100.
16 Aslanbeigui (1990).
17 Pigou (1932), 332–3.
18 Ibid., 334.
19 Coase (1960).
20 Coase (1988), 14.
21 Ibid., 26.
22 Ibid., 182–3.
23 Coase (1974).
24 See also: Liroff (1980); Tietenberg (1985); Liroff (1986).
25 Baumol (1972).
26 Pigou (1932), 192.

27 Bromley (1991).
28 Hardin (1968).
29 Majone (1989), 95.
30 Baumol and Oates (1971).
31 Kneese and Bower (1968); Kneese and Schultze (1975).
32 Baumol and Oates (1979), 357.
33 Weizsäcker (1989); Weizsäcker and Jesinghaus (1992); Wicke (1986).

3

How to approach the analysis of environmental policy

Introduction

Institutions, economic and political, are in the broadest sense a core concern for political science. The questions raised by political science on environmental policy have focused not as much on the use or efficiency of individual policy instruments as on general policy styles and applied intervention strategies. It has been established that countries with comparable levels of industrialisation and urbanisation have designed quite different environmental policies. However, political science has not limited itself to explaining why different states have chosen so diverse strategies. Attempts have also been made to assess country performance so as to reveal whether differences in policy design have been reflected in environmental performance. The ultimate question has been: 'Why have some countries been relatively more successful than others in the pursuit of environmental policy?' Although no country can be said to have had absolute 'success' with regard to environmental policy, there are important relative differences.

Lundqvist's now classic air pollution study analysed the differences between the command-and-control policy of the United States and the more consensual Swedish policy.[1] Vogel compared the achievements of the United States' more aggressive environmental policies with those of Great Britain.[2] Although Lundqvist found that the two approaches had been equally effective in reducing air pollution, the Swedish policy style revealed smaller political costs in terms of a business community more prone to accept public regulation. Vogel found that the aggressive American policy style had not led to more environmental improvements as compared with the more conciliatory British style. Still, neither of these studies provides a firm answer to the question of success, although both affirm that the command-and-control policy was less effective than more consensus-seeking policies. The absence of firm answers may be partly explained by the limited use of statistical data to assess the impacts of environmental policies. Both Lundqvist and Vogel belong to a tradition that has focused more on cultural and historical explanations for differences in environmental policies, rather than on identifying differences in policy outcome.

A second approach has placed more emphasis on policy design and problems of implementation. The comparative air pollution study carried out by Knoepfel and Weidner in the EC member states and Switzerland looked at whether differences in policy design were reflected in policy outcomes.[3] The research focused specifically on institutions and policy instruments of implementation, by adopting the 'bottom–up' approach of implementation research.[4] The unit of analysis used by Knoepfel and Weidner was the regional implementation system, and they found that improvements in air quality varied considerably among regional implementation systems within each of the countries studied. Knoepfel and Weidner did not, however, assess the technological response, but accepted any decline in environmental quality or in emissions as an indicator of the outcome, regardless of possible problem-shifting techniques.

A third approach to the comparative analysis of environmental policy aims to identify the basic capacity for ecological modernisation. Jänicke's theoretical work is the first attempt to construct a coherent, intelligible theory on environmental policy within political science.[5] It presents a theoretical framework for the analysis of environmental policy that incorporates many of the political and institutional variables usually ignored by economists. Jänicke's general hypothesis is not only that institutional capacities affect the ability of state regulatory agencies to achieve environmental protection, but that national policy style is of major importance for effective environmental policy. Jänicke seeks to explain why some countries are relatively more successful than others in environmental policy.[6] The approach, which is inspired by the work of Manfred Schmidt, is quite similar to that used within the neo-corporatist tradition for the study of national economic policy-making.[7] Indeed, Jänicke's work shows that countries with relatively successful economic and labour market policies also tend to have relatively successful environmental policies.

Using aggregate data, the industrialised countries are ranked with regard to environmental performance, and the findings are used to validate the theory. Jänicke reveals that Japan has the highest score on performance, but also that the smaller European states, such as Sweden and the Netherlands, tend to have more successful environmental policies than the larger, federal states, such as Germany and the United States. In the following, Jänicke's theory is used to construct an analytical framework for the study of particular environmental policy programmes to investigate whether the use of economic policy instruments does make a difference in terms of relative success.

The ecological modernisation capacity theory

According to the ecological modernisation theory, a country's environmental performance depends on the basic preconditions for its ecological modernisation (see Figure 3.1). A country's 'modernisation capacity' refers to its achieved level of institutional and technological problem-solving capabilities, and this capacity is seen as critical to achieving effective environmental protection and to the transformation to more sustainable structures of production. Ecological modernisation capacity depends on four basic variables: (1) problem pressure, (2) consensus ability, (3) innovation capability and (4) strategy proficiency.

(1) *Problem pressure* is primarily a question of economic performance. The impact of economic performance is two-fold. Countries with adequate economic performance, while willing and able to pay for environmental protection, are also subject to heavier pollution loads. The economic performance of a country is thus an important precondition both for managing environmental problems, but also for their permanence.

(2) *Policy style (consensus ability)*. The national style of policy-making affects the potential for ecological modernisation. Countries where neo-corporatist structures prevail are characterised by policy styles more amenable to new interests and ideas, and they enable a more open decision-making process. In such countries, environmental issues will, according to the theory, more rapidly become subject to public policies than

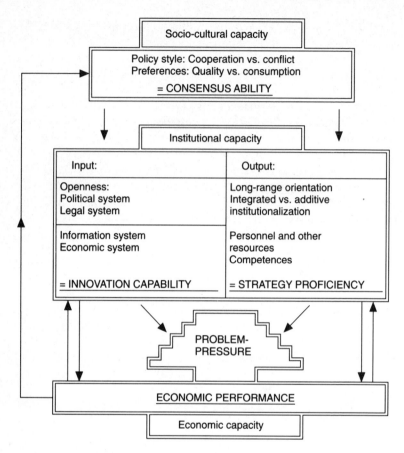

Figure 3.1 Ecological modernisation capacity

in countries dominated by closed coalitions that are seeking to safeguard their interests against new challenges. According to Jänicke, the high scores on environmental performance in Sweden, the Netherlands and Austria have been reached owing to their alleged consensus-seeking approach to decision-making. In Japan, the distinctive concertation of interests between industry and the government has assured a comparable, and even more successful, effort to control pollution. The common denominator of these very different policy styles is the search for broad consensual solutions.

(3) *Innovation capability*. Institutional innovation capability reflects the policy style as it has become institutionalised over
time. Institutional innovation capacity is a property of both
state and market institutions, and it determines the degree
of openness to innovations and new interests in the political
and judicial system, the media and the economic system. The
established constraints on or prospects for innovative behaviour help to filter the political and economic inputs. None the
less, a proper innovation capacity is only a necessary, but not
a sufficient, condition for successful environmental policy.

(4) *Strategy proficiency*. Environmental policy will have to be
institutionalised in terms of new administrative organisations,
programmes, planning, resources and personnel. If institutionalisation is weak, e.g. owing to a powerless ministry or
to an environmental policy remaining a sector issue rather
than a cross-sectional one, the institutional capacity on the
output side will be modest. To implement complex policies
and programmes is difficult and requires unambiguous competence and responsibilities. This is especially problematic for
federal states, which face potential fragmentation and delay
during implementation. If environmental policy is weakly institutionalised, the 'additive' environmental bureaucracy may
result in similar additive end-of-pipe solutions, rather than
broader, preventive policies.

As an analytical model the theory is a complicated tool; in spite
of four main variables it in fact offers more than twenty variables
to be investigated. Furthermore, it lacks clear distinctions with
regard to what the dependent variable(s) and the independent
variable(s) are.

A disputable relationship

Before the causal relations claimed by the theory are discussed, it
is worth considering whether the theory is actually validated by
Jänicke's performance ranking.

The performance ranking is established on the basis of aggregate data. It should be noted, however, that the variables that
affect the ranking appear somewhat arbitrary and comprise such
diverse parameters as specific air pollution emissions, the oxygen

quality of selected rivers and the capacity of sewage works. The aggregated data used for validation are in practice highly dependent on these, which are incidentally available in international environmental statistics.

The independent variable, interest mediation, is even more intricate. Jänicke operationalises interest mediation presumably using the classification proposed by Manfred Schmidt. Jänicke's findings apparently indicate a close relationship between environmental performance and countries with consensus-seeking policy styles.

However, there appears to be an inconsistency in the classification of countries. While Schmidt designates Germany as a consensus-seeking country, but places Sweden and the Netherlands in the middle group, Jänicke reverses the order, classifying Sweden and the Netherlands as consensus seeking and Germany in the middle group. In Figure 3.2, Jänicke's environmental quality ranking is shown with Schmidt's original classification of interest mediation, and the result seriously conflicts with the claimed causality. Since Jänicke does not justify his characterisation of the countries with reference to research on the nature of their political systems, it is difficult to assess whether his operationalisation of the variable should be preferred to Schmidt's. The main problem, which this inconsistency underlines, is that there is hardly any authoritative or even meaningful classification of political systems with regard to the degree of interest mediation.

It should also be noted that other researchers, who have done more detailed environmental policy studies, have been unable to confirm the importance of consensus-seeking. Knoepfel and Weidner, despite their detailed case study of air pollution in seven European countries, were unable to make an association between patterns of consensus-seeking and more successful environmental policy in the field of air pollution.

The small European states
Although the environmental policy sector is quite different from the peak-level system of organisational bargaining that has evolved around labour market policies and national economic policies, the link suggested between consensual policy style and environmental policy is never really substantiated by Jänicke, who, following Katzenstein, merely stipulates that the 'small states of Europe' are the trendsetters in environmental policy: 'the distinct democratic

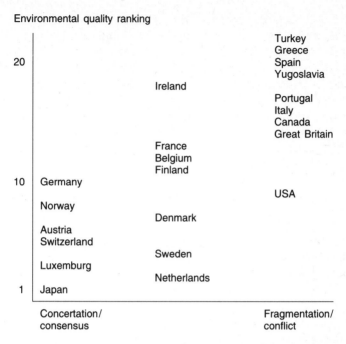

Environmental quality ranking

		Turkey
20		Greece
		Spain
		Yugoslavia
	Ireland	
		Portugal
		Italy
		Canada
	France	Great Britain
	Belgium	
	Finland	
10	Germany	
		USA
	Norway	
		Denmark
	Austria	
	Switzerland	
		Sweden
	Luxemburg	
		Netherlands
1	Japan	

Concertation/   Fragmentation/
consensus   conflict

Figure 3.2   A disputable relationship. Ranking of environmental changes, 1970–85, and integration of interest mediation in Western industrial societies

institutions of these small countries generate a stronger political pressure for accommodation and provide better training for an active reform policy.'[8]

However, there are substantial differences between the patterns of bargaining that have evolved in the sector of economic policy-making and environmental decision-making. The environmental organisations, the counterpart of polluters, tend to be organisationally weaker than the labour market trade unions, and their means of influence are more dependent on the media than on negotiations with the government. Consensus-seeking in the environmental policy sector is typically directed from government bureaucracies towards polluters, and it is only infrequently that it includes the environmental organisations in actual negotiations. In Scandinavia, the environmental non-governmental organisations (NGOs) have had less influence on pollution control policies compared with the peak interest organisations of industry and commerce.⁹

The ecological modernisation capacity theory suffers from a deterministic view of environmental policy and fails convincingly to link the external variables of environmental policy with the internal institutional variables. Furthermore, it exaggerates the importance of integration and consensus mechanisms. Since national policy styles are deeply rooted in the history and traditions of individual countries, such an approach attributes *a priori* some countries with success and others with failure. However, it is unable to reveal the dynamics that cause success in some environmental policies and failure in others even within the same country. For instance, whereas Japan has been relatively successful in air pollution control, its water pollution control policy has produced mediocre results. And whereas Dutch water pollution control policy has been successful, manure problems have undermined the value of the achievements.

The analytical framework

Jänicke's initial research design was in fact more promising. He sought patterns that could explain experiences of partial success, and tried to construct a theory on the basis of the patterns found in the mosaic of various case studies:

Environmentally positive experiences with sector measures are . . . not only to be found in certain front-running nations. They are found, rather scattered, in countries with very different gross environmental performance . . . I stress this type of partial success (under otherwise disadvantageous circumstances), because a concept of environmental policy based on the mosaic of partial successes is conceivable.¹⁰

The cases of relative success in pollution control are limited, and consist of a small number of countries in specific sectors. For instance, Japan has been relatively successful in air pollution control, whereas its water pollution control policy has produced mediocre results. Denmark's air pollution control policy has been inadequate, but achievements within energy policies have had far-reaching impact on air quality.¹¹ Rather than making a loosely defined consensual policy style the primary requirement, even for countries without the traditions of the small, predominantly social democratic states of Europe, a theory concerning the criteria for successful environmental policy must explain under which circumstances environmental programmes will succeed.

Much literature on public regulation seems to agree with economics that regulation by incentive will improve effectiveness as well as efficiency. Whereas economics has put most emphasis on efficiency, regulation theory has focused more on effectiveness; i.e. the ability to implement politically set targets.[12] As pointed out by Wilson, environmental policy belongs to a category of regulation where costs are concentrated but benefits are spread.[13] In contrast to traditional welfare state regulation, which relies more on transfers from the general tax revenue to specific clients, the potential gains from impeding implementation of pollution control to actors subject to that regulation can therefore be considerable. For that reason, the requirements placed upon policy instruments and institutions are quite different from those placed upon traditional forms of regulation.

A successful environmental policy, therefore, will depend, to a considerable extent, on the specific policy design for pollution control programmes and the specific choice of policy instruments. This relationship is also what we find on the 'output' side in Jänicke's model, and, if one overlooks the unsubstantiated assumptions in the model about the character of the national policy style, Jänicke in fact provides a useful framework for the analysis of environmental policy. National policy style should simply be seen as a contextual variable that only partially affects the operation of sectoral policies.

This study focuses more specifically on the relationship between the policy instruments of specific national environmental programmes and the outcomes in terms of environmental performance. The primary focus of interest is not so much the background to the choice of specific policies and policy instruments, but rather how such choices affect environmental performance. The goal of this study is to examine how differences in policy designs and the use of policy instruments are reflected in the outcomes of policies.

The central hypothesis is that the use of economic policy instruments, in terms of Pigou-taxes, potentially increases the chances of successful outcomes of environmental policies, as compared with policies relying mainly on administrative policy instruments, whether command-and-control or the more consensus-seeking type. However, since environmental policies must confront both market failures and state failures, economic instruments are not per se expected to lead to a successful environmental policy. The effects of economic instruments should depend on how they are placed in the policy design as a whole, and how they are linked to existing political and administrative institutions. The essential question to be analysed is whether the application of economic instruments in practice promotes the innovation and application of non-waste, clean technologies, and under what circumstances such a policy will lead to a more anticipatory, preventive and cost-effective pollution control.

Because economic instruments are implemented not in free markets but in highly regulated contexts, an econometric study of the level of the charges and the output in terms of emissions is not likely to be a useful method of analysis. That studies of electricity taxes, for example, have been unable to prove a relationship between the level of the taxes and the consumption of electricity can be explained by the intervening influence of the general regulation of electricity utilities, as well as the regulation of the energy supply of production units.

The analytical model employed here is shown in Figure 3.3. The model takes environmental performance as the dependent variable and environmental policy as the main independent variable. A specific sectoral policy design for pollution control consists of a set of policy instruments and policy agents, and it is necessary to map and analyse all the policy instruments and policy agents employed for environmental policy in order to better assess the precise role of economic instruments in policy design. By successful environmental performance is meant preventive, cost-effective outcomes, based on non-waste, clean technology rather than end-of-pipe solutions.

It is important to control the relationship between environmental policy and environmental performance for intervening or external variables. Among the most evident intervening variables are the economic and technological preconditions. The public support available during implementation may also affect final outcomes. Gratis effects, in terms of reduced emissions, may arise from industrial decline, which will have to be taken into consideration as well.

Background factors:

Problem pressure and situative preconditions
National policy style and regulatory failures: administrative and historical background

Independent variable:

Environmental policy programme	
– Policy instruments	– Policy agents
– Planning – Guidelines – Norms – Subsidies – Effluent charges	– Ministry – Local authorities – Special-purpose agencies – Research facilities

Intervening variables:

– Economic preconditions – Technological know-how – Public opinion – Industrial decline

Dependent variable:

Outcome: Emission reductions (chemical oxygen demand) – by problem shifting – by structural changes
Costs: Public investments Private investments
Technological impact: Public response: sewage treatment Industrial response: end-of-pipe solutions or cleaner technology

Figure 3.3 Analytical framework

Choice of research design

In his comprehensive review of environmental policy studies, Vogel concludes that assessing the effectiveness of public policy in the environmental area presents several serious challenges to researchers.[14] However, because of the variety of national approaches to regulation, analysing the outcomes of differences in policy design enables us to gain valuable insights.

The comparative method offers an attractive means of eliminating some of the most obvious obstacles, since studying a group of countries with similar economic and technological preconditions makes it possible to eliminate external variables. The method applied for this study, however, is the multiple case study design as developed by Robert K. Yin. Yin has made the assumptions of the comparative method, as traditionally employed by political science, more transparent and articulate.[15] By definition, a case study 'is an empirical enquiry that investigates a contemporary phenomenon within its real-life context, when the boundaries between phenomenon and context are not clearly evident, and in which multiple sources of evidence are used'.[16]

The *multiple* case study design is based on the logic of replication. Each case must be carefully selected so that it either predicts similar results or produces contrary results but for predictable reasons.[17] Consequently, it is necessary to have a more comprehensive theory to interpret findings. The replication logic of the case study design implies that each of the cases be considered as what medical science might regard as a rare, clinical syndrome. From each 'patient' there is something to be learned. If similar results are obtained from selected cases, replication is said to have taken place. In evaluating environmental policies we may, owing to the limited record of success, be able to learn more from the few 'successful patients' than from the many 'fatal' cases. In this sense, 'successful' is as theoretically interesting as 'failure'.

The cases studied are not to be confused with a sample drawn from a larger population. They are not representative, and there is no 'population' about which to make generalisations. Rather, the research design should be regarded as experimental, and findings are to be generalised to the 'theory' in question. Just as the natural scientist does not select representative experiments, neither can the political scientist do more than test the theory by studying actual policy experiments. On the basis of such experimental results, the theory may be re-evaluated or modified, and it is for its potential contribution to theory-building that the case study methodology usually is acknowledged.

The case study design does not mean that statistical data cannot be employed in the analysis. Within each of the cases studied, it is possible to employ highly quantitative data, for the analysis of embedded units for instance. In the present study, the national environmental programmes represent the cases, but within each case the policy instruments constitute embedded units of research. The data are primarily used to interpret each individual case. Although environmental statistics have improved, differences in time-series and data techniques tend to impede pooling of data, which makes the case study design well suited for analysis of this subject. Furthermore, a case study will typically focus more on the context of the programme studied than on particular quantitative data.

Choice of cases

The initial reason for selecting France, Germany, the Netherlands and Denmark for the analysis was the wish to compare the experiences of Danish water pollution control policy, which has been without the use of economic instruments, with three countries where such instruments have been applied. Previous studies have pointed to an 'implementation deficit' in Danish environmental policy, but it appears that such implementation problems have been inherent in virtually every nation's attempt to undertake pollution control.[18] This phenomenon has been neatly captured in the expression 'different styles, but similar content'.[19]

Inasmuch as economic instruments have been applied in the water policies of Germany, the Netherlands and France since the 1970s, these countries can be usefully compared with Denmark. Are clean water policies marked by similar outcomes in spite of different policies? Or have these countries accomplished a relatively more successful environmental policy by having employed economic policy instruments?

We know little, however, about the relative merits of water policies in Denmark as compared with the three other countries. Experts are typically experts in the policies of their own country, and few, if any, have the breadth of outlook to venture a

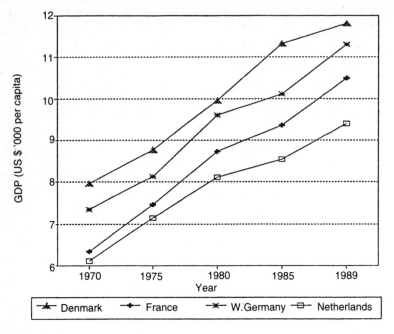

Figure 3.4   GDP per capita at 1985 prices and exchange rates, 1970–89

comparative estimate of the merits of national surface water policies. The few pooled data in the OECD environmental statistics confirm, however, that there are marked differences in the performance of the four countries. Although the four countries are the most affluent in the European Community (besides Luxemburg) and have had similar growth rates of GDP (see Figure 3.4), their performance in water policies has varied considerably (see Figures 3.5 and 3.6).[20]

OECD statistics show that Denmark is a world leader in sewage treatment, closely followed by Germany and the Netherlands, whereas France has lagged far behind (see Figure 3.5). In terms of environmental quality, however, the Danish Gudenå has deteriorated as compared with the considerable improvement in the German Rhine and the Dutch Meuse, while the French Loire has the highest oxygen content (see Figure 3.6). Nevertheless, relative difference in oxygen content is a disputable indicator of regulatory effectiveness, and reflects merely the basic contrast between the

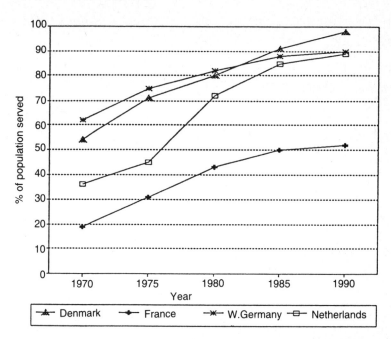

Figure 3.5 Percentage of population served by public sewage treatment plants, 1970–90

roaring Loire and the quiet Gudenå, which in fact is a large water course rather than a river. However, the absolute deterioration in Denmark's water quality is evident compared with the other countries, none of whose most important interior waters have deteriorated since 1970. Even the Rhine, once nicknamed 'the sewer of Europe', was slightly cleaner than the Gudenå in 1989 measured in terms of oxygen content.

Considerable priority was given to environmental policies in the 1970s, and public support was relatively strong and has remained so, even after the recession began. In spite of the increased attention to economic issues, citizens have placed pollution control between 'important' and 'very important' (see Figure 3.7). Hence we may assume that the environmental programmes initiated around 1970 were implemented under quite similar – and favourable – conditions of public support. Although regulatory programmes were in place and public support available, performance seems to

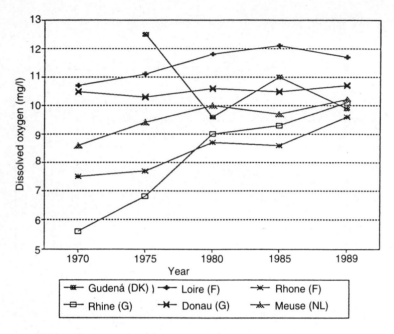

Figure 3.6   Dissolved oxygen (mg/l) in major rivers, 1970–89

differ, which indicates that possible deficiencies in the design of environmental regulation may have affected performance.

One or two additional countries could have been included in the analysis, but relatively few comparative studies of environmental policy have previously been undertaken. In an overview of the literature, Vogel found that 'the relatively small number of countries examined in the typical study is apparently a function of the dominance of the case-study approach, which tends to be very labour-intensive. Thus, only two of the studies comparing policies in two or more political units were written by individuals; the remainder were collective efforts.'[21]

In these circumstances, the three countries where economic instruments were applied seemed the most interesting candidates for examining successful regulatory policies.

Focus areas of the cases
Water pollution control has been the major target of public and private investment for pollution control since 1970, and therefore

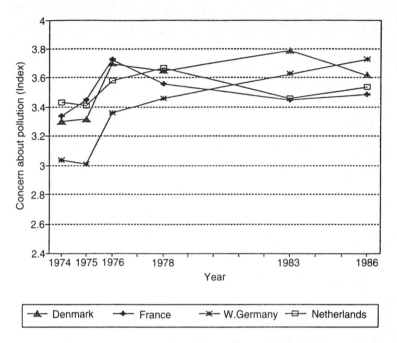

Figure 3.7 Concern about pollution, 1974–86

presents a case of considerable economic interest. As a result of large investments in this sector, some of the relatively best environmental statistical data are available in the area of water pollution control. Water pollution has now been an 'issue' for approximately fifteen to twenty years, which is a sufficiently long period over which to assess the impact of economic instruments. It is a paradox that most of the previous comparative environmental policy research has focused on subjects other than clean water policy. Since Johnson and Brown reviewed the water policies of six European countries in their *Cleaning up Europe's Waters*, no systematic effort has been undertaken to evaluate the different policy approaches, although a number of publications have praised the policies based on effluent charges.[22]

Water can be affected by a broad range of pollutants (human, industrial and agricultural), both diffuse and from point sources. Hence, a clear demarcation of the study has been necessary. The most recent water pollution control problems are related to diffuse

sources of pollution, and even though one country, the Netherlands, has introduced a levy on surplus manure, the introduction
of this levy was too recent to be included in the study. In general,
control strategies for agricultural nutrients and other diffuse sources
of pollution are still in a very early implementation phase, and are
difficult areas for performance evaluation. Control of point sources
of pollution (discharges from manufacturing industries and cities)
has been at the core of water pollution policy for fifteen to twenty
years, and focus will be on pollution control with regard to surface waters. The insights to be gained from this core area of
pollution control, twenty years after the start of modern environmental regulation, can shed light on the performance of regulatory policies in other areas of water control and pollution control
generally.

Presentation of case studies
Each case study begins with a short introduction to the environmental, administrative and historical background to the water
pollution control policy. Policy instruments employed by policy-
makers are described, as are the achievements. Policy instruments
'at work' are analysed so as to clarify their role for implementation,
and special attention is devoted to the role of economic policy
instruments with regard to effluent charges. The term 'pollution
tax' is not used in the case studies, which distinguish between
effluent charges (also called levies) and user fees. An effluent charge
is a financial obligation that must be borne by some entity discharging waste, treated or untreated, into a natural water course.
The size of the bill for the effluent charge varies with the amount
of pollution produced, at least in principle. In contrast, firms and
households are charged for sewage and sewerage services received.
These user fees are related to the service received.[23]
   Analysing the role of various policy instruments is essentially a
qualitative judgement, based on the sources of evidence used for
the study. The available empirical evidence varies considerably
among the cases. Germany, France and the Netherlands publish
excellent environmental statistics. In both Germany and the Netherlands, social science researchers have conducted surveys and
statistical tests on the effects of economic instruments. This means,
however, that the empirical evidence available for each case is not

strictly comparable, and, since economic instruments also differ, interpretation and analysis must be specifically related to each country. In the case of Germany, the specification of data has improved markedly with the advent of the Statistisches Bundesamt, and, in the three other countries, communication with environmental authorities and national census bureaus has also been undertaken to secure data.

For each case study, a search for secondary literature on water policies was carried out using national and international databases. On the basis of the description of the regulatory systems and the most important institutions involved in implementation, each case study country was visited both in the start phase of the project and later on. Interviews with key officials were carried out in ministries and other relevant public institutions and interest organisations. Since the project's emphasis is mostly on implementation, no attention was paid to policymakers during these interviews. The interviews were originally assigned an important role in the project but, since career patterns mean that few officials have been occupied with the same tasks for decades, it was generally not easy to find interview subjects who had experience matching the twenty years studied. Thus, the interviews were used as a source of information for present problems with regulatory systems, and to obtain archived data such as older ministerial reports, previous annual reports and other relevant policy documentation. In each country, interview partners were chosen from the responsible ministry and, in the cases of France and the Netherlands, from the specific institutions responsible for water management. Furthermore, specialists at universities were interviewed to obtain information and evaluations on existing regulatory systems and problems of implementation.

It is not possible to assess the impact of an economic instrument through interviews, since interview partners may not have adequate knowledge about impacts, or may be biased in information because of national pride in the chosen regulatory system. Generally, however, it is my impression that interview partners have been quite frank about defects as well as advantages. Being a foreign researcher in three of the four countries might have proved an advantage, in that officials talked more openly than perhaps would have been the case with a domestic researcher.

Measuring the dependent variable

The most serious problem with the evaluation of environmental policies, also apparent in Knoepfel and Weidner's air pollution study, is how to take basic differences in the natural environment into account when measuring the outcome of environmental policies. Different environmental qualities can be explained by different absorption capabilities of the natural environment, and emission values thus provide a preferable basis for performance evaluation, depending, however, on the exact subject to be studied. Yet, differences in emissions, for instance of air pollution, may reflect not only different energy supply systems, but also differences in the need for heating due to climate, and one would for instance have to assess emissions in relation to total energy consumption.[24] Regarding water pollutants, comparable emission data are less complicated to achieve, at least in principle.

The primary pollution indicator used is organic pollution, which is the classical emission parameter. The strength of this indicator is that it represents a basic non-hazardous pollution parameter and it has been the primary focus of interest since the 1970s. The weakness of organic pollution as a key indicator is that heavy metals and chemical substances have also been subject to regulation, and that different policies have been applied to different pollution parameters. Data on these substances are extremely limited, however, and often reflect discharges by particular firms, whereas the organic indicator, comparable with basic mass pollutants such as CO_2, corresponds better to the general level of industrial activity.

The indicators for emissions can provide means of assessing the application of cleaner production technologies. Employing cleaner production technologies can result in reduced discharges, but so will the application of end-of-pipe technologies. Consequently, it is necessary to estimate the effects of sewage plants as compared with initiatives undertaken by industry itself. Structural changes within industries may also consist of traditional end-of-pipe techniques applied at the level of the firm. At the aggregate level it is difficult to estimate the exact technological response. Figures for industrial investments and the capacity of industrial sewage plants may provide hints as to the nature of the technological response. At the methodological level, emission data are, however, the best available indicator of structural changes.

Since the project was initiated, the international (and national) environmental statistics have improved considerably. The principal problem that arises when comparing data from different national statistics is differences in specifications, but international statistics issued by the OECD are encumbered with similar problems.

Control for intervening variables
As the four case studies concern four countries with similar economic and technological preconditions, we assume that some intervening variables affecting the way policies can influence emissions will also be similar.

Research into technological solutions to pollution control has become highly international, and methods and technologies have been presented and intensively discussed in a number of international research journals.[25] Although there are differences in national research strategies, and different amounts of resources have been allocated for such purposes, results and experiences are well communicated and marketed. Japan and the United States have been front runners in scrubber technology and catalytic converters for automobiles, whose lack of application in Europe until the mid-1980s was a result more of lack of political commitment to air pollution control than of technological impediments. We may thus assume that the potential technological options in pollution control are quite similar in the Western industrialised countries, and particularly that the four countries in this study have access to a more or less a common technological basis.

The economic preconditions for environmental policies have been less similar, even within the OECD and EC. Within the European Community, there are marked differences in annual GDP. The dual character of the economic precondition variable, noted by Jänicke, applies very well, and differences in GDP impede meaningful comparisons not only between Northern and Southern Europe, but also between the United States and West European countries; per capita GDP of the United States was 50 percent higher than the German GDP in 1989. Although comparisons of environmental policies between the United States and other countries certainly can be informative, they become less reliable if one seeks to investigate the effect of certain policy instruments, where economic preconditions may cause a bias. A cluster of countries at a similar level of economic development provides the soundest basis for comparison with regard to the effects of policy instruments.

In spite of similar levels and growth rates of GDP, national industrial structures vary tremendously. Industrial structures may influence not only the level of emissions but also their evolution, since technological breakthroughs relevant to pollution control may occur in only certain sectors. For instance, developments in the pulp and paper industries and food-processing industries have caused the most considerable innovations in water pollution control. The general implication is that emissions must be analysed separately for various industrial sectors.

For each sector, where data are available, a de-linkage index is calculated. The de-linkage index is an indicator of the possible gap between production output and emission output for each sector in the period studied. In principle, the goal has been to construct a de-linkage index for the most water-intensive sectors in each of the four countries, and to compare these indexes across cases. Such indexes will ease pattern-matching between the cases, and at the same time control the most obvious external factor – structural changes in industry.

Whereas it is difficult to draw conclusions about the effectiveness of certain policy instruments on the basis of a single case, the multiple case study method provides a better foundation for building and refining theories of policy instruments. Differences in policy design and policy outcomes may tell us something about the effectiveness of various regulatory approaches. Emission profiles of the individual countries thus serve as a litmus test for the effectiveness of applying economic policy instruments. If economic instruments are as effective as claimed by the Brundtland Commission and many others, we should expect to find three cases of relative success and one of (relative) failure (Denmark). The following chapters present a case-by-case examination of the reasons for relative differences in success in implementing clean water policies.

Notes

1 Lundqvist (1980).
2 Vogel (1986).
3 Knoepfel and Weidner (1985).
4 See Sabaticr and Mazmanian (1981).

5 Jänicke (1990a).
6 Jänicke and Mönch (1988); Jänicke, Mönch, Ranneberg and Simonis (1988).
7 See Schmidt (1986).
8 Jänicke (1990), 224, my translation; Katzenstein (1985).
9 Lundqvist (1980); Andersen (1989a).
10 Jänicke (1990a), 214, my translation.
11 Krawinkel (1991).
12 See Mitnick (1980), 321–412.
13 Wilson (1980).
14 Vogel and Kun (1987).
15 Yin (1989).
16 Ibid., 23.
17 Ibid., 53.
18 Andersen (1989a); Downing and Hanf (1983).
19 Knoepfel et al. (1987).
20 OECD, *Environmental Data* (1979, 1985, 1987, 1989, 1991); OECD (1991a).
21 Vogel and Kun (1987), 141.
22 Johnson and Brown (1976a); Bower et al. (1981).
23 See Johnson and Brown (1976a), 14.
24 See OECD, *Environmental Data* (1979) for an attempt on SO$_2$.
25 Among such journals are: *Pollution Prevention, Industry and Environment, Water Pollution Control, Water and Environmental Management, Research Journal of the Water Pollution Control Federation* and *Water International.*

4

Denmark: Consensus-seeking as best available technology

Introduction

In 1986–87 water pollution became a political issue of the utmost importance in Denmark. The pictures of dead lobsters, broadcast to all Danes on television in the autumn of 1986, made clear what occasional fish mortality had been indicating for some time, namely that Denmark's coastal territorial waters and straits had deteriorated seriously. Dispute about the subsequent Plan for the Aquatic Environment nearly caused the government to resign, and in the following years the issue frequently generated political turmoil.[1] Although environmental problems in general had been subject to public attention during the 1980s, it was surprising that so much focus was suddenly directed towards water pollution. Since the environmental reform in 1973, billions of Danish crowns had been invested in sewage treatment, and the water pollution sector had accounted for more than 50 percent of total environmental investment. The Danes had been convinced that the country possessed 'the world's best environmental law' – a phrase frequently used by Danish politicians. However, world leadership in sewage treatment is not, as will be demonstrated, tantamount to world leadership in water pollution control.

For reasons already suggested in Chapter 1, Denmark did not introduce economic incentives in 1973, although the 'polluter pays' principle was applied to some extent. In this respect, the Danish approach corresponded to that chosen by Sweden, Norway and Great Britain.[2] The Environmental Protection Act of 1973 was a comprehensive piece of legislation with a rather ambitious cross-sectoral approach. It was not devoted to a specific pollution sector, but was intended to regulate all types of pollution within a common legal framework. Most of the policy instruments employed were similar to those of the command-and-control scheme, but it is perhaps more adequate to characterise the Danish approach as one of 'consensus and delegation'. A consensus was accomplished with the most important peak interest organisations before legislation was passed, and during implementation there was further room for negotiation, especially with the influential Federation of Danish Industries. The delegation of considerable discretionary powers to local authorities was another feature of the Danish Environmental Protection Act.[3]

The approval of the Plan for the Aquatic Environment, in 1987, was a turning point in Danish water pollution control policy. Optional guidelines and case-by-case approval of discharges were now replaced by mandatory guidelines.[4] There were also elements of continuity; the general emphasis remained on end-of-pipe solutions provided and financed by the public sector.

The context of water pollution control policy

Environmental background

The aquatic environment is of prime importance to Denmark. With more than 500 islands and the peninsula of Jutland, Denmark's coastline exceeds 7,000 km. No Dane lives more than 50 km from the sea, and within Denmark there are no rivers, but only streams, brooks and lakes. Denmark is a small country, with a moderate population density (119 inhabitants/km^2). Plenty of high-quality groundwater is available, and Denmark relies almost exclusively on this source for water supply. Leakage of nitrates, oil spills and hazardous waste has made inroads into groundwater resources, but surface waters are not in question for future water supply.

Food-processing industries, related to intensive agricultural production and fishing, account for a large share of the manufacturing sector. There are few traditional smoke-stack industries such as steel or mining. Recently, pharmaceutical products, plastics and chemicals have become more important, and industry is now spread out over all of the country, with the highest growth rates in Jutland.

Situated between the North Sea and the Baltic Sea, Denmark

appears to be affected by international marine pollution. While
Denmark exports pollution to the North Sea, it imports pollution
from the Baltic Sea. Still, as far as coastal territorial waters and
straits are concerned, national sources of pollution remain the
most important, and are larger than the combined Swedish and
German contribution. Furthermore, because the waters from the
Baltic Sea exchange very slowly (approximately thirty years) and
because pollutants are transformed, the direct effect of marine
pollution from Eastern Europe is in fact not very significant,
although substantial scientific uncertainties remain.[5]

Administrative background
Denmark's Ministry of the Environment, initially named the Ministry for Pollution, was established in 1971, and from the very
beginning the government had a separate Minister of the Environment. Although well-staffed, the Ministry and its agencies have
institutionally been in a difficult position with regard to the local
authorities, who have responsibility for implementation.

In spite of its modest size, Denmark is very decentralised. The
14 counties and 277 municipalities enjoy an almost unprecedented
autonomy in comparison with other local authorities in the European Community. The local authorities charge their own taxes
and, although they receive grants from the state, local taxes are
their most important source of revenue. Local taxes make up
approximately one-third of all taxes and no other local authorities
in the European Community have such a large direct share in taxation. One important reason for policy traditions being inclined
towards decentralisation is found in the farmers' co-operative
movement, which emerged in the nineteenth century under the
leadership of the cleric, poet and educator Grundtvig, and which
was strongly opposed to rule by decree from Copenhagen.[6] This
libertarian preference has since then been strong in Denmark and
was reinforced in the late 1960s; during the 1968 administrative
reform, municipalities and counties came to play a more important role in all policy sectors, including environmental policy.

The newly established Ministry of the Environment recruited its
leading staff members from the Ministry of the Interior, which
had just completed the reorganisation of municipalities. The leading officials were trained mainly in law, and they brought with
them their concepts of public regulation from the Ministry of the
Interior. Although the scheme they designed for pollution regulation

may have looked neat on the legal drawing board in Copenhagen and although it respected the autonomy of local authorities, it was rather complex and sophisticated for a small country where only a few large factories were responsible for the bulk of discharges. The Environmental Protection Act was designed to promote a consensus-seeking policy. Throughout the 1960s, Denmark had witnessed an unprecedented growth of public services under the aegis of social democratic governments. Policy making in the Danish welfare state was shaped through close co-operation between the government and major interest organisations, and this was also true of environmental policy. The Environmental Protection Act was passed in 1973, shortly before the oil crisis and the elections to the Danish parliament that brought an end to a relatively stable, majority government rule. In several ways 1973 marked the culmination of the social democratic welfare state.

Historical background[7]
It was the cholera epidemic in Copenhagen in 1851, which caused more than 5,000 deaths, that led to the first regulations concerning hygiene and water. In the late nineteenth century, a liability and compensation scheme for industrial discharges was established, and in 1907 the Sewer Act vested the municipalities with the authority to establish sewer networks and charge the polluters. In 1949 a major reform was undertaken with the passing of the Water Course Act, which endowed the authorities with the competence to require licences for urban industrial dischargers into both fresh and marine waters. The Water Course Act mandated the treatment of discharges so as not to spoil the natural conditions of water courses or cause general inconvenience in marine waters. It gave special Farmers' Commissions (*landvæsenskommissioner*) the competence to issue permits, as these bodies were traditionally used to settle conflicts between neighbours.

Concern for the environment increased during the 1960s, and several motions were put forward in parliament. In 1969 the government established the Pollution Council to analyse Denmark's environmental problems and make recommendations. Only two years later, a Ministry for Pollution was established and asked to draw up proposals for modern environmental legislation. After lengthy negotiations, especially with the Federation of Danish Industries, the Environmental Protection Act was passed in 1973 and took effect on 1 October 1974.

The Environmental Protection Act[8]

The delegation principle

The reform of the municipal structure resulted in fewer and presumably more effective local authorities, and, within the framework of the Environmental Protection Act, power in most practical matters was delegated to the local authorities. Traditional institutions, such as the Health and Farmers' Commissions, were abolished. The municipalities were made responsible not only for public sewage treatment but also for inspection of industry.

Suggestions were made to establish independent water authorities, as in Britain and France, but the proposals were never seriously considered. Although Denmark has no large rivers, its many water courses are linked to the vulnerable fjord systems and, as Figure 4.1 shows, it was possible to draw consistent administrative borders on the basis of hydrological principles.[9] Nevertheless, the proposal of Professor Harremoës, a committed member of the Pollution Council, was turned down. Instead it was preferred to allow the counties, reorganised by the Ministry of the Interior, to play an important role.

The Environmental Protection Act was based on a 'water quality principle' that did not require polluters to meet national effluent standards. The water quality principle meant that the requirements for the treatment of waste water should be balanced against the sensitivity of the local aquatic recipient to discharges. It appeared reasonable to set up stricter requirements for discharges into fresh waters than to the fjords or open sea, especially from an economic point of view. The logic of the delegation principle was to allow counties to set requirements on a case-by-case basis according to the quality and capacity of local surface waters.

The Danish approach was to aim at more or less common qualities of the surface waters, rather than to impose similar emission guidelines on industries. Hence, extensive 'recipient quality planning' was undertaken, very much in accordance with the European Community directives.* A comprehensive planning system

---

* The EC water directives are based on a dual approach (76/160/EEC; 76/464/EEC). For non-toxic substances they prescribe a recipient quality approach as well. The member states are to designate waters for various purposes (bathing, shellfish, etc.) and set targets in terms of water quality standards. For toxic substances, guidelines are or will be prescribed. The dual approach was a compromise between the British/Danish and the Continental traditions.

Figure 4.1 A comparison between counties and hydrological water basins

was set up, and local authorities were required to present plans for their future efforts in sewage treatment and with regard to water quality. All plans were tied into a comprehensive planning system under the regional plans and were subject to approval by the counties and the Minister for the Environment.

The Act also included among its formal aims a much disputed 'balancing principle'. Environmental authorities were required to balance the requirements of pollution control against the costs incurred to industries.* The balancing principle was one of the most important concessions made to the Federation of Danish Industries. Together with the 'water quality principle' it formalised the possibilities for local authorities to deviate from the national guidelines.

The consensus principle
The second cornerstone of the Environmental Protection Act was the bargaining between the authorities and industries about everything from guidelines to individual cases. The Act was a framework legislation, which meant that parliament and government delegated the setting of detailed guidelines and standards to experts within the Danish Environmental Protection Agency, Miljøstyrelsen. The experts participate, however, in a bargaining system of their own. Every guideline issued under the law is negotiated with the relevant interest organisations. Thus, basic guidelines on water were negotiated with the Federation of Danish Industries.[10] The guidelines were not mandatory, however, but merely recommendations to local authorities.

Furthermore, the Environmental Board of Appeal has played a key role in the case-by-case reviews of dischargers. This board functions as the administrative 'high court' of the environment, and was in fact set up in response to concern from business organisations that the environmental bureaucracy would become too powerful. Decisions taken at the local level, concerning permits to polluting firms for instance, can be taken to the Board of Appeal.

The Board of Appeal is headed by a judge, but its members are appointed by the peak business interest organisations and Miljøstyrelsen.[11] In practice, the Board of Appeal functions as a delicate mix of expertise and consensus-seeking. Although it decides on the basis of existing legislation and available scientific evidence, most environmental issues are marked by the 'crisis of proof' situation and are open to some interpretation.

The Danish system is thus characterised not only by a high degree of adaptation to local preferences, but also by an institutionalisation of the traditional Danish consensus-seeking policy style. The fundamental position of local authorities allows for adaptation to local environmental problems and preferences

* The balancing principle was annulled as part of the amendments in 1987.

concerning the choice of solutions, and even the national system of standard-setting is permeated by a balancing of requirements against the acceptance of those subject to regulation. Furthermore, implementation is subject to the review of the Environmental Board of Appeal, a corporatist body per se.

The 'polluter pays' principle

In contrast to Sweden, Denmark was not prepared to support industry or municipalities through comprehensive subsidy schemes, although a limited subsidy scheme was set up for older firms. Generally, the rhetoric on the 'polluter pays' principle was strong, but on the other hand proposals to extend the 'polluter pays' principle to include state levies or taxes on pollution were rejected. Ideologically, the Social Democratic government did not want to give polluters the chance to avoid controlling pollution by being able to pay instead. Pragmatically, such taxation could also have disturbed the fragile compromise that had been reached with the Federation of Danish Industries. Furthermore, the experts of the Pollution Council recommended against such taxes.

The Pollution Council had analysed the properties of different policy instruments, including pollution taxes. The Council was well aware of the economic advantages of this policy instrument, but pointed out that a number of practical obstacles impeded its application. The Council thus concluded,

As a system of state pollution taxes implies a considerable administration and also specific information about water quality and discharges, which is not currently available – making it difficult to set taxes in a rational way – further application of the taxation method [other than user fees for public treatment] will for the present hardly be expedient.[12]

The Pollution Council was more concerned about the system of user fees for provision of public sewage treatment, which it found insufficient to provide incentives. It pointed out that the municipalities, by contributing financially to this service, provided indirect subsidies for local firms, and that the system could be misused in order to attract new firms to a municipality.

The reluctance to use levies as economic incentives, however, meant that industries discharging directly into fresh or marine waters obtained substantial advantages compared with firms served by public sewer networks and sewage plants. Whereas indirect dischargers had to pay user fees for public treatment, direct dischargers simply needed to obtain a permit from county authorities. This procedure could incur costs for pollution control equipment but, once discharges had been authorised and a license obtained, there were no further costs.

Because local sewage plants were partly subsidised, and because levies were not imposed on direct discharges, economic incentives to Danish industry became weak or even absent. In particular the group of industries discharging directly into the surface waters can be viewed as a control group compared with countries where economic policy instruments have been applied.

A first account

Public sewage treatment
Although sewage plants were widespread already in 1970, a large proportion of them were providing only simple mechanical treatment.* Under the Environmental Protection Act, biological treatment became the prevailing method, although mechanical treatment was maintained at many discharge points into the sea. In 1986, however, the year of the dead lobsters, 75 percent of the population were provided with biological treatment and 18 percent with mechanical treatment. More than DKr 10 billion has been invested in sewage treatment since 1973.

Industrial effluents
Figure 4.2 shows direct and indirect discharges from industries prior to the effects of public sewage plants. Surveys of industrial emissions have been carried out by Miljøstyrelsen in selected years.[13] The available data on industry's organic discharges have been converted into inhabitant equivalents (IE), and an index figure has been calculated in order to compare with the trends in net industrial production.† As Figure 4.2 depicts, the relationship between

---

* Definitions: mechanical/primary treatment – removal of gross solids; biological/secondary treatment – removal of organic material by bacteria under aerobic conditions; tertiary treatment – removal of nutrients (phosphorus and nitrogen) by chemical or biological treatment.
† The survey figures are not very precise, especially the figure for 1972. The figures are typically based on the emissions sanctioned in the permits, rather than on measurements. Non-compliance with permits was very common in the early 1980s, so they probably represent a conservative estimate. On the other hand, some companies have not discharged fully what they were allowed to. Still, for an estimate of the level and trend of discharges, the data must be regarded as sufficient.

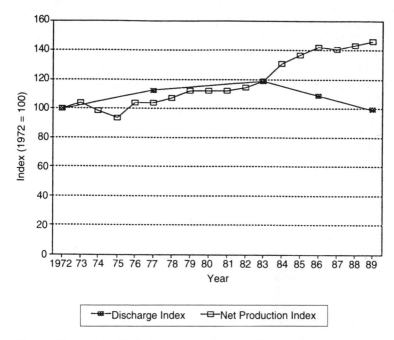

Figure 4.2 Industrial discharges of organic pollutants before treatment (estimate) and net production index

net industrial production and emission outputs in terms of organic discharges has been quite close, until a modest de-linkage appeared in the mid-1980s. Owing to public sewerage, 63 percent of the total industrial pollution was removed in 1991, but it appears that until 1986 industries had hardly reduced pollution at source.

The policy instruments at work

The role of the municipalities
The construction of sewage treatment plants was in keeping with the general expansion of local public services in the early 1970s, and the Danish municipalities were generally keen to undertake this task, although they partly disagreed with the technological ambitions of the national planners.

In its final report of 1971, the Pollution Council had given recommendations on the quality of waste water treatment. The

Council advised that discharges directly into the sea should be treated mechanically, whereas discharges into water courses flowing into the sea should be treated biologically. Discharges into more sensitive waters, such as lakes, water courses and inlets, were to be treated both biologically and chemically. In 1972 the Pollution Ministry drew up a ten-year plan for the extension of sewage treatment plants. It was based on plans prepared by the municipalities, and it was evident that the municipalities were reluctant to equip those treatment plants that had outflows into fresh water with the most advanced treatment methods. Similarly, 10–20 percent of the outflows to other waters were not planned to be sufficiently treated.[14]

Moreover, the municipalities were overtaken by the economic recession. The government's concern for the environment waned, and in 1975 it recommended that the municipalities consider limiting the planned extension of treatment plants, so as to reduce public expenditure. The government encouraged the municipalities to consider treatment measures in relation to the water quality and to balance costs against the possible improvement of environmental quality. Waste water treatment was subordinated to economic policies, and the water quality principle became a convenient tool for this exercise.[15] The result was that mechanical treatment methods retained a rather large share of Danish waste water treatment.

To many smaller and middle-sized municipalities, sewage treatment was a technically complicated task. Sewage plants have generally been operated as an integrated part of municipal services and have not been delegated to independent utilities, such as water and electricity supply. The result was a lack of professionalism, and in 1984, after its first national survey, Miljøstyrelsen found that 46 percent of the plants did not meet the requirements set in their individual permits. Many were simply too small, but a general problem was a lack of well-trained staff.[16]

Permits, planning and standards
For twenty-five years, direct industrial discharges were subject to a permit procedure, the 1949 Water Course Act. The general requirement of the 1973 Environmental Protection Act was that every discharger obtain a permit, but permits granted under the old scheme remained in force. In 1972, fewer than ten firms were

responsible for 80 percent of direct industrial discharges of organic pollutants, but several of these, as well as other major polluters, had already been licensed under the 1949 Act.[17]

According to the 1973 Act, county-based recipient quality plans were supposed to have provided the basis for the permit procedure. By classifying individual water courses, lakes, inlets and sea territory, the counties would be able – in theory – to decide how much pollution could be absorbed without undesirable deterioration. In practice, the counties were novices in environmental protection and had insufficient knowledge about the quality of the waters. They knew even less about how much the waters could absorb.[18] The companies, on the other hand, only occasionally knew what they actually discharged and had even less knowledge about previous discharges.

Damage to fresh waters was well known, but there was more uncertainty with regard to the sea. Thus, the general policy became to restrict discharges into fresh waters, whereas discharges into the sea proceeded more or less unchanged, except where problems with bathing waters occurred. Because of the 'balancing principle', authorities abstained from requiring pollution control, and were ready to license discharges if they were equipped with longer outlets to the sea, and if industries undertook more precise monitoring programmes.[19]

Drawing up recipient quality plans was a lengthy procedure, which was sometimes extended by conflicts between the county authorities and the municipalities, of which especially the latter were eager to protect local firms and jobs. The first recipient quality plans were passed in the late 1970s, with considerable delay, and it was only in 1985 that most of the counties had completed their planning. In the meantime, more firms had already obtained discharge permits, and it was often a pragmatic exercise to set targets for water quality. If a firm had already been licensed, and if the recipient was of poor quality, it was certainly most realistic not to classify the waters for salmon or trout. The optional guidelines issued by Miljøstyrelsen in 1974 were balanced not only against water quality but also against the potential costs incurred by industries.

Among the environmental inspectors in both Miljøstyrelsen and the local authorities, there was a well-developed sense of what ought to be done to restrict emissions, but the planning procedure had its own tedious logic, and planning had to be completed before new demands to dischargers acquired a legal base.

The very idea that discharges could be dissolved in the open sea was undermined as most of the recipient quality plans approached their final approval around 1985.[20] A few months before the dead lobsters appeared in the Danish Kattegat Strait, separating Denmark and Sweden, a research report clearly showed that the diffusion policy had failed. Fornæs, at the eastern tip of Jutland, had become host to a number of large dischargers, since that part of Kattegat, owing to strong currents, was regarded as perhaps the most robust recipient in Denmark. Treatment was not required by the authorities when discharging from industries in the nearby town of Grenå, but less than ten years later marine researchers could prove that the sea bed was severely damaged and even occasionally biologically dead.[21] When even the most robust recipient, the Kattegat, could not dissolve pollutants, what could one expect for other waters?

The Environmental Board of Appeal

If the recipient quality planning had delayed decision making on permits, complaints procedures served to extend the final date for implementation of the necessary pollution control measures. Miljøstyrelsen was the first authority to review local decisions but, if this did not satisfy the plaintiff, a second appeal could be directed to the Board. A significant effect of the complaints procedure was to postpone the final decision on the permit conditions. The average time for considering a case has been one year, but certain delicate cases have been deferred for several years, usually because additional technical inquiries have been necessary.

The existence of the Environmental Board of Appeal provided a check on the discretion of local authorities and a departure from the general decentralisation principle. The intention was to establish an independent body to review cases, but the appointment of members from selected interest organisations also provided a forum for qualified negotiations between experts from Miljøstyrelsen and representatives of interest organisations on a case-by-case basis.

The Board did not acknowledge every plaintiff, only those with an interest in the decision in a narrow juridical sense. Thus, firms could complain about decisions taken by local authorities, and local authorities could complain if they disagreed with Miljøstyrelsen's decision. Until 1984 environmental interest groups were not recognised as plaintiffs, and have still not been entitled to appoint members to the Board. The Board is therefore an asymmetric forum for consensus-seeking, since only bureaucracy and industry are represented.

Subsidies
The legal framework was not very helpful in promoting pollution control, and there were only weak economic incentives to supplement it. A few direct subsidies were offered to industry through a state subsidy programme. All significant measures were eligible for a 50 percent subsidy, a figure changed to 25 percent around 1980. Still, the total sum was modest, amounting to less than DKr 0.5 billion through the 1970s. Approximately 90 percent of the investments were granted in connection with permit procedures, and the subsidies did not provide an independent incentive. They were used to support firms when these could not escape the demands of the authorities.

Since the 1907 Sewer Act, user fees had been charged to cover expenses for public sewers and sewage treatment, but the system had evolved in varying ways in the municipalities. There were no mandatory guidelines, and in practice each municipality engineer designed his own user fee system. In some municipalities, such systems were abolished and the costs covered through general tax revenues. This was the case in Copenhagen up to 1977.

The Sewer Act obliged municipalities to contribute financially to the construction of sewage treatment plants, if these were in the 'general interest'. On average, municipalities covered around 30 percent of the operating costs, thus providing a much more important indirect subsidy to industry than the government's modest subsidy programmes. A survey among municipalities revealed that the total annual subsidy for operating costs was around DKr 300 million in 1977, and that DKr 135–150 million was allocated in favour of industry. The annual indirect subsidy for capital costs to industry was around DKr 85 million, which was more than the approximately DKr 70 million invested annually in the period 1972–81 by industry itself. On a twenty-year basis (the depreciation period for sewage plants), the indirect subsidy to industry from the municipalities accounted for approximately DKr 1.5 billion.*[22]

From the early 1970s and up to 1987, user fees for the discharge of waste water were moderate. Even in 1988 the average fee was below DKr 10/m³. Furthermore, Danish water supply prices have been very low owing to the readily available resources of pure groundwater. The average Danish water supply tariff of DKr 2.67 is one of the lowest in the European Community, and a factor 3 times less than the average German water supply tariff.[23] We may conclude, then, that Danish industry has had access to cheap resources of water.

Industry's response

The importance of policy instruments

In a survey carried out among factories discharging directly into surface waters, and thus subject to the permit procedure, it was asked whether pollution had been controlled and for what reasons. The questionnaire was mailed to all direct dischargers, and 48 percent of the companies, responsible for nearly 70 percent of the discharges, replied.

Since 1974, 66 percent of the firms have reduced organic pollution. These firms (N = 31) were asked to specify the most important reasons for undertaking pollution control, and Figure 4.3 shows the percentage of respondents who responded positively to the individual factors. It is evident that public regulation has played a major role, since 90 percent of the firms surveyed mention it as the reason for pollution control. However, external factors such as company responsibility and concern about reputation have also had significant influence.

The companies were then asked about the formal background of the authorities' requirements, and Figure 4.4 shows the distribution

---

* A further subsidy is provided by the pricing method employed. The user fee unit is typically calculated per cubic metre. Industrial discharges, which usually contain more concentrated pollutants than those from households, have in principle been subject to a surplus user fee, but municipalities have often abstained from imposing this fee. If the municipality does not collect the surplus fee, the result is a de facto additional discount of approximately 50 percent. Technically, the method is cross-subsidising, since households are charged with a bill that should have been imposed on industry.

Reasons for pollution control	No.	%
Public regulation	28	90
Pollution control is a company responsibility	18	58
Safety and considerations for workers' health	2	6
To avoid bad reputation	8	26
Influence from neighbours	3	10
Influence from environmentalists	1	3
Influence from consumers	0	0
Profitable investments	5	16
As part of regular production monitoring	6	19

N = 31

Figure 4.3   Reasons for pollution control

Policy instrument	No.	%
Water quality targets	18	58
Plan for aquatic environment	5	16
Best-available technology	4	13
Non-compliance with permit	5	16
Other reasons	7	23
Do not know	1	3

N = 31

Figure 4.4   Impact of policy instruments

on different policy instruments. The survey was carried out in 1992, and it was necessary to ask also about the impacts of the Plan for the Aquatic Environment and the possibility of requiring best available technology, a stipulation added to the 1973 Environmental Protection Act in the same year.

Of the firms surveyed, 58 percent point to recipient quality planning as the most significant formal reason for the demands of the authorities. Failure to comply with permits is mentioned by 16 percent, while 23 percent point to a broad category of other instruments, such as regional or international conventions, political circumstances, an increase in production or the construction of a public sewage plant, as leading to requirements from the authorities. The Plan for the Aquatic Environment is mentioned by 16 percent, but only 3 percent indicate the requirements following from this plan as the only reason for pollution control, which in any case must have been undertaken later than 1987.

Technological response	No.	%
Diffusion	2	6
Primary treatment	8	26
Secondary or tertiary treatment	17	55
Cut-off of waste streams to public sewers	10	33
Adjustments in the production process	13	42
New technology applied	6	19
Major categories:		
Diffusion	2	6
End-of-pipe	27	87
Clean technology	15	48

N = 31

Figure 4.5   Technological responses

Technological responses

When it comes to the technological response to regulation, Figure 4.5 shows what the respondents who controlled organic pollution did. Since the survey was undertaken in 1992, measures taken in response to the latest changes in policy are also included.

End-of-pipe measures were the response of 87 percent of the firms. At the same time, however, 48 percent indicate that they have also made changes in production processes or installed new production technologies to prevent pollution. Most of these, however, pertain to adjustments of the production process; only 19 percent mention the introduction of new, clean production technology, and it appears that all firms in this group except one had their permit reviewed in 1991–92. The application of clean technology appears to be a more recent phenomenon, whereas end-of-pipe measures have been more prevalent until recently.

The findings confirm the general picture in Figure 4.2: Danish industries have to only a limited extent reduced pollution at source. A major reason for this might have been that most companies were served by public sewage plants, and that only approximately 100 firms, most quite large dischargers, were allowed to continue with direct discharges.

Because of subsidies to public sewage plants, user fees did not reach the level that they stimulated efforts at pollution control before 1987. Because of lax permit procedures, the reduction of pollution into the sea has been modest. Authorities focused on the few dischargers into fresh waters, and as a result, for instance, two large paper mills were still discharging the same amounts of pollutants in the late 1980s as they had in 1973. When the Plan for the Aquatic Environment was passed, it was 'discovered' that the fish-processing industries, especially in northern Jutland, were a considerable source of organic discharges and had not been subject to any restrictions since 1973, because of the water quality principle. The local authorities had not even included these factories in their planning, because, as they said, they were situated in the harbour areas.

Conclusions

The policy approach chosen by Denmark for water pollution control in 1973 was in many ways exemplary. Fragmented water regulations were replaced by a general Environmental Protection Act, which ensured an integrated permit procedure. A separate Ministry of the Environment, with substantial resources, was institutionalised very early. In fact, the Environmental Protection Act was a pronounced example of the Danish policy style: the most essential implementation decisions were contracted out from parliament to negotiations between major interest organisations and public officials from the Ministry of the Environment. Emphasis on consensus-seeking and the importance attributed to achieving informal understanding with those being regulated were major elements of this style.

Effluent charges failed to win any acceptance in Denmark (or in any other Scandinavian country) because such policy instruments were out of step with the prevailing Danish policy style. It was incompatible with the ruling welfare ideology to abstain from public planning, or to allow someone to pay a charge rather than clean up as government required.* The Danish national policy style resulted in the public sector assuming responsibility for pollution management by constructing public sewage plants. Extending public institutions fitted nicely into the standard operating procedures of Danish policy-making.

---

* It is curious how different this 'welfare ideology' was from Pigou's welfare economics (cf. Chapter 2).

What was never questioned was the issue of whether public operation of end-of-pipe solutions would be much more expensive in the long run than control at source. Even economic considerations were applied at 'end-of-pipe' with the water quality principle. The amount of discharges was not questioned, but faith in the diffusion principle, explicitly expressed as late as 1979, led to the toleration of considerable untreated discharges into the sea.

The delegation principle tempted the autonomous municipalities to use the environment as a competition parameter in order to attract new firms, secure jobs and increase tax revenues. Firms were granted discounts on waste water treatment, and controls exercised by the municipalities relaxed. The ideal approach with regard to water quality led to water pollution control being managed by counties without much experience of water management, and required the compiling of data and evidence before pollution could be controlled. Although the large direct dischargers, accounting for more than 80 percent of total discharges, were quite few, national authorities were unable to penetrate the municipal 'shield' and deal with essential problems. The national agency, Miljøstyrelsen, was cut off from negotiating agreements with the large polluters owing to the delegation principle, which vested authority in the counties.

In fact, the policy represented a very indirect and complicated approach. Miljøstyrelsen issued guidelines on planning and effluent standards, and it was then up to the counties to undertake planning and issue permits. Before the counties could issue permits on the basis of the recipient quality plan, these had to be drawn up. When permits were issued, these could be appealed to Miljøstyrelsen and to the Board of Appeal. Finally, there was a technical implementation phase. Perhaps the number of steps was logical, but for a small country with a limited number of polluters, the method was amazingly complex. Miljøstyrelsen proposed in the late 1970s to take over control of the major polluters, but this was opposed by the Federation of Danish Industries, which preferred local administration, and the proposal was withdrawn.

Consequently, from 1974 to 1987, Danish water pollution control took place hardly at all at source, but by a combination of diffusion and end-of-pipe solutions. This is reflected in Figure 4.2, which shows that structural changes in industry have been modest. The actual decrease in discharges is mainly due to the fact that a large number of industries have been linked to public sewage plants. Thus, the regulatory response has essentially been that the public sector has acceded to receiving and taking over responsibility for industrial discharges, but not charging industry the true costs of treatment. It should therefore not come as a surprise that the Environmental Protection Act, modelled on the consensus-seeking policy style, has proved to be an expensive and essentially problem-shifting choice.

Environmental policy basically implies an offensive against well-established 'rights' to pollute, but the policy model applied was taken from policy areas, such as labour market policy, that have been more concerned with distributing the benefits of a growth economy. In the immense bargaining and planning scheme that was constructed for this new policy sector, there were no incentives for those being regulated to participate by taking measures themselves.

Notes

1 For an account of the Plan, see Andersen and Hansen (1991); Dubgaard (1991); Akademiet for de Tekniske Videnskaber (1990).
2 See Waage (1984); Johnson and Brown (1976a).
3 Andersen (1989a).
4 Kristensen et al. (1987).
5 Richardson and Ærtebjerg (1991).
6 Mørch (1982).
7 Nue (1980).
8 Von Eyben (1989); Haagen-Jensen (1982).
9 Harremoës (1970).
10 See Miljøstyrelsen (1974b).
11 See Basse (1987).
12 Forureningsrådet (1971), 145, my translation.
13 Miljøministeriet & Miljøstyrelsen (1974); Miljøstyrelsen (1981b, 1984, 1990).
14 Miljøministeriet (1974b).
15 Miljøstyrelsen (1976).
16 Miljøstyrelsen (1985b); DIOS (1987).
17 Miljøstyrelsen (1981b), 58.
18 Fenger and Jensen (1977).
19 For case studies of direct dischargers, see Pedersen (1987); Gamby et al. (1988); Nielsen (1985).

20 Hansen and Rask (1986).
21 Århus Amtskommune (1986).
22 See Hjorth-Andersen (1978).
23 International Water Supply Association (1988).

5

France: River basin management

Introduction

For practical and economic purposes, engineers and environmental economists have for many years advocated an integrated approach to water management.[1] In this context, French water policy is an interesting case, because France has apparently practised river basin management since the late 1960s. In the technocratic state that evolved in de Gaulle's France it was quite logical to apply such a strategy for water management. The creation of the new river basin agencies (Les Agences Financières de Bassin) provided the administrative framework for an integrated approach, although local authorities were still left with some formal tasks. Nevertheless, by applying effluent charges to all discharges and by setting up an appropriate administrative structure, France seems, at least at first sight, to have been 'going by the book'. The achievements of this regulatory strategy have thus attracted considerable international interest.

France contains the European giants in water services. The vast majority of local water utilities are privately managed, a paradox in a country otherwise characterised by a large share of nationalised industries. The French water companies, with an annual turnover of more than Fr 70 billion, have now expanded their activities not only to Southern Europe, but also to Britain, Germany and Denmark.[2]

However, France has lagged behind in the construction of public sewage plants. In 1990, coverage was still moderate with only 52 percent of the population served. This level is well below the OECD average and comparable to that of the former German

Democratic Republic.[3] The much heralded system of water pollution charges has mainly been effective with regard to the direct
discharges of industry, whereas local authorities have hesitated to
undertake public sewage treatment.

The context of water pollution control policy

Environmental background

Owing to its ambitious nuclear programme, France has relatively
clean air. Other environmental problems, including water pollution,
remain, however, quite significant. Many rivers are without fish,
and the leakage of nitrate from agriculture has caused eutrophication and has already spoiled the water supply for approximately
2 million inhabitants.[4]

France's population is concentrated in the northern half of the
country and along the large rivers. With 102 inhabitants/km², the
average population density is modest.[5] Industry, too, is concentrated in the northern part of the country, in the Parisian region,
Ile-de-France, and in the northeastern former mining region. Still,
industry can be found in all large cities, including Lyon and
Marseilles. Among the principal sectors are the chemical, steel and
food-processing industries. Agriculture is predominant in central
and southern France, which are also the less developed regions.

Since central and southern France are plagued by aridity, water
supply has historically been given high priority. Less attention has
been paid to water pollution, even though the French problems
are mainly internal and could be solved on a national basis. There
are few transboundary rivers and only the Rhine forms part of the
French–German border. However, it is French pollution that has
drawn protests from other countries along the Rhine.[6] The French
access to robust waters, such as the Mediterranean, the North Sea
and the Atlantic Ocean is probably the reason why most focus has
been on the larger rivers: the Loire, Garonne, Seine, Rhône, Meuse
and to some extent the Rhine. Conflicts among water users along
the rivers apparently triggered French regulation.

Administrative background

Ministry of the Environment   The Ministry of the Environment
was set up in 1971, but has been in a weak position compared

with traditional ministries such as Industry and Agriculture. The Ministry of the Environment has remained small, with fewer than 500 employees. For almost twenty years it did not even have its own minister, being instead led from the office of the Prime Minister through a state secretary. Furthermore, the ministry has had only a very small and insignificant branch administration in the regions and the *départements* (fewer than 420 persons for all of France). In practice, the ministry has been dependent on the external services provided by other ministries and on contracting with these units for the implementation of environmental legislation.

The fundamental problem of the Ministry of the Environment is that its staff are not recruited from a specific institution of higher education in the French tradition of engineer corps.[7] The established ministries are each staffed with employees from a specific corps (e.g. the Ministry of Industry with mining engineers corps, the Ministry of Agriculture with water and forest corps engineers, etc.). The Ministry of the Environment, however, has been divided into four sections, each of which recruits staff from separate engineer corps. Thus, the Ministry of the Environment has not only been weak vis-à-vis other ministries, but also subject to dominance by the long-established socio-administrative cultures of other ministries. As a result, the other ministries have been able to keep a number of environmental tasks away from the Ministry of the Environment and within their own jurisdiction.

Local authorities   The French administrative system is a four-level system with '*communes*', *départements*, regions and the state level.* The distinctive feature of the French system is the relatively powerful state authority and the dependency of local administrative units on state directives. The special traditions of the French executive and the problems pertaining to the interplay between the local administrations and the state have to some extent made it difficult to assign responsibility. This complicated administrative structure has itself become an important obstacle to effective regulation of the environment.

France is divided into ninety-six *départements*, and each *département* has a dual administrative function: it is responsible both for its own tasks financed on a separate budget under the

* The French term for municipality, '*commune*', is used here.

control of the popularly elected Conseil Général, and for tasks performed as a local unit of the central administration.[8] The chief executive of the département is the prefect, who is appointed by the central administration.* The most important ministries have their own branch offices in the *départements*, and together with various expert councils they play an important role in consultations with the prefect. The ninety-six *départements* are grouped into twenty-two regions, which have the same dual character as the *départements*, and which are also led by a regional prefect. The *département* is the most important sub-national unit, since many tasks have been delegated to it.

The communes, constituting the lowest administrative level, have formal responsibility for water supply and sewage treatment. The administrative division of the communes is centuries old, and France still has more than 36,000 communes, which is more than one finds in the rest of the European Community altogether. Most French communes are very small, with 90 percent having fewer than 2,000 inhabitants.[†] Although a council is elected, its primary task is to appoint the mayor of the town. The mayor is responsible both for carrying out the directives of the state and for ensuring a sufficient level of local public services. However, a local mayor is usually faced with a small and tight budget that has to be balanced.

The French Ministry of the Environment has expressed the view, in a rather bitter tone, that the environment has remained a concern of the state, but not for the rest of society. One can question, however, whether the state has provided local authorities with sufficient instruments to meet the ambitions of the Ministry of the Environment.

Historical background
The first regulation of water pollution in France was passed in 1898. In 1917 this Act was replaced by more comprehensive legislation that provided a framework for water pollution control of manufacturing industries. The 1917 law established the basic

---

* Since Mitterand's decentralisation reform, the title of Prefect has been changed to Commissionaire of the Republic. In practice, however, the original title is still applied.
† Only 2 percent have more than 10,000 inhabitants; 30 percent have less than 200 inhabitants; 4,000 communes have fewer than 100 inhabitants, and there are even 100 communes with no population at all (Wright, 1989: 309).

principle, still in force, that discharges from factories into surface waters require a permit from the prefect. From 1917 to the 1960s, despite severe increases in pollution, no major changes occurred in the water pollution control scheme. The 1917 law did not regulate local authorities, or municipal or household discharges, and sewage treatment facilities were not installed outside the Parisian region until the end of the 1950s.[9]

Generally, the 1917 Act was poorly implemented. Funds and political support were inadequate and public concern about water pollution was lacking. Although pollution increased considerably after World War II, the permits issued came to be regarded as permissions to pollute, and were almost impossible to withdraw or change without raising conflicts regarding the economic development of a department or region.[10] Over half a century, factories had obtained a vested interest in discharging into surface waters. Even when permits were violated, as occurred often, companies were usually sufficiently powerful to impede or evade enforcement.

In 1959 a commission was formed to prepare new water legislation under the auspices of the Commissariat Général du Plan. The commission consisted of representatives from ministries, industries, agriculture, fisheries and the scientific community. In 1964 it presented its proposal for a 'Loi de l'Eau' to the National Assembly. The draft Water Act rested on two principles: integrated river basin management and integrated planning of water management. However, it did not change the principles of the 1917 Act, instead building on the existing permit system. Whereas the proposal made it possible to allow specialised agencies to take over the entire water management system, the Senate altered the draft so as to limit the powers of the proposed water basin agencies and to maintain the role of the local authorities in the domain of water pollution control. Members of the Senate and the National Assembly were not prepared to allow specific-purpose agencies to take over water management completely. The resulting law was a more fragmented scheme than that originally proposed.[11]

Loi de l'Eau – The Water Act

Still, the Loi de l'Eau has been the cornerstone of water pollution control over the last two decades.[12] The most significant element of the 1964 reform was the possibility of establishing regional water authorities that could impose levies on polluters to finance the treatment of waste water and related activities.

Agences Financières de Bassin (AFBs)
Following the 1964 Act, new administrative units in the field of water management were established by decree in 1966. Six Agences Financières de Bassin were drawn up on the basis of a hydrological division of the country, although on the basis of purely hydrological principles only five agencies should have been created. Since there are three *grands corps* of engineers, equal treatment meant allocating two AFBs to each. Hence, six agencies were chosen.*[13] Each agency is responsible for a comprehensive river basin including tributaries and groundwater. The six agencies shown in Figure 5.1 were set up in 1967–68.

The most important tasks of the agencies are the setting and collecting of environmental levies, redistribution of funds, supervision and collection of data as well as general planning and overall co-ordination of the activities in the river basin. The priorities are set in special five-year intervention programmes.

The agencies are public special-purpose agencies, ruled by independent boards (named Comités de Bassin) for each agency. In principle, the governing board sets priorities for its river basin agency. However, the agency is only a financial and technical advisory institution; it does not itself manage sewage treatment plants or water supply. Rather, the agency collects levies on water pollution and water supply, and redistributes the funds to communes and industries, which contract with the agency. The activities of the river basin agencies are supervised by the Ministry of the Environment, but there is no formal hierarchical relationship between the two.

The river basin agencies have often been characterised as corporatist bodies in which the various interests reach agreements through dialogue and negotiation.[14] The six governing boards are composed of representatives from ministries, regions, départements, communes, industry and environmental organisations. The composition, which is fixed, is independent of the financial contributions. Since the river basin agencies are in practice often overruled

---

* The creation of special financial–technical agencies has also been used within other environmental areas, e.g. air pollution management, thus providing France with a five-level system of environmental administration.

LA FRANCE DES AGENCES DE L'EAU

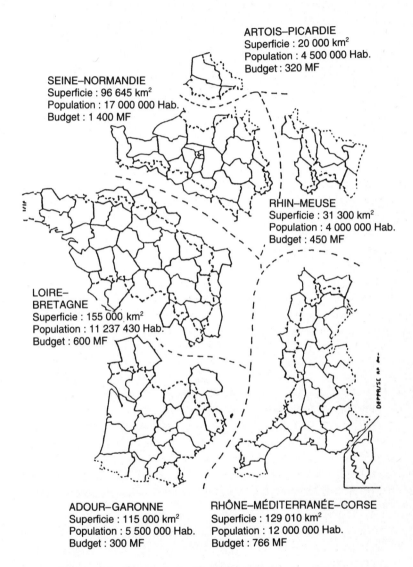

ARTOIS–PICARDIE
Superficie : 20 000 km²
Population : 4 500 000 Hab.
Budget : 320 MF

SEINE–NORMANDIE
Superficie : 96 645 km²
Population : 17 000 000 Hab.
Budget : 1 400 MF

RHIN–MEUSE
Superficie : 31 300 km²
Population : 4 000 000 Hab.
Budget : 450 MF

LOIRE–BRETAGNE
Superficie : 155 000 km²
Population : 11 237 430 Hab.
Budget : 600 MF

ADOUR–GARONNE
Superficie : 115 000 km²
Population : 5 500 000 Hab.
Budget : 300 MF

RHÔNE–MÉDITERRANÉE–CORSE
Superficie : 129 010 km²
Population : 12 000 000 Hab.
Budget : 766 MF

Figure 5.1 The Agences Financières de Bassin of France

by ministerial decisions, and since most of the negotiating takes place among various public authorities, calling them 'corporatist' is something of an overstatement. Rather, the agencies seem to have become an eloquent solution to excessive co-ordination problems caused by the complicated French administrative system.

The three main principles of the Water Act rest on the implementation of a feasible administrative structure, user influence and financial solidarity. The last term refers to the principle that all dischargers of waste water should contribute to the funds, regardless of their individual benefits in terms of subsidies, etc.[15]

The water pollution levies

The levy scheme is actually a closed tax-bounty scheme that allows the river basin agencies to impose levies to finance the activities scheduled in the intervention programmes on the basis of the principle 'qui pollue paye; qui épure est aidé'.[16] The levy is thus 'earmarked', and accounts for only a smaller share of the total water bill. It is a supplement to the water tariffs and user fees for waste water treatment.

The water levies are the only financial source of funding for the river basin agencies. They are based on a sophisticated formula using water supply and water pollution discharges.* The exact amount of the levies is set by the boards of the river basin agencies, which results in differences in the levies among the six agencies. Furthermore, it is possible for an agency to differentiate the levy within its own territory. The water supply fee is set on the basis of supplied water, whereas the discharge surtax is set on the basis of a pollution parameter measured in inhabitant equivalents (IE).†

Levies are paid by all dischargers, public sewage plants and industries. From the levies are deducted a so-called '*prime*', i.e. a bonus for pollution that has been eliminated. The funds are used for subsidies to communes and industry, and subsidies are offered for traditional treatment techniques as well as for cleaner technology projects.[17]

Standards and water quality planning

The Water Act is based on a principle of water quality. Dischargers are required by the law to apply for a permit; the law sets no

---

* Water supply management is not treated in this analysis.
† Levies are imposed according to the following parameters: oxidisable matter, suspended solids, equitoxics and dissolved salt.

mandatory guidelines for discharges of water pollution. Instead, prefects of the *départements* may establish limits on discharges in accordance with the pollution load and the quality of the water in question. The law thus provides the prefects with broad discretionary powers. Even though the Water Act was passed in 1964, it took more than ten years before a number of ministerial decrees gave the prefects the necessary competence to license dischargers. The decrees set neither targets nor guidelines, however. According to most sources, the licensing procedure has been of very little significance for pollution reduction, since firms usually obtain the permits they have sought.[18]

A first account

Public sewage treatment

As already mentioned, the coverage of public sewerage has been modest, in spite of considerable French know-how in the water sector. While the recent Plan National de l'Environnement claims that 64 percent of the population is connected to public sewage treatment, OECD data indicate that the figure is only 52 percent.[19] The standard of treatment is relatively high, since more than 90 percent are served by units that provide biological treatment. Public treatment is especially inadequate in the larger cities, such as Paris, Marseille, Lyon, Lille, Bordeaux.[20]

Figure 5.2 shows that the total load of both households and manufacturing industries served by public sewers has been quite constant, at approximately 70 million inhabitant equivalents (IE). Until recently, the treatment capacity has been insufficient compared with the discharges into the public sewer network, but this deficit has now been remedied, at least on paper. The major problem is the poor condition of the sewer networks, which allow only little more than half the discharges to reach public treatment facilities. Pollution equivalent to 30 million IE leaks from the sewers directly into the groundwater. The half-empty facilities perform reasonably, eliminating 70 percent of the sewage that reaches them, but remaining leaks push the gross discharge up to unacceptable levels. In spite of approximately 7,800 treatment plants, many of which provide secondary treatment, only 35 percent of the discharges are eliminated. Furthermore, many works do not perform according to set standards. The former director of the

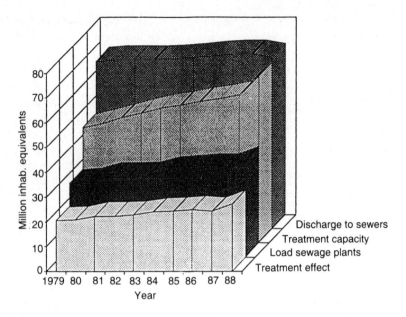

Figure 5.2 Discharges of organic pollutants from households and connected industries to public sewers and effect of sewage treatment, 1979–88

Seine–Normandie agency lamented that many communes fail to fulfil their role after the initial construction of a sewage plant: 'Construire une station d'épuration, c'est bien, faire en sorte qu'elle fonctionne à plein, c'est mieux!'[21]

Annual public investment in water pollution control has been Fr 1.5–2 billion, and paradoxically 80 percent of these funds have been spent on sewer networks. A rather high investment volume in the late 1970s was followed by a recession in the 1980s, although investment in the water sector accounted for 40 percent of total public environmental investment during this period.

The modest disbursements for the environment are often attributed to the Mitterrand administration's economic policies. In the early 1980s a decree from the Finance Ministry restricted the increase in the environmental levies to a mere 2 percent above the annual rate of inflation. This brought to a halt the more ambitious plans for extending public water treatment plants. Moreover,

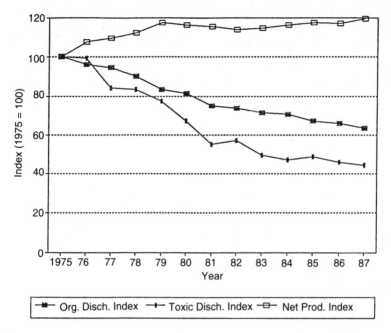

Figure 5.3 Industrial discharges and net production index, 1975–87

diminishing revenues due to improved pollution abatement narrowed the possibilities for action of the river basin agencies.

Industry
Developments have been more favourable when considering the discharges and effluents from industry. Toxic discharges were reduced by more than 50 percent from 1975 to 1986, and discharges of organic pollution were reduced by nearly 40 percent in the same period, compared with the achieved increase in output (see Figure 5.3). Figure 5.4 shows how discharges of organic effluents have evolved in the most pollution-intensive industrial sectors.

It is notable that industrial investment in water pollution control exceeded that for public sewage. Nevertheless, of the Fr 2 billion annual investment (compared with Fr 1.5 billion for public disposal), a large share has been subsidised by funds made available through the river basin agencies, which include both low-interest

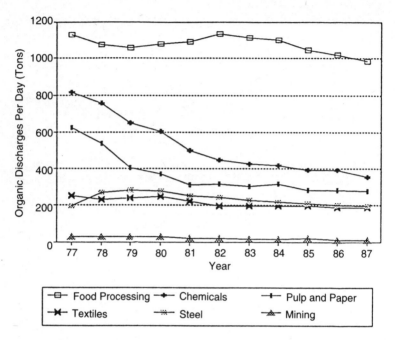

Figure 5.4   Organic discharges by the industrial sectors, 1977–87

credits and pure subsidies. In the first decade, 1969–79, subsidies from the river basin agencies accounted for 52 percent of total industrial investment, with only minor variations among the sectors.[22]

Overall, environmental investment by industry has accounted for approximately 2–3 percent of total industrial investment, but there remain significant variations between the sectors. While the energy sector allocated only 1 percent of investment for environmental purposes in 1987, the chemical industry allocated 7 percent.

The policy instruments at work

Water pollution control in the 1970s was characterised by a gradual upgrading of public sewage plants to include biological treatment. The 1980s was a period of stagnation, while the period beginning around 1987–88 has been marked by an increased interest in cleaner technologies.[23]

The permit and planning system

Water quality planning was supposed to have been the backbone of the system. Through comprehensive planning and designation of surface waters, as required also by the European Community, the *départements* would have the administrative tools to issue individual permits.[24] Hence, the task of water quality planning was originally assigned to the *départements*. However, since the administrative borders of the *départements* differed from the hydrological ones, they were requested to co-ordinate their planning with the regions as well as with the river basin agencies. It is hardly surprising, therefore, that several years elapsed before planning was initiated.

It was not until the late 1970s that the Ministry of the Environment issued the first guidelines concerning water quality planning, and it soon became evident that the *départements* were insufficiently staffed to meet the requirements. In practice, planning came to be executed by a river basin agency. Via the imposition of levies, the river basin agencies had generated the data necessary for planning. The river basin agencies typically worked out a plan and presented it to the Conseils Généraux of the *départements* for confirmation.[25]

Until the mid-1970s, discharge permits were issued by the prefects on the basis of the original 1917 Water Act. These permits were issued without time limits and administered on lenient terms. As the Ministry of the Environment did not have its own branch agencies, the actual task of issuing licences was carried out by the staff of the Ministries of Agriculture or Industry.[26] The personnel concerned with environmental issues were generally too few in number and had too few resources to enforce the requirements laid down in the permits. Little wonder, then, that the permit procedure has been described as a policy of tolerance towards the polluters. Public treatment plants required no permit by the prefect. Generally, very little attention was paid to the permit system, whereas the existence of river basin agencies, water pollution levies and the possibilities of subsidies meant that both industry and communes directed their attention towards this system. The water quality principle, supposedly the backbone of water regulation and a requirement of the EC, has been superseded by other policy instruments.[27]

Economic instruments

With each river basin agency setting its own levies, rates differ from one agency to another. The lowest levies are found in the agencies of Artois–Picardie, Rhine–Meuse and Adour–Garonne, which are also economically the least developed regions. The differences have been most noticeable concerning the organic pollution levy, which is currently 30 percent lower in the two northeastern agencies than in the rest of France. The highest levy is found in the Seine–Normandie river basin, which also accounts for the highest concentration of manufacturing industries. Even though the levies have gradually been increased since their introduction, this has partly been offset by inflation (see Figure 8.2).

National research on the impact of the French levies has not been identified, but generally their direct impact on pollution is regarded as rather modest:

Undeniably, with but few exceptions in certain industrial sectors, the levies have not yet reached the level of at least neutrality; it is more profitable for example for the polluter to pay his levy than to carry out investment in pollution control.[28]

There has been only a modest reduction of discharges from food-processing industries, even though this is the sector where reductions are known to require the least amount of investment. However, some sectors – most notably chemicals and pulp and paper – display considerable reductions. This is apparently the result of the successful utilisation of revenue generated by the levy, rather than of simple price incentives.

Voluntary sector contracts

The tax-bounty scheme has been organised by means of a number of industrial sector contracts. These voluntary sector contracts were introduced in the early 1970s as a pragmatic and concerted step to ensure pollution control over the most significant polluters. Through such sector contracts, water-pollution-intensive industrial sectors were exempted from paying pollution levies, provided that they introduced specified pollution reductions. The state contributed with subsidies for these contracts, but, generally, the bulk of the funds derived from the river basin agencies. While the state contributed Fr 59 million from 1971 to 1980, the river basin agencies contributed ten times this amount for the sectors in question.[29]

The sectors with which contracts were concluded had been responsible for most of the industrial effluents. In 1972, for example, 51 percent of the total discharges came from three sectors: paper, sugar and distillation industries. Contracts were made between the Ministry of the Environment and the individual sectors, resulting in seven sector contracts: pulp and paper (1972), sugar (1973), yeast (1975), potato flour (1975), distillation (1975), cement (1977) and wool–textile (1977). Most of the sector contracts were executed during the period 1974–76.

The paper industry was the most significant discharger of organic effluents, and the main recipient of subsidies. Half the state subsidies were spent in this sector. According to some observers, the contracts resulted in the application of traditional end-of-pipe technologies, whereas little or no attention was paid to changing the production process.[30] The river basin agencies were critical of the sector contracts, partly because too little attention was paid to local water quality problems, but probably also because the contracts appropriated most of their funds. The sector contracts were a rather expensive solution and were phased out in the late 1970s.[31] Furthermore, the contracts were criticised for impeding the 'polluter pays' principle, although the direct state subsidies were limited.

River basin agency personnel found that contracts absorbed a large part of available funds, thus obstructing regional priorities. Officials of the Ministry of the Environment were more enthusiastic about the contracts, concluding that they had fostered considerable improvements.[32] It is tempting to interpret the sector contracts as a shortcut by which the ministry could gain influence over the funds and priorities of the river basin agencies.

River contracts and city contracts

In the 1980s, the contract system came to be used with local authorities and selected rivers, in the form of 'river contracts'. Since local authorities are not subject to mandatory guidelines, and since the river basin agencies are not allowed to subsidise sewage treatment up to 100 percent, such contracts have been a stimulant in persuading local authorities to invest in pollution abatement measures.

Since 1983, more than 27 river contracts have been concluded.[33] A river contract includes all dischargers, both industrial and public sewage plants, and is often concluded on the initiative of the Ministry of the Environment for a five-year period. A 'river committee' is established to inspect the implementation of the contract. Funds are provided from the ministry, the river basin agencies (up to 30 percent), and the local authorities (up to 50 percent). On average, each river contract has generated Fr 40 million in investments.

Through such a contract, consensus is reached about co-ordinated action to improve water quality, and the river contract principle has now been adopted by the river basin agencies. In its sixth framework programme, AFB Seine–Normandie has launched a 'Seine-Propre' action, resulting in increased levies in the communes along the Seine and an expansion of investment for treatment.[34]

The five-year plans of the river basin agencies

Each of the six regional river basin agencies operates on the basis of five-year plans passed by the boards of the river basin agencies. The plan, being the result of a bargaining process, where needs are presented and funds allocated, is an important tool in the work of the river basin agencies. The plan contains a status report on the state of the aquatic environment in the region, and goes on to establish specific targets for the plan period. On basis of the targets, concrete action is proposed within each field of pollution abatement and water supply. The need for funds is estimated, and the plan determines the level of water pollution and water supply levies for the entire plan period. The plan also sets eventual zone coefficients for those special zones where the average levy is multiplied. Typically, the extra revenue is spent within this zone as well.

When the agencies allocate funds for various purposes, there is a tendency for the contributing groups to attempt to get a hold on 'their' share. In AFB Seine–Normandie, industry contributes Fr 200 million annually, and the representatives of industry carefully see to it that this money reappears as subsidies for industrial pollution abatement. It appears that the earmarking of the revenue was a very important reason why industry accepted the creation of the levy system at all.

One of the most serious problems confronting the river basin agency is ensuring that its funds are redistributed. Even though the Finance Ministry has put restrictions on the increase in levies, the river basin agencies have had difficulties spending all their revenue. Over the years, considerable sums have been accumulated within the river basin agencies, and a visitor to the elegant headquarters of the AFB Seine–Normandie in a Parisian suburb gains the distinct impression that this is a well-consolidated financial institution. As the director of the section in charge of levy raising stated: 'It is no problem to collect the levies, but to give them away – that can be very difficult.'[35]

In AFB Seine–Normandie (the largest of the six agencies), the accumulated assets are Fr 700 million, compared with an annual turnover of approximately Fr 1,600 million. According to the recent Plan National pour l'Environnement, the levies will be doubled, which has placed some pressure on the river basin agencies to ensure that the funds will be spent. In fact, the Ministry of Finance regards it as very unlikely that the river basin agencies will succeed in initiating a sufficient number of projects on which to spend all this money, and has therefore only provisionally consented to the doubling of levies. If the river basin agencies continue to accumulate funds, the Ministry of Finance has threatened to reduce the levy rates again.

The role of the communes

Technically, many French communes are too small to run their own sewage plants, and around 50 percent of the service is privatized. The large water companies, being historically responsible for water supply, have therefore extended their activities into this sector. Privatization of the water supply has not been to the benefit of the consumers. A survey has shown that private companies generally provide their services at higher cost than public companies.[36] The alternative, however, may be no service at all, as the inadequate sewage treatment in many French cities indicates.

The problem of extending public sewage plants pertains especially to the communes. It is a question not just of lack of commitment to water pollution control, but also of a lack of financial resources. The heavily indebted communes must contribute at least 20 percent of the necessary investment, and it is quite difficult to convince the communes to do so.[37] It must be recalled that 90 percent of the French communes have fewer than 2,000 inhabitants, and their individual share of public tax revenue is, even after Mitterrand's decentralisation reform, insignificant.[38] Little more than 30 percent of their limited income derives from local taxes, with the remainder provided through block grants and specific-purpose programmes from the state. State subsidies and loans are numerous and complex; in 1979, fifty separate types of specific grants were operated by ten ministries. The 1988 annual report of the Court of Accounts noted that state financial assistance to the local authorities was massive, highly complex, not very coherent, distributed according to unclear criteria and inadequately monitored.[39]

If a commune or a local water authority is unable to undertake adequate sewage treatment, the alternative is to pay the levy. However, local authorities already charge users for water supply and sewer systems, so that paying the levy does not greatly increase the total water bill. According to a national survey, the water pollution levy accounts for only 6 percent of the total water bill on average, and this extra cost may be included in the water bill in advance.[40]

Concern among the French population about water pollution problems has not been any less than in the other countries in this study, and the French have certainly not been satisfied with the results of the water pollution control policy. In 1983, 71 percent stated that France was 'rather badly' equipped to control water pollution.[41] The failure of the French communes must be interpreted in terms of the absence of institutional reform of local authorities in France, and the preference for a centralised state. If one prefers centralisation, one must question the wisdom in decentralising important environmental services. During the current reform of the Water Act, the question was raised whether the river basin agencies should be permitted to take over responsibility for technical services as well, but this idea was dropped again. Clearly, institutional conflicts explain the mediocre condition of public sewage treatment facilities.

Summary
The most important function of the French water pollution levy has been to create revenue. The pure price signal from the levy has been modest. Nevertheless, the levy has had an impact on discharges from industry. In relation to public sewage plants, the levy

has not been very effective with regard to reductions in the pollution load. Even though a bonus is offered to communes that reduce pollution, many of them prefer to pay the levy. Rather, it is the funds offered for river contracts that have promoted public sewage treatment.

Technological responses

Since 1987, increasing attention has been paid to cleaner technologies, but the general picture is still marked by a few prestige projects rather than large-scale application. Very early on, some firms, helped by public funds, changed their production processes so as to limit emissions. A wood fibre factory in the Adour–Garonne region used cleaner technologies to reduce its discharges by 99 percent as early as 1973, but, in spite of the well-developed French water industry and the presence of considerable know-how, investment in cleaner technologies has generally been at a minimum.[42] Of environmental protection investment in industry, less than 10 percent has been allocated for cleaner technologies. Since total environmental investment account for 2–3 percent of total industrial investment, the result is that French investment in cleaner technologies represents less than 0.3 percent.[43]

The trends vary greatly from sector to sector. Interest in cleaner technologies has been most significant in the chemical industry, where 35 percent of all investment for this purpose has been undertaken, and this line of thinking has prevailed since the early 1980s. Since the mid-1980s, investment in cleaner technologies has also been undertaken in the paper and pulp industry, in tanneries and in the electro-plating industry.

The river basin agencies have started to fund the innovation of cleaner technologies. Support is given as low-interest credits, and may comprise up to 70 percent of such investments. In AFB Seine–Normandie, the chemical industry has been the main recipient of this funding, but the electro-plating industry has also received such support. In the latter, however, funding has primarily been provided for the application of an already developed cleaner technology, with consequent limited innovative spin-offs. In the new five-year intervention programme of AFB Seine–Normandie, it is planned that 30 percent of all waste water funds will be spent on projects with cleaner technologies.[44]

Most of French industry regards cleaner technologies with scepticism. In particular, the smaller and middle-sized companies with limited means for research and development are far away from such thoughts. The large water companies, Compagnie Générale des Eaux (CGE) and Lyonnaise, on the other hand, have undertaken extensive research into traditional water pollution technologies.[45] The exceptionally strong position of these firms is backed by the privatisation of water supply and sewage treatment, as well as by the French provision of water supply systems to former African colonies. The eco-industrial complex in France is thus quite well established, and CGE is the second largest company in the country, with an annual turnover of more than Fr 50 billion. The predominance of traditional end-of-pipe technologies in French industry appears to be supported by the presence of strong suppliers of such technologies.

Conclusions

The administrative system of the French surface water pollution regulation is extremely complicated, something admitted by most French people. On the one hand, a formal system of institutions, laws and plans has been established; on the other hand, these have been applied in a fashion quite far from the intentions.

France does not represent a 'true' case of integrated water management, although the existence of river basin agencies provides a loose framework for a more co-ordinated effort. Nevertheless, the continued reliance on local authorities causes fragmentation of water management activities, and it is therefore perhaps not so surprising that the general performance of public water pollution control is somewhat mediocre.

The regional river basin agencies, while formally autonomous, have seen their sovereignty reduced. The Ministries of Finance and of the Environment in particular have challenged their status as independent decision-making bodies. The river basin agencies reflect the dilemmas of French centralism, and there have been numerous measures to control the river basin agencies and to gain influence over their priorities, e.g. by sector and river contracts. However, the lack of mandatory standards, poorly staffed *département*-level environmental administrations and the shortcomings of the communes have led the institutions and water pollution levies of the 1964 Act to become the most significant policy instruments.

Without the activities of the river basin agencies and the introduction of the financial instruments, the results would probably
have been even more mediocre than is the case. It is worth recall-
ing that French industry has in fact reduced its organic discharges
by 35 percent, but that result has been achieved mainly through
earmarking revenue and using sector contracts.

However, the very poor state of public sewage treatment demonstrates that the levies have generally been too low to induce
sufficient action. Generally, the levy has been a fund-raising instrument that has not offset much more than could be financed
out of the levy itself. Regarding cleaner technologies, the French
experience is not very promising. Even though France is renowned
for its technical know-how, there are indications that it may face
serious problems as environmentally friendly technology becomes
a new parameter of competition.

According to the Plan National de l'Environnement, approved
in 1991, total environmental investment is to be tripled in the
1990s, and investment in the water sector will still account for
approximately 50 percent of this. The plan states frankly that
France has lagged fifteen years behind Germany, the Netherlands
and Denmark. It will, of course, not be inexpensive to keep up
with these countries. This seems to be the French ambition, at
least if the Plan National and other French statements are to be
taken seriously.[46]

As outlined in the Plan National de l'Environnement, the Ministry of the Environment has been strengthened. Its staff will be
tripled, it is provided with its own branch agencies at the
département level and the Water Act has been amended to meet the
new challenges. Furthermore, protection of surface waters has been
allocated its own section in the ministry. Yet, if France does not
solve the problems of the communes, it will face serious problems
in implementing its policy. If the communes do not have sufficient
financial autonomy to respond to increased levies, France might
find itself replicating an experience comparable to that of the
previously 'planned' economies, where effluent charges were in
fact applied but neither companies nor local authorities were able
to respond to them, simply because they were embedded in the
institutional constraints of the command economy.*

---

* The French experience will, of course, not be similar. However, as Wolf
Biermann once said, 'If something is identical, you cannot compare it.'

Notes

1   Kneese and Schultze (1975); OECD (1989c).
2   Hayward (1982); Lorrain (1991); *Hydro+ (International Water Review)* (1991).
3   OECD, *OECD Environmental Data* (1991); Petschow et al. (1990).
4   *Annales des Mines* (1988), 18.
5   Noël (1991).
6   Bennett (1992).
7   Interview with Thierry Lavoux, Director, Institut pour une Politique Européenne de l'Environnement, 11 October 1991, Paris, Also Larrue (1992).
8   Wright (1989).
9   WHO (1954); Johnson and Brown (1976b).
10 Johnson and Brown (1976b), 35ff.
11 Nicolazo (1989), 31–7.
12 Loi no. 64–1245, see *Journal Officiel de la République Française* (1981, 1982). For a more detailed description of the law, see Nicolazo (1989); Johnson and Brown (1976b); Bower et al. (1981); Despax and Coulet (1982); Holm (1988); Wulff (1988).
13 Nicolazo (1989), Chapter 3; Hansen (1991).
14 Buchot (1991).
15 Interview with Claude Truchot, Deputy Director, Division of Water Quality, Ministry of the Environment, 24 October 1989, Paris; Truchot (1989).
16 See Nicolazo (1989), 113.
17 Interview with Georges Pauthe, Chef du Service Industries Chimiques et Métallurgiques, Agence de Bassin Seine–Normandie, 11 October 1991, Nanterre.
18 For instance, interview with Thierry Lavoux (1991); Wulff (1988); Johnson and Brown (1976b).
19 Lalonde (1990); OECD, *OECD Environmental Data* (1991).
20 See Ministère de l'Environnement, *L'Etat de l'environnement* (1990), 119.
21 Nicolazo (1989), 84.
22 Ministère de l'Environnement, *Données économiques sur l'environnement* (1981), 29.
23 Interview with Georges Pauthe (1991).
24 Interview with Claude Truchot (1989).
25 Holm (1988).
26 Wulff (1988).
27 Lavoux (1986).
28 According to Nicolazo (1989), 7.

29 Ministère de l'Environnement, *Données économiques de l'environnement* (1982), 28–9.

30 Harrison and Sewell (1980).

31 Wulff (1988).

32 Johnson and Brown (1976b), 61.

33 Larrue (1992), 10; Ministère de l'Environnement (1987), 101.

34 Agence de l'Eau Seine–Normandie (1991).

35 Interview with Eric Kepes, Chef du Service Mesures et Redevances, Agence de Bassin Seine–Normandie. 8 October 1991, Nanterre.

36 Lorrain (1991).

37 Interview with Eric Kepes (1991).

38 Ministère de l'Intérieur (1991).

39 Wright (1989), 312–15.

40 Direction de l'eau et de la prévention des pollutions et des risques (1989).

41 See Eurobarometer, *Public Opinion in the European Community* (1982, 1986, 1988); and Crampes, Mir and Moreaux (1984), 387.

42 Ministère de l'Environnement (1978), 17.

43 Ministère de l'Environnement, *L'État de l'environnement* (1989).

44 Interview with Georges Pauthe (1991); Agence de l'Eau Seine–Normandie (1991).

45 Drouet (1987).

46 See: Lalonde (1990, 1991); Tavernier (1990); Romi (1991).

6

Germany: The sector guideline approach*

Introduction

Pollution of surface waters was not one of the most urgent environmental issues in Germany in the 1980s, nor is it likely to become so in the near future. In 1991, *Die Welt* reported that after twenty years' effort the Rhine is 'breathing' again, and contains more than 40 different fish species, including trout and salmon.[1] Not water pollution, but acid rain, dioxins and hazardous waste pushed environmental issues to the top of the political agenda in Germany in the mid-eighties. The pollution of the Rhine by the Sandoz incident in 1986 proved how vulnerable Germany was to transboundary pollution, and thus intensified the international theme in the environmental discussion. Among the national water pollution problems, the deterioration of ground- and drinking water due to leakage of nitrates from agriculture and pesticides has been the primary focus of interest.

Founded upon initiatives from the early part of this century, and strengthened by the environmental reform of the 1970s, water pollution control of surface waters has been an area of routine policy, neither disturbed nor severely altered by sudden political initiatives. Still, this single area has been privileged with 30 percent of industrial environmental investment and more than 66 percent of public environmental investment. Germany perhaps has Europe's strongest tradition of water pollution control. The

* Fieldwork for this chapter was largely undertaken during a stay at the Wissenschaftszentrum Berlin in the autumn of 1990. For helpful comments on various drafts I would especially like to thank Dr Heinrich Pehle of Erlangen-Nürnberg University and Bernd Mehlhorn, Umweltbundesamt. The responsibility for any errors or omissions remains mine. For financial support I am grateful to DAAD (Deutscher Akademischer Austauschdienst).

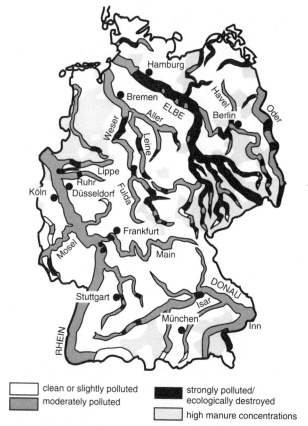

Figure 6.1 Water quality map of Germany

heavily industrialised Ruhr valley was the cradle of the sewage treatment technologies around the turn of the century. The immense public investment schemes of the thirties also included completion of sewage treatment, e.g. for Greater Berlin.

In 1960, international co-operation began to protect the valuable Lake Constance, on Germany's border with Austria and Switzerland. Soon afterwards the International Committee on the Protection of the Rhine also gained official status. At the time of the amendments to the Water Household Act in 1976, many German cities and municipalities had already acted to ensure treatment of point sources through sewage plants. Surface water pollution became an issue only in connection with international problems such as the sudden death of North Sea seals in 1988 or the pollution of the river Elbe by the former German Democratic Republic.*

German surface water policy is based on an emission limit principle and is unique for its emphasis on uniform industrial sector guidelines. It is mainly a command-and-control scheme, but economic incentives are used as a supplementary instrument. The interesting aspect of German surface water policy is the delicate interplay between guidelines and economic incentives that has been designed. Yet German industry has undergone only few structural changes since the 1976 amendments to the Water Household Act with regard to water pollution, and the complicated water regulations appear to have caused a persistent implementation deficit.

The context of water pollution control policy

Environmental background

Germany is highly industrialised, even compared with its neighbour countries. There is a very large concentration of heavy industry (chemical and metallurgical), which produces considerable volumes of liquid effluents. Among the members of the European Community, it is in Germany that industry accounts for the highest share of employment and economic activity. With its high population density of 220 inhabitants/km², pollution control is subject to considerable concern. The Ruhr region used to be the industrial heartland of Germany, with more than one-third of its total industrial capacity. In the last ten to fifteen years, the mining and steel industries have been declining, and the southern *Länder*, especially Baden–Württemberg and Bavaria, have had the highest growth rates.

Germany has limited access to the sea, and industrial centres are located along its rivers. Perhaps one of the reasons for the early priority given to water pollution control is the interwoven and vulnerable system of rivers and water resources. The main river, the Rhine, passes northwards through the country and receives several large tributaries: Maine, Moselle, Neckar, Ruhr, Emscher

---

* Serious problems of water pollution have been revealed in the five new *Länder*. This study concerns only the policy implemented in the western *Länder* from 1970 to 1990.

and Lippe. In fact, 80 percent of all domestic and industrial waste water is discharged directly into the Rhine or reaches it through the tributaries.

Although precipitation is high, groundwater reserves are not sufficient to meet the demands for water supply. Of the drinking water delivered by public water works, 27 percent stems from treated surface water. There are potential conflicts not only between industries and water supply companies, but also between industries upstream and downstream on the same river.

Administrative background

Germany was very late in establishing a federal environmental ministry and in appointing its first environmental minister. In 1974, as a consequence of the first pollution control programme, Umweltbundesamt (the Environmental Protection Agency) was set up under the auspices of the Ministry of the Interior. However, it was not until 1986, in an initiative taken as a direct response to the Chernobyl accident, that a separate Ministry for the Environment was established. Germany is a federal state, and the delayed institutionalisation reflected the fact that the German constitution formally did not vest the federal authorities with much more than framework legislative power before 1970, while there has been an ongoing conflict over the extent of federal supervision of the *Länder*.

According to the 1949 constitution, certain tasks rest almost exclusively with the *Länder*, and this applied to most environmental issues. In the early 1970s the constitution was changed, and the issues of air pollution, noise and nature conservation were transferred to the federal level. With regard to water pollution, however, there was resistance. Water policy is still a matter of almost exclusive *Länder* competence, although the federal level has in practice succeeded in passing fairly detailed framework legislation. However, the framework legislation must be transformed into *Länder* laws by the individual *Länder* parliaments, causing both delays in implementation and differences in the final versions owing to amendments.

The constitutional restraint on federal environmental policies was clearly perceived when the government wrote its first environmental programme in 1971. Several attempts were in fact made in the early 1970s to ensure the necessary majority to change the constitution and assign competence in water policy to the federal level. However, the proposed changes were blocked by the Bundesrat (the German second chamber), which consists of delegates from the *Länder* governments, in order to retain their competence in pollution control. The *Länder* have established their own environmental ministries, and their autonomy in water policy necessitates extensive consultations between the federal authorities and the *Länder*. Germany is traditionally said to practise a rather imposing policy style, but the constitutional problem of water policy has created a situation with more consultation than normal.

The considerable hierarchy of public authorities – from federal level to local municipality – may cause certain implementation problems, and there has been considerable concern in Germany about the possible 'implementation shortfall' in environmental policies. In the late 1970s a study published by the Council of Advisors on the Environment, an independent advisory board, highlighted significant implementation problems in most areas of environmental policy. The report was, however, prepared on the basis of experiences in the period before the Water Household Act had been amended in 1976.[2]

Historical background
The development of German water pollution control has been shaped and penetrated by constitutional problems for more than a century. In the late nineteenth century, water pollution had become severe and, from the first German federation in 1871, scientific and agricultural associations pressed for national water legislation. In 1912, Prussia, situated downstream from several large rivers and the most important state, called for negotiations on a draft for federal water legislation. There was considerable resistance from states situated upstream, and because of World War I the work was never finished. Only after the National Socialists had dissolved the *Länder* in 1934 was a new National Water Law presented, but again work stopped because of war. Consequently, until 1960 water pollution was regulated by laws passed by the individual states, most of them in the period 1878–1913.

In 1949, German industry, which had opposed a national water law in 1912, was ripe for a reform of water management. Because of the fragmented development, more than 119 laws and circulars regulated various parts of the reorganized German *Länder*, and 70 of these applied to different stretches of just one river, the Rhine:

The division and heterogeneity of water legislation has always proved to be a restraint on business life. This condition will continue . . . indefinitely, if the *Länder* do not decide, in the interests of a common law, to abstain from such regulations, which are not absolutely necessary due to specific regional circumstances.[3]

Because of the constitutional restraints, the conflict of competence caused the negotiations to make slow progress, in spite of the fact that surface waters were too polluted in some areas even for industrial purposes. The Water Household Act was finally passed in 1957 on the lowest political denominator, and was to become effective in March 1960. Despite the lack of federal legislation, the *Länder* laws had given water pollution control an early start in Germany. In 1963, approximately 50 percent of the population was served by sewage plants, and secondary treatment was provided to three out of four of these citizens. The problem was clearly that the requirements for industrial discharges were so different in various parts of Germany. The 1957 Act provided little more than a loose framework for federal water pollution control, and it was not until 1976 that the sector guideline approach was introduced. Curiously, the principle of uniform industrial sector guidelines had also been included in Prussia's 1912 proposal for a national water act, but it appears to have been almost a century of pollution control experiences, rather than a Prussian taste for order, that finally caused the introduction of this principle.

The water pollution control laws[4]

The Water Household Act
The foundations of modern environmental legislation were laid down in the early 1970s, during Willy Brandt's social–liberal coalition. The starting signal was the government's 1971 environmental programme, which outlined a comprehensive policy for pollution control and stated three general principles to govern its environmental policy: the prevention principle, the 'polluter pays' principle, and the co-operation principle. Whereas declarations on co-operation and 'polluter pays' were quite common in similar policy statements from other countries, the strong emphasis on prevention was perhaps somewhat unusual in the early 1970s. However, it did not result in a very strong emphasis on prevention in the subsequent environmental laws, but it probably contributed

to a higher awareness of the prevention approach in Germany. Generally pollution control did not receive much attention from 1973 to 1982, a period now regarded as the 'Ice Age' of German environmental policy. Comparisons between the ambitious 1971 programme and actual policies formed a straightforward starting point for the critique raised by the German Greens in the early 1980s.[5]

As an offshoot of the 1971 programme, a revision of the Water Household Act was prepared by the government, and passed as the fourth set of amendments in 1976. The 1957 Act had established a permit scheme, which required that discharges be licensed by the public authorities, but the innovative contribution of the fourth set of amendments was to establish a common set of guidelines for such permits. Besides amending the Water Household Act, a law on detergents was also introduced. The Detergent Act, the result of an individual proposal in the Bundestag, required producers of detergents to reduce the phosphorus content in their products. In contrast with most other European countries, there has been very little emphasis on the quality of the receiving waters. Germany practises an emission approach, which implies that common guidelines are set for the discharge of effluents.

The most important change of the 1976 Water Household Act was the inclusion of article 7a, which enables federal authorities to prescribe maximum emission standards for each industrial sector (so-called 'Mindestanforderungen'). The insertion of article 7a was a confirmation of the practice since 1970, when so-called 'LAWA-normalwerte' had been issued (LAWA stands for Länderarbeitsgemeinschaft Wasser), but the fourth set of amendments to the Water Household Act made such guidelines mandatory. Initially, the sector standards were set with reference to the principle of 'allgemein anerkannte Regeln der Technik' (generally accepted technological standards – GATS). The GATS principle refers to a control technology that is the 'general' norm within the industrial sector in question. The setting of such a standard is open to negotiation, and in 1986 the fifth amendments of the Water Household Act, largely in accordance with the demands for more pollution control, abandoned GATS and introduced the principle of 'Stand der Technik' (best available technology – BAT), which increased the demands of the control technologies to the level of the 'best available'. In theory, BAT means that the firm with the most advanced control technology will set the norm for its sector, since the guidelines will prescribe the norm on the basis of the best available technology. However, the BAT principle does not apply to all pollutants; organic pollutants are covered by the GATS principle.

Because the federal level has only framework law competence, each emission standard must obtain formal approval in the Bundesrat. The formal approval follows extensive consultations among the *Länder* and the federal authorities. Although experts and officials play a key role in the setting of standards, the German policy is unique in the sense that a political body determines the final technical standards that are set. The setting of national emission standards ensures, at least in principle, that the *Länder* do not compete with each other by setting lax standards to attract industry, and that a firm cannot obtain a less restrictive licence by moving from one *Land* to another.

The federal Waste Water Levy Act

The fourth set of amendments to the Water Household Act were supposed to have included a section on a new waste water levy. In its 1974 report, the Council of Advisors on the Environment had strongly recommended the use of economic incentives to decrease pollution, rather than traditional regulatory measures. The wording of the Council was quite clear on this matter, and deserves to be quoted:

The instruments previously applied, primarily traditional regulations, cannot eliminate, even if tightened, the widespread practice of saving money by postponing or abstaining from sewage treatment. As long as self-interest is lacking, many obstacles may appear. The 'polluter pays' principle and the ensuing charges would not just provide the missing incentives for pollution control. If correctly applied they would also make it possible to reduce total costs.[6]

The Council recommended that the permit procedure not be relied upon as the basic instrument, but to use this merely as a supplement to a waste water levy that was to become the cornerstone of the Water Household Act. The Council also found that a projected levy of DM 40 per 'damage unit' would be too low to have an impact on discharges. However, the levy became a controversial political issue, since the *Land* of Bavaria questioned the federal competence to establish such a levy. As a result, the issue of the levy was removed from the Water Household Act and was passed as a separate act, the federal Waste Water Levy Act (Abwasserab-gabengesetz – AbwAG). The recommendation of the Council was reversed, and the levy instead became a supplementary instrument to the licences. The initial rate of the levy was set at only DM 12 and the implementation postponed for five years to 1981. However, from 1981 to 1986 the levy was gradually to be increased to DM 40 per 'damage unit'.

The levy applies to direct discharges – by industry as well as by municipal sewage treatment plants. Indirect discharges, i.e. from households and industry to the public sewers, are not subject to the levy since it is calculated only for the amount of pollution that is discharged after public treatment. The basic unit for determining the levy is a special German 'damage unit' calculated on the basis of various pollution parameters listed in an annex to the Act. The most important parameters are organic pollution and certain heavy metals.* The levy is an earmarked levy, and is collected and disposed of by the *Länder* authorities.

The AbwAG has been changed several times. In 1986, simultaneously with the revision of the Water Household Act, some exemptions were inserted, and the incentive of the levy was connected directly to the new technological guideline principle of best available technology.[7] Since 1986 the levy can be reduced by 80 percent if a firm is able to comply with the 'best available technology standard'. Also since 1986 municipal authorities extending or constructing sewage works are eligible for three years' exemption from the levy, provided that the new plants are able to meet the guidelines. The amendment was designed to meet the criticism that the levy puts a strain on the municipal treasury in a period of conversion. Furthermore, the amendments even allowed for complete annulment of the levy in certain circumstances. Generally, the 1986 revision was perceived as a downgrading of the waste water levy.[†8]

---

* One damage unit represents: 50 kg chemical oxygen demand (COD), 25 kg nitrogen, 3 kg phosphorus, 2 kg organic halogens, 20 g mercury (Hg), 100 g cadmium, 500 g chromium, 500 g nickel, 500 g lead (Pb), or 1,000 g zinc per year.

† The set of amendments passed in 1990 removed some of the most serious exceptions and added new parameters to the calculation of damage units. Phosphorus and nitrogen are now included, which has to do with the new guidelines for public treatment of waste water. Furthermore, it was decided to increase the levy to DM 60 by the end of 1992 and to DM 90 by 1998.

The levy is often praised in German literature on environmental economics as the country's first environmental levy, but most authors do not ascribe a strong regulatory effect to the levy.[9] The most important instrument in German surface water policy has been the sector guideline and the issued permits. As such, German water policy rests on a traditional 'command-and-control' philosophy, and the German version, with its emphasis on national emission guidelines, seems even more rigorous than the average approach.

A first account

Public treatment

The Water Household Act of 1957 was the starting point for the extension of treatment plants to cover most public discharges in Germany. From 1960 to 1970 more than DM 10 billion were invested in sewage works, and extensions continued during the 1970s. In 1976, at the time of the fourth set of amendments to the Water Household Act, public sewerage was in fact already widespread in most of West Germany. Approximately 75 percent of the population was connected to public sewerage, and more than 80 percent of the sewage units provided biological treatment of waste water – a high standard compared with Germany's neighbours at that time.

From 1975 to 1987 the share of the population connected to sewerage rose to 90 percent, and mechanical and biological treatment was extended with more advanced techniques, especially phosphorus removal. Since the early seventies, public investment in the water sector has remained at a fairly stable level of DM 5–7 billion per year, with perhaps something of a 'recession' in the early 1980s.[10]

Industry

Between 1977 and 1987, industrial discharges of waste water, including water for cooling purposes, declined by 14 percent, while production increased by 14 percent. However, if one excludes cooling water and looks at the category of production-specific waste water, discharges declined by 20 percent in the same decade (see Figure 6.2).

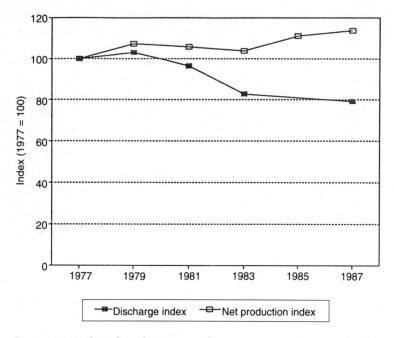

Figure 6.2 Index of production-specific waste water and net production index for manufacturing industry and mining (1977 = 100)

Unfortunately, the national statistics tell us nothing about the pollution load, so the above figures are all based on cubic metres. However, figures from the *Land* of Nordrhein–Westfalen for the period 1981–87 show that organic pollution also decreased.[11] The industrial load decreased by around 30 percent but, since Nord-rhein–Westfalen includes the Ruhr district, the decrease must be seen as partly a result of the phasing out of sunset industries. Still, the German account of the achievements pertaining to in–house facilities is generally optimistic:

Although industrial production has increased considerably, the amount of industrial sewage has been decreasing for many years. The decrease is due to the introduction of water saving processes and of water recycling. The most important advice to industry and the general trend is towards the retention of pollutants in industrial processes. Sewage treatment down to the effluent standard is quite often so costly that changes in the industrial processes are more economical.[12]

German industry only to a limited extent relies on public sewage plants for treatment of its discharges. Only 18 percent of the production-specific waste water is discharged into public sewers; 82 percent is either discharged directly or passes through an industrial treatment plant. Five thousand German firms, 10 percent of German industry, have their own treatment facilities, but they nevertheless account for almost 70 percent of the waste water. In the decade studied, mechanical treatment was gradually phased out and replaced by biological and advanced treatment techniques. Industry's investment in pollution control declined in the late seventies, but has since increased dramatically, reaching nearly 8 percent of total industrial investment. Investment in water pollution control has been fairly constant, at around 1.0–1.5 percent during the entire period.

The policy instruments at work

The sector guidelines
Since the sector guidelines of 1976 have been the cornerstone of German water pollution control, it is remarkable that the first guidelines based on GATS were so long in being enacted. From the passing of the Water Household Act in 1976 it took four more years before the first sector guidelines were approved. Since 1980, however, more than 50 sector guidelines have been issued. Until 1980 the authorities were not completely without instructions, but could rely on the preliminary LAWA standards. Following the 1986 revisions of the Water Household Act, revised guidelines, all based on the BAT principle, had to be negotiated. In a sense the process had to start all over again.

The reason for the lengthy procedures in issuing sector guidelines has to do with the negotiation procedure. A negotiation committee is formed under the auspices of the Ministry for the Environment, and contains members of all the *Länder* as well as a single representative of industry. However, the positions of the *Länder* are often connected to the importance of the sector in question in the particular *Länder* and, as such, the representatives substitute for the moderate industrial representation. The different importance of industrial sectors in the different *Länder* explains why particular representatives see dragging their feet in the negotiations as being in their interests. This bargaining game was one of the reasons for abandoning the previous GATS scheme, as the term 'generally accepted' was obviously open to differing interpretation. The new BAT principle leaves much less discretion to the committee, since it is simply the 'best' within a sector that sets the standard.[13]

Generally, this principle creates a dynamic situation. A firm that chooses to go ahead and introduce new control technologies will also be sure to benefit. Furthermore, the Umweltbundesamt has introduced a modest subsidy for pilot projects to persuade firms to innovate. Since the mid-1980s, 44 projects have received a total grant of DM 197 million. Within a sector, introducing a new technology is not always welcomed, since this imposes extra costs on all other firms in applying the same technology. In 1990 a small Danish petrol service station company extended its activities to northern Germany, causing annoyance among German petrol stations because it owned an oil spill control technique that was regarded as a BAT solution, and thus imposed additional costs on its competitors.

Officials in the Umweltbundesamt claim that the implementation period of the sector guidelines is around two years.[14] This does not mean that all firms must meet the requirements within this period, but only that the officials at the *Länder* level have begun to apply the guidelines in their permits.

Uniform targets for water quality

The fact that the principles of the Water Household Act are so different from the European Community directives has brought Germany into conflict with the European Commission.[15] The water directives of 1976 require that member states designate their surface waters and set targets for water quality standards. Germany opposed the directives even in the decision-making process, primarily because of a general incompatibility of the EC approach with the German emission approach. It was stated that the EC requirements would be too strict, but they were also criticised for their relationship to the biological indicator of fish. It was stated that Germany 'does not wish to have imposed on it a water protection policy through the intermediary of fish'.[16]

Some attempts were commenced to meet the EC requirements, but the planning requirements were generally a stepchild of German surface water policy.[17] Germany actually neglected the directives until the late 1980s, which demonstrates the persistence of the German policy style. Proceedings against Germany at the European Court were withdrawn following consultations in 1988, when Germany reached compliance by the decision to classify all the surface waters of all *Länder* in one single category – the so-called Gewässergüteklasse II. In this way Germany managed to achieve compliance without seriously changing its regulatory policies.

Apart from the historical experiences, the preference for a sector guideline emission principle must be understood as a feasible solution in a country with limited access to the sea. Strict application of a water quality principle in Germany might have been more difficult to manage in cases where discharges, even in the case of best available technology, clearly exceed the assimilative capacity of the environment.[18]

Authorities in water management
The task of ensuring public treatment of waste water has in practice been divided among a number of authorities. In the three city *Länder*, it has been a task for the *Land* administration itself. In the eight other West German *Länder*, water management has generally been a task for the municipalities. However, in the Ruhr district (covering large parts of the *Land* Nordrhein–Westfalen) and in Saarland the task has historically been delegated to special 'Wasserverbände' (water boards).

The first of these water boards, the Emschergenossenschaft along the river Emscher, was established in 1904. It was the result of a court decision that prohibited the discharge from certain upstream towns of waste water, which had contaminated the drinking water of other towns downstream. The water boards were set up to try to solve the problem, and the method became to levy industry and towns for their discharge of waste water and to use the funds for treatment works. Today, eleven water boards still function in some of Germany's most heavily polluted areas.[19]

In most of Germany, however, it is the municipalities that are responsible for sewage. The dominant mode of organization is the municipal authorities (Regie-Betriebe), which means that the services are run as an integrated part of the municipal administration. Recently, however, some authorities have created autonomous authorities (Eigen-Betriebe), independent municipal utilities that have a larger degree of autonomy in relation to city authorities and the municipal assemblies. In 1988, for example, *Land* Berlin created the Berlin waterworks as an independent company for both sewage and water supply.[20]

Subsidies

In principle public sewage is financed by user fees, but a substantial share of the investments as well as some of the operating costs have been financed through direct and indirect subsidies, and virtually all public authorities seem to have contributed. The municipalities have covered approximately 13–18 percent of the operating costs by means of the general tax revenue. This is only the local subsidy, however, since the federal authorities, and more importantly the *Länder*, have also provided subsidies for investment in public sewage works.

In the period 1976–88, municipalities invested more than DM 67 billion in sewage works while receiving subsidies of approximately DM 16 billion, or 22 percent of total investment. The direct subsidy from the federal level was modest, less than DM 1 billion, and was focused on special programmes to control pollution of the Bodensee and the Rhine; it ended around 1981. At the federal level, too, the European Recovery Programme has been used to back investments, with subsidies and loans of more than DM 5 billion from 1976 to 1988. Still, the *Länder* have been the most important source of subsidies. The subsidy from the *Länder* since 1981 has been partially offset by revenue from the waste water levy, which has accounted for DM 3–4 million of a total *Länder* subsidy of more than DM 10 billion.

The fine-meshed net of subsidies follows from the 'fiscal equalization principle' (Finanzausgleich Prinzip) of the constitution, which seeks to provide citizens everywhere with equal levels of public services (e.g. schools and public transport). Most local services are supported by numerous subsidies from the federal and *Land* level in Germany. As regards pollution control, however, the subsidies clearly work to violate the 'polluter pays' principle. The subsidies are both general and specific. Specific infrastructure grants from the *Länder*, to which sewage works are subject, have been criticised for distorting the priorities of the local authorities. When local authorities subsidise sewage works to keep user fees low, however, it may simply be inertia, to retain or to attract new business, since the business tax (Gewerbesteuer) is the most important local tax. As a consequence of both local, *Land* and federal subsidies, it is estimated that German user fees for waste water treatment cover only 65–75 percent of the true costs of pollution control.*[21]

International agreements

Although not prescribed in the Water Household Act, international agreements play an important role in German water policy. Generally, it has been in Germany's interest to limit transboundary pollution, which is most pronounced from France (the Rhine) and the former German Democratic Republic (the Elbe), but with practically all its other neighbour countries Germany has negotiated environmental matters either directly or through various multilateral conventions.[22]

The most successful agreement has probably been the Lake Constance convention, signed by the riparian countries of Austria, Switzerland and the FRG. In order to protect this renowned lake, a wide-reaching agreement was concluded in 1960 to eliminate phosphorus discharges. This agreement also became the framework for innovation of this particular treatment technique. While the general German (and international) standard for phosphorus elimination is 1.0 mg/l, the Bodensee commission recently lowered its standard to 0.3 mg/l for large works.[23]

The International Committee on the Protection of the Rhine, which gained official status in 1963, has been less successful, especially because of resistance from France. The Sandoz incident in 1986 led to some action, but in practice attention has switched to the North Sea convention, where Germany has been among the more active participants.[24] In spite of numerous conventions with its neighbours, their impact on Germany's domestic water pollution control has been modest. In the near future they will probably provide a more important incentive for control with a number of chemicals.

* An alternative, but curious, approach to low-cost provision of sewage treatment was practised in West Berlin, where almost half the city's waste water used to be exported and treated by works in the former GDR at a very favourable price. The economic gains from this export of sewage are difficult to calculate, but could be nearly 80 percent of corresponding West German prices.

The impact of the levy

Incentive structure

The waste water levy has been imposed since 1981 and in some *Länder* only since 1982 or 1983. The passing of the federal Waste Water Levy Act in 1976 provided an exceptionally long warning period enabling industry and public authorities to familiarise themselves with the guidelines, and to consider measures to reduce pollution rather than paying the levy. Several studies were carried out by the Umweltbundesamt to estimate the considerations and reactions of the regulated.[25] One study showed that the levy accounted for less than 2 percent of total annual costs in all industrial sectors except one. Nevertheless, the warning period was used by the political opposition in parliament to commence new offensive movements against the levy, and, just before it was to be introduced, proposals were in fact presented to abandon the law.

Municipalities   For the public authorities the levy is meant as an incentive to make them comply with national guidelines for sewage treatment, issued under art. 7a of the Water Household Act. Since the levy was enacted in 1976 but not implemented until 1981, it gave the municipalities a chance of achieving compliance by extending treatment.

A survey conducted in Nordrhein–Westfalen showed that, in those cases where the authority complies with the guidelines, the levy accounts for only 1–2 percent of total costs for sewers and sewage.[26] In one case where an authority did not comply, the levy accounted, however, for 10 percent of total costs. The levy is to be paid even in cases of compliance with guidelines, but the rate per damage unit is then reduced by 50 percent. If the authority performs even better than the guidelines, the levy is gradually reduced to zero.

The levy depends not only on the pollution emitted, however, but also on a statement, prior to the monitoring period, of the target value for the treatment. If an authority is careful and sets a high emission target value, it will not obtain the same reward by performing better as it would if a realistic low emission target value had been set and fulfilled. Figure 6.3 indicates the relations between target values and actual emission performance. In this

Target value (mg COD/l)	Waste water levy ('000 DM/y) (performance value)				Risk interval	
	65	100	130	140	DM	%ª
65	0	216	561	605	605	3.5
100	117	117	561	605	488	2.8
130	280	280	280	605	325	1.9

Note:
a. Percentage of total sewer costs.

Figure 6.3 Financial risk for the sewage works' manager when setting the target value (city with 45 percent industrial discharges)

particular case, the risk interval is between 1.9 and 3.5 percent of the total costs of sewage and sewers. In another case, the risk interval was found to be between 1.0 and 9.0 percent.

The levy accounts for only a small percentage of total costs, but a share of 9–10 percent in the event of non-compliance is not insignificant. If the sewage works sets a target that it is unable to meet and subsequently has to pay the levy, it will usually have to request further support from the municipal treasury. Those in charge will have a strong incentive to avoid such a situation. As a result, more than 80 percent of Germany's public works comply with the guidelines (1987 data). Of those that fail to comply, a large proportion are mechanical works, which would not be able to meet the guidelines without funds for expansion. This is a remarkable improvement from the mediocre conditions of German sewage works found by Renate Mayntz and her team in the mid-1970s.[27]

Industry To industrial dischargers, the levy is meant as an incentive to reduce discharges.* One of Germany's largest companies, BASF, is said to have paid DM 15 million in waste water levy annually.[28] During the first implementation phase, 1981–86, the

* In an illustration of the principles used to calculate the waste water levy, the Umweltbundesamt showed that a company annually discharging 84,000 m³ of waste water containing 4.2 kg of mercury and 16.8 kg of cadmium would pay a total of DM 8,388 in 1981, and DM 27,960 in 1986, when the levy had increased to DM 40/damage unit (ATV, 1982, p. 154). By respecting the sector guidelines, the firm would be able to reduce the levy by 50 percent.

annual revenue of the levy, despite successive increases, was less than expected and only moderately increasing. This reflected the fact that companies did what they could to reduce effluents.*

National evaluations

Surveys carried out by the Financial Research Institute in Cologne indicate that the mere decision to impose a waste water levy provided a warning phase that led to reactions among the regulated.[29] In 1978, 60 percent of the surveyed communities planned to improve their sewage treatment to a standard exceeding the national guidelines; 46 percent of the industrial direct dischargers were considering additional initiatives. Of the industrial pollution abatement initiatives under concurrent implementation, 65 percent were pre-treatment initiatives and 31 percent consisted of changes in the production process, preferably by establishing recirculation of process water.[30] At the beginning of 1980, 66 percent of the industrial direct dischargers were found to have implemented better treatment. In an evaluation of the levy, the Umweltbundesamt claimed that the mere collection of the levy had provided for improved transparency concerning the exact amount of water pollution, since, in order to impose the levy, discharges had to be accurately measured. This increased interest among firms and municipalities for better monitoring of discharges.[31]

Sector study

In the following, a closer look at the trends in selected industrial sectors is provided in order to estimate whether the levy has produced structural changes in German industry. Unfortunately, and much to the regret of German water experts, data have not been compiled that allow for a systematic assessment of the effects of the waste water levy on discharges.†[32] The census bureau in Wiesbaden, Statistisches Bundesamt, has compiled data on the discharges of waste water from all German firms with more than 20 employees since 1977. Since cooling water is not liable to charges, the category of production-specific waste water must be

---

* In 1984, the levy revenue accounted for DM 349 million and in 1987 for DM 478 million (Umweltbundesamt, 1989).

† While the levy is paid according to polluting damage units, the environmental statistics measure waste water in m^3. One cannot conclude very much about the pollution from the number of damage units, since firms can achieve levy reductions in cases of good technological performance.

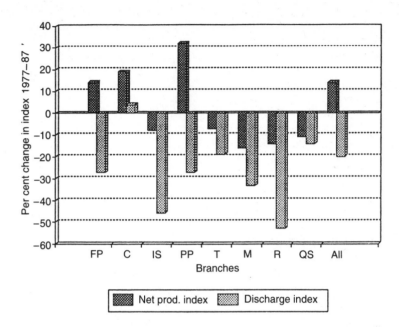

Figure 6.4 Change in discharge and net production index, 1977–87 (1977 = 100)

FP: Food processing   PP: Paper and pulp   R: Refineries
C: Chemistry   T: Textiles   QS: Quarry and soils
IS: Iron and steel   M: Mining   All: All industry

regarded as the most useful aggregate parameter to indicate the effects of the waste water levy.*

Trends Figure 6.4 depicts developments for the eight most water-intensive sectors, accounting for 85 percent of total discharges, as well as the average of all sectors. For each sector the change in production-specific waste water discharges and net production index

* Previously the measurements were published without specifying production water versus cooling water. In its 1987 compilation, the Statistisches Bundesamt specified the category of 'production-specific waste water'. Statistisches Bundesamt has for the purpose of this project helped provide data for this category for the preceding years 1977–83. It is theoretically possible to discharge exactly the same pollution load with less water. However, previous studies have shown that reductions in one water pollution parameter tend to correlate closely with reductions in other parameters and in water use (Hudson et al., 1981). Still, one must take this fact into consideration when drawing conclusions.

is shown.* While the proportion of production-specific waste water declined 20 percent in the decade 1977–87, there were remarkable differences between the sectors. The eight water-intensive sectors can be divided into three categories:

(1) *Stagnation, no de-linkage.* In one sector, quarry and soils, production declined, and the waste water discharges followed the decline very closely. Thus, the reduced discharge simply reflects the decline of the industry.

(2) *Stagnation, but de-linkage.* Four sectors – iron and steel, mining, textiles and refineries – were the typical sunset industries of the period, but were able to reduce production-specific waste water over and above the reduction reflected in the decline of the net production index. De-linkage was especially strong in the steel industry.

(3) *Growth and de-linkage.* Two industrial sectors – chemicals and paper and pulp – achieved high growth rates, while waste water discharges were stagnant (chemicals) or even declined (paper). A third sector, food provision, demonstrates a more confusing, but still similar trend. When the sugar industry, because of its unusual development, is separated from the other food-processing industries, these present moderate economic growth and at the same time reductions in waste water. The sugar industry separately shows strong de-linkage.†

Since production-specific waste water is measured in cubic metres, it is clear that the decline must be interpreted as an indicator of the application of cleaner technology processes, since, by definition, cleaner technology implies less use of water. If pollution abatement is provided merely through end-of-pipe treatment, this would not affect the amount of water used, but only the individual pollution parameters.

Figures on environmental investment do not, however, indicate any strong relationship between environmental investment and

* The development in water supply has been controlled to check for any extreme deviations between water supply and waste water. To avoid paying the levy, firms could have reclassified 'waste water' into 'cooling water', and unusual fluctuations could reflect such efforts. At the aggregate level this is not the case.

† Among nine other less water-intensive sectors, seven exhibit growth in net production combined with large decreases in discharges. For example, the synthetic fibres industry has achieved a 50 percent increase in net production and at the same time a 50 percent decrease in discharges.

pollution control. Investment for clean technology purposes has been modest, accounting for less than 15 percent of water pollution control investment. In general, total investment in cleaner technology within all sectors of pollution control accounts for approximately 1 percent of total industrial investment, and has been almost constant in recent years, despite the general increase in pollution control investment.

Zimmermann has interpreted the modest share of clean technology investment as a decline for source-related pollution control, but this conclusion is probably too pessimistic.[33] In practice it is quite difficult to specify the environmental share of a new production process with lower discharges, and the interest in specifying the cleaner technology share is apparently connected to the possible tax deductions for such investments, which serve to bias the official figures.*

The interplay of policy instruments It appears obvious that the 1976 amendments helped curb discharges from German industries, and it is curious that the decline began in 1981, precisely when the waste water levy was introduced. However, it was also around 1980–81 that the first sector guidelines were introduced, so it remains uncertain whether the levy has contributed anything to the sector guidelines, or whether the permit procedure has by itself been responsible for the development achieved.

In Figure 6.5 the relationship is shown between the de-linkage achieved in the various sectors and the regulatory system. As payment of the levy is connected to the attainment of the specific emission limits set in the sector guidelines, Figure 6.5 indicates the

---

* Especially in the three sectors with the greatest de-linkage between discharges and net production index (chemicals, paper and pulp industry and food-processing industry) clean technology investment has been moderate. Among the sunset sectors, it is particularly within the three sectors with medium de-linkage indexes (steel industry, mining and refineries) that one sees a larger share of clean technology investment. Within textiles and quarry and soils, the share of clean technology investment is more moderate, although not so insignificant as among the three growth sectors. In growth industries, the interest in achieving tax reductions by doing the paperwork to specify the cleaner technology share cannot be expected to be very great, since the technologies are probably applied for reasons other than purely environmental ones. The interest in obtaining a share in such tax deductions can be expected to be more prevalent in sunset industries, which might explain the paradox that investment in clean technologies is apparently more widespread in such sectors.

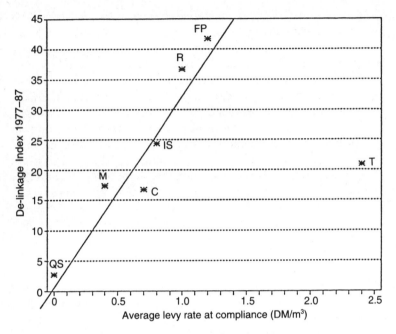

Figure 6.5 Average waste water levy rate per cubic metre discharged in compliance with the requirements of sector guidelines (COD damage parameter only) and de-linkage index, 1977–87

levy to be paid per m³ waste water discharged in accordance with the guidelines (before reductions in the levy rate).[*][34] This is, of course, only a rough indicator of the relationship between the regulatory system and the de-linkages achieved. It must be interpreted carefully since de-linkage is calculated on the basis of production-specific waste water, which is a pooled parameter, whereas the COD value is a single damage parameter, although the most significant.

Production processes are different for each sector, and the marginal costs in treatment must also be expected to differ. Hence,

* For some sectors there is more than one guideline owing to the classification of the Umweltbundesamt, and the average guideline value is used in the figure. For simplicity, it is assumed that the waste water contains only organic pollution, and the border value for mg COD/1 is converted into damage units per m³ and recalculated to DM/m³. It is not possible to depict the relationship for pulp and paper, since the guidelines are set on a different basis from mg COD/1.

there is no strong *ex ante* expectation that the relationships should all fall within the same parameter line. It appears, however, from Figure 6.5 that there is a relationship between the waste water levy pertaining to the sector guideline and the de-linkage achieved in each sector. The fact that textiles exhibit a smaller de-linkage than could be expected can be explained by the combination of an economically stagnating position and small environmental investment. In contrast, the food-processing industry has managed strong de-linkage with little investment, probably because of general economic growth and low marginal abatement costs. The relationship found in Figure 6.5 could benefit from more detailed sector studies but, as an indicator of the close interplay between guidelines and levy, it presents sufficient evidence. While the general impact on discharges remains modest, there is a general structure in the decreases that is in accordance with the incentive of the levy.

Conclusions

The present German command-and-control policy reflects the experiences of a tedious process of learning from the time when water pollution control was first introduced in the late nineteenth century. In spite of federalism and constitutional problems, national authorities have gradually tightened their hold on regional and local authorities through the use of sector guidelines. In this case it is worth noting that industry has tended to act as a political entrepreneur and has pushed for a modernised and uniform water legislation.

The uniqueness of German water pollution control policy lies not only in the sector guidelines but also in the German attempt to integrate economic incentives into a traditional command-and-control policy. Germany does not practise a true standard-pricing solution of the Baumol and Oates type, since standards are mandatory and clearly have priority over the levy. Yet the structured interplay between sector guidelines and the waste water levy seems appropriate in light of possible implementation deficits. It is obvious that the mere imposition of the levy necessitates monitoring and thus assures a minimum of surveillance from the authorities.

The pronounced improvements in water quality in the Rhine and other rivers are mainly a result of immense investments in public and industrial sewage works, supported by heavy subsidies.

The structural changes achieved in German industry, however, are hardly impressive. Only a limited number of less water-intensive production processes have been introduced, and industrial pre-treatment has been the most important response to regulation. German industry continues to treat pollution at the source, in the sense that few industries are connected to public works.

The sector standard approach is very sensitive to the updating of permits, which will have to ensure that the standards set on paper will also be implemented in practice. The immense and growing numbers of rules and guidelines are hard to digest for the local environmental inspectors. Although they seem to be quite precise, they leave often numerous legal and practical questions unanswered. The collected set of guidelines relevant to water pollution control fills six loose-leaf binders, and for each permit the inspectors have to go through a veritable labyrinth of regulations. Where toxic discharges also have to be considered, the requirements differ according to whether the waste is solid or fluid, hazardous class I, II or III, and according to flame point, quantity and recipient. According to Gertrude Lübbe-Wolf, a former water administration official and professor of law at the University of Bielefeld, the implementation shortfall is serious, and is increasing with the myriad of guidelines and regulations.[35]

The policy framework surrounding the levy is indeed also extremely complicated, but Germany in fact seems to have been quite successful in designing an incentive structure despite its rather small levy. While the waste water levy was initially controversial, in the last few years it has become an accepted instrument, which has been refined and extended. The findings indicate that the effects of the levy could very well be reinforced.

Notes

1 Thierbach (1991).
2 Mayntz et al. (1978).
3 Quoted from Wey (1982), 177, my translation.
4 Roth (1977, 1991); Salzwedel and Preusker (1982); Umwelt-bundesamt, *Act Pertaining to Charges Levied for Discharging Waste Water into Waters*, English translation.
5 For a general account of German environmental policy, see Müller (1989); Weidner (1989); Pehle (1990); Johnson and Brown (1976e).

6 Rat von Sachverständigen für Umweltfragen (1974), 62, my translation.

7 *Umwelt* (1986).

8 Benkert et al. (1990), 177–85. See Umweltbundesamt (1990a).

9 Friege (1984); Maas (1987); Bongaerts and Kraemer (1989); Bayreuther (1990); Benkert et al. (1990); Mayer-Renschhausen (1990); Nutzinger and Zahrnt (1990); Vos (1990). For a different account, see Johnson and Brown (1984).

10 Statistisches Bundesamt (1988), 157.

11 Minister für Umwelt, Raumordnung und Landwirtschaft des Landes Nordrhein–Westfalen (1989).

12 Bucksteeg (1991).

13 Interview with Bernd Mehlhorn, Scientific Official in the Waste Water Treatment Section, Umweltbundesamt, 12 October 1990, Berlin.

14 Interview with Herr Ross, Head of Waste Water Section, Umweltbundesamt, 5 October 1990, Berlin.

15 Kromarek (1986).

16 Ibid., 54.

17 Berendes (1981), 15.

18 Weizsäcker (1989), 43–5.

19 Holm (1988).

20 Kramer (1990).

21 Sources: *Bundeshaushaltsplan*, 1976–88; Statistisches Bundesamt, *Rechnungsergebnisse der kommunalen Haushalte*, 1976–88; Gemeindefinanzbericht (1989); Gunlicks (1986), 119–42.

22 Umweltbundesamt (1990b).

23 Ibid., Bucksteeg (1991).

24 Sætevik (1988).

25 Bundesminister des Innern (1977, 1983); Ewringmann, Kibat and Schafhausen (1980); Ewringmann et al. (1981); ATV (1982); Umweltbundesamt (1985a).

26 Rudolph (1989).

27 Mayntz (1978).

28 *Wirtschaftswoche* (1986).

29 Bundesminister des Innern (1977); Ewringmann et al. (1980).

30 Bundesminister des Innern (1983), 35.

31 Lühr (1984).

32 See ATV (1988).

33 Zimmermann (1988).

34 See 'Übersicht über die geltenden Verwaltungsvorschriften zu art. 7 a WHG', *Korrespondenz Abwasser*, 6 (1990), 660–7.

35 Thoms and Uebel (1992).

7

The Netherlands: The legacy of water management

Introduction

Compared with Germany and Denmark, the Netherlands was initially quite reluctant to take even the most simple steps toward water pollution control. The first Dutch sewage treatment plants were built in the 1930s, but the extension of such works proceeded slowly until the passing in 1969 of the Surface Waters Pollution Act.[1] Up to 1970, the Netherlands had achieved very little in the way of water pollution control. Situated in the Rhine delta, the Dutch were reluctant to spend money in light of the effects of transboundary pollution. In 1969, however, after many years of preparation, the Dutch parliament approved the Surface Waters Pollution Act, and the Netherlands soon emerged with Western Europe's most prominent and comprehensive scheme of water pollution control. During the first decade, the Netherlands had not only caught up with its most advanced neighbours, but had also experienced a considerable reduction in industrial emissions.

Dutch water pollution control policy assigns a key role to the use of effluent charges, and two important works by Dutch scholars have already demonstrated the importance of this policy instrument (see below). Originally Dutch environmentalists vigorously opposed the use of effluent charges and organised a boycott campaign among households against their payment. Only ten years later, however, they had to acknowledge the substantial impacts of this policy instrument and reversed their position completely.[2] Nowadays, environmental pressure groups advocate the extension of economic instruments to other fields of pollution control, and the Netherlands has recently introduced a levy on surplus manure.[3] The Dutch achievements deserve attention, not only for their environmental and technological implications but also for their cost-effectiveness.

One can hardly understand the Dutch experience, however, without clarifying the role played by the traditional water authorities. Rooted in centuries of water regulation, the autonomous water boards, together with the national water authorities, provide an exceptional infrastructure for integrated water management. It is not the environment ministry that is in charge of water pollution control, but the powerful Ministry of Transport and Public Works and its operational wing, the Rijkswaterstaat. The Rijkswaterstaat has for almost a century been a 'state within the state' in the Netherlands because of its central position in water management, and its responsibility for the implementation of Cornelius Lely's renowned plan to reclaim the Zuidersee. It is no coincidence that water quality management has been assigned to the Rijkswaterstaat along the lines of traditional water quantity management, nor that RIZA, its research institute for sewage technology, has played a key role in the supervision of water boards and manufacturing industries.

The context of water pollution control policy

Environmental background

It is said that Napoleon once justified the French occupation of the Netherlands by claiming that the low countries consist merely of sludge from the great French rivers. The Netherlands' location in the Rhine delta certainly subjects the country to transboundary water pollution, as well as to substantial air pollution exports from the adjoining, well-populated regions of neighbouring countries, such as the Ruhr district, south-east England and Flanders. Still, with 364 inhabitants per km^2, the Netherlands has the highest population density in Europe. Most of the population is compressed in the Randstad area, which consists of the adjoining metropolitan areas of Rotterdam, The Hague, Amsterdam and Utrecht, causing a population density of 700–1100 per km^2 in the central provinces.

Both main Dutch rivers have their sources outside the Netherlands, and, although the Rhine cuts through the most populated parts of the country, the pollution imported by the Rhine into the Netherlands matches the pollution discharged by the Netherlands itself. The Schelde originates in Belgium and transports untreated sewage from Antwerp and other large cities into the Dutch delta area in the south. Since the Netherlands depends on surface water for its drinking water (approximately one-third of the piped water delivered by the waterworks is produced by water from the two largest rivers, the Rhine and the Meuse), there are substantial reasons for concern about water quality. When drinking a glass of water in The Hague, one might reflect on how many times this water has been purified, used and polluted again before it reaches the Dutch waterworks.

Water has been regulated since the early Middle Ages in the Netherlands, since one-third of the country lies below sea level, and another third faces possible flooding if dikes and canals are not properly maintained. The complicated interplay between tide, surface waters and the groundwater level requires meticulous and conscious water management, and there is an unusual degree of interest attached to the way waters are managed. The thousands of canals that traverse the country are used for both traffic and irrigation purposes, and water management is not only a complicated technical task but also an intricate trade-off between different interests. Crop growers are in need of water for irrigation, but groundwater is scarce, and intrusion of saline may damage the soil if the water level is too low. The canals no longer function as open sewers, but their often stagnant waters are still vulnerable to pollution and exposed to problems of eutrophication.

Administrative background
Although the Dutch Ministry for the Environment was established in 1971, it was headed by a state secretary and did not have its own minister. Water pollution control has from the beginning been delegated to the Ministry of Transport and Public Works, whose policy has been to pursue integrated water management within the framework of its own organisation. Although a certain reluctance about environmental management has been maintained in the conservative Rijkswaterstaat, and although tensions exist between water quantity and water quality staffs, the ministry has generally been committed to the same degree of professionalism in undertaking water pollution control as in the other fields under its jurisdiction. The Ministry of Transport and Public Works has traditionally been an influential ministry, able to control the resources necessary for its responsibilities. It has a profile commanding

somewhat more respect than the joint Ministry of Housing, Planning and Environment, especially in the eyes of industrialists and local authorities. The water administration has a tradition of financial autonomy, which explains not only why effluent charges were introduced, but also why the economic ministries do not interfere in this sector.

The Netherlands is a unitary state with three administrative levels: state, provinces and municipalities. The degree of decentralisation is more limited than in the German or Scandinavian administrative tradition. Some scholars claim that Dutch centralisation dates back to the period of French occupation, and the position of the Dutch municipalities is certainly also more similar to the French tradition. They depend on the state for most of their incomes, and impose only few and modest taxes themselves. As a consequence of their weak position, the municipalities have not been assigned the task of water pollution control, although some municipalities originally had been active in this area. The twelve provinces, however, play an important role in most fields of environmental protection, but, even though water pollution control is formally a competence of the provinces, most of them have delegated their tasks to the water boards.

It is the water boards that attract most attention in this context, although they enjoy a stable position in the tranquillity of Dutch politics. The water boards also date back to the early Middle Ages, when peasants and landholders carried out drainage and reclamation of land. Their existence was once constitutionally prescribed, but it was only in 1990 that the first Act, which actually defined their tasks and made them subject to public regulation, was passed.

Traditionally, the boards have been headed by a 'Dike Count', and the members of the board elected by those who contributed financially to the activities of the board. Since water quantity management was their original task, they tend to be dominated by farmers. The public also regards them as 'peasants' clubs', or, as less sympathetic observers prefer to label them, as the 'Boer Republics' of the Netherlands.[4] The inclusion of water quality management has caused some changes in the composition of the water boards, but user groups, having traditional water quantity interests, have generally maintained a dominant role. The number of seats on the boards has been fixed among the different groups of contributors, each group having their own principles of election. The water quantity interests elect their members by open ballot, while the water quality interests are appointed by municipalities or manufacturing associations.

Although the water boards are composed of the various user groups, they cannot be regarded as truly democratic institutions. Representation has to some extent followed the principle that whoever pays decides. When the first Water Board Act was passed in only 1990, a proposal to allow environmental interest groups a seat on the boards was turned down. Furthermore, on many of the boards, such as the Rijnland water board, the inclusion of water quality management has permitted the quality users a representation of only one-third of the seats, with the other two-thirds remaining with the classical quantity users. Revenue from water quality management constitutes 75 percent of total incomes, so the 'whoever pays decides' principle is in fact grossly violated. Farmer dominance is maintained, however.[5]

In 1970, the Netherlands still had more than 800 water boards, many of them very small. The boards did not always administer a single hydrological basin, and they were often inadequately staffed. Following the conclusions by a Study Commission on Water Management, the water boards were either merged, or principal water boards, combining many smaller water boards, were established. A water basin management principle was implemented, although some of the new water boards did not overlap with the provincial administrative borders. Today twenty-seven water boards carry out water quality management.

The existence of water boards is so self-evident that most Dutch do not pay much attention to them. They are regarded as public institutions, but their functions have evolved gradually, and with due respect to local circumstances and traditions. The water boards are in fact quite wealthy and their organisation, the Union of Water Boards, is an influential interest organisation, with its own bank and an impressive headquarters in The Hague.

Historical background

As in Germany, France and Denmark, water pollution in the Netherlands was already perceived as a problem at the turn of the century. As early as 1897, the Dutch government set up a Royal Commission, which a few years later presented a complete report of the situation and a proposal for a water act, but the proposal failed to receive sufficient support. A second unsuccessful attempt was made in 1921 to pass a water act but, as a result of the initial debate on water pollution control, the government then established the scientific centre of the Rijkswaterstaat, known as RIZA, the National Institute of Sewage Technology.[6] When the government established a new study commission in the 1950s, it discovered that many of the water pollution problems had been well described in the earlier reports.

It was not until the post-war period, in response to increased industrialisation, that concrete policies took shape. In 1952 an important amendment to the Public Nuisance Act was passed that made control of industrial water pollution possible, but more important were the initiatives taken independently by the water boards. Just before the amendment of the Nuisance Act, in 1950, the small Dommel Water Board was reorganised as the Dommel River and Purification Board, in order to manage the problems of water pollution as well. During the next few years seven other water boards made a similar transition, among them the Rijnland Water Board, which covers a large part of the Randstad area. The water boards extended their traditional activities of water quantity management to include water quality. As with water quantity, quality control was also financed by user payment.

The proposal for the Surface Waters Pollution Act, first presented in the Dutch parliament in 1964, had adopted the management system that had evolved among the water boards, and prescribed a system of pollution levies to finance sewage plants. The proposal generated discussions of the effluent charge system, however. The water boards asked for the establishment of a subsidy scheme, which would allow general tax revenues to be used for water pollution control. This request was rejected by the government.[7] Long experience with water control had led the Netherlands to establish one of the first coherent systems of effluent charges in the world. Still, the decision-making process was lengthy, and it was not until 1969 that the Bill was approved by both chambers, the Act taking effect on 1 December 1970.

The Surface Waters Pollution Act[8]

The Surface Waters Pollution Act (SWPA) was the first modern environmental act passed in the Netherlands. It provided an important political starting signal for the construction of public sewage plants and required all dischargers of waste water to obtain a permit from the authorities. The SWPA made a distinction between provincial waters, to be managed by either provinces or water boards, and state waters, to be managed by the Rijkswaterstaat. In practice, the large rivers, part of the Zuiderzee/IJsselmeer and the North Sea have been classified as state waters.

Explicitly based on the 'polluter–pays' principle, the SWPA prescribes a detailed system of levies to finance water pollution control. The ruling principle of SWPA is to treat all polluters in the same way, regardless of what they discharge to. Thus, if a company or household discharges into a water course or canal, it will have to pay the same levy as if it were connected to the public sewerage system.

The 'polluter–pays' principle applies within the framework of the individual water authorities, which means that the levies differ from one authority to another. The water boards are allowed to impose levies only to cover their costs for public sewage treatment, and the amount of the levy thus depends on the historical costs and depreciation rates for water pollution control. The Rijkswaterstaat imposes levies both on water boards and on companies that discharge into state waters, but the Rijkswaterstaat does not actually operate sewage plants. Instead, revenue from the state waters is used in what appears to be a closed tax-bounty scheme to subsidise firms that undertake pollution control. In practice, considerable differences exist in the amount of the levies. In 1992 the highest levy for organic pollution, 120 guilder per inhabitant equivalent (IE), was imposed by the Het Vrije van Sluis Water Board, while the smallest levy was the state water levy for salt waters at 39.50 guilder. Rijkswaterstaat distinguishes between fresh and salt waters, but the difference is very small. The average water board levy was 60–70 guilder – an increase from 8–10 guilder in 1972. It must be noted that a separate charge is levied by the municipalities to cover the costs of sewers. The water pollution levy thus covers only treatment costs.

The levies must be paid according to the quantity of pollution discharged, although fixed values are used for calculating the levy for dwellings and smaller firms. The most important pollution parameter, with which the law operates, is that of oxygen-binding substances, but it allows for the use of other 'noxious' parameters as well. Most water authorities also impose levies on discharges of heavy metals. Recently, the Dutch parliament has decided to include phosphorus and nitrogen in the basis of the levy. According to Section 17 of the SWPA, levies may be imposed on polluters both for the purpose of public sewage treatment and for prevention. The water boards have only very seldom offered local companies subsidies for pollution control, but the companies discharging into state waters were eligible for such funds.

The administrative system of levies can be compared with a nest of Chinese boxes. A special 'insufficiency' clause of the SWPA is used as a stick against those water authorities disinclined to spend money on water pollution control. The clause states that if the waters of a local water authority are insufficiently treated, and thus transport pollution into the waters of the authority downstream, the Rijkswaterstaat may issue an insufficiency declaration. Such a declaration forces the delinquent water authority to pay levies on all pollutants leaving its waters. The clause was disputed when SWPA was passed but, although not yet applied, it cannot be neglected. It has been used in negotiations between at least one local water authority and the Rijkswaterstaat.[9]

Permits for discharges are issued by the water authorities on the basis of national standards. Unlike Germany, there is not a strict system of sector guidelines. Instead, there exists a mixed system of mandatory and optional guidelines, and with regard to organic discharges guidelines are optional. The principle of 'best available technology' applies to discharges of toxins, heavy metals, chemicals, etc., whereas discharges of organic pollution, phosphorus and nitrogen are linked to the quality of the water. When the provinces delegate water quality control to water boards, this includes the permit procedure.

There is, however, central supervision of the permit procedure through RIZA, the National Institute of Sewage Technology. According to the provisions of the SWPA, all permits must be reviewed by RIZA. The permit is issued by the relevant water authority, but RIZA gives advice, and the advice must be stated in the text of the permit, even if not followed. RIZA thus accumulates an overview of the available abatement technologies in the whole country, and can provide a firm basis for approving permits for similar firms. However, RIZA does not formally take part in the permit decision making by the local water authorities. The overview and progress in pollution control is supported by a

comprehensive planning scheme in which RIZA has been responsible for the elaboration of five-year plans, the so-called indicative
multi-year planning (IMP).

A first account

Public treatment

During the implementation of the SWPA, the Netherlands experienced a comprehensive extension of public sewage plants, offering
primarily biological treatment, and a major effort by manufacturing industries to control pollution at source. From the very beginning it was a deliberate policy to keep control of industrial pollution
separated from public sewage works, and this is also reflected in
the successful control of industrial pollution. In 1970 the total
capacity for both households and industry amounted to 8.4 million IE, compared with a population of 14 million.[10] In 1975,
despite nearly doubling capacity, only 45 percent of the Dutch
population were provided with sewerage, compared with 70 percent
in Denmark and 75 percent in Germany. Between 1975 and 1988
the share of the population provided with public sewerage increased
to 92 percent, thus surpassing western Germany.

Industry

It is in Dutch industry that one finds the most remarkable developments since the introduction of SWPA. Figure 7.1 shows the evolution of organic discharges by Dutch industry from 1965 to 1986,
and includes both discharges into public sewers as well as direct
discharges into surface waters, but without considering the effects
of public treatment on industrial discharges. Thus, the intention is
to depict the gross amount of industrial organic discharges as
compared with production output in the same period. The outcome
has been a reduction in pollutants by nearly 80 percent since
1970, while economic growth has been maintained. The impact of
the SWPA is evident from the reductions in discharges.

The policy instruments at work

The water authorities

In most parts of the Netherlands, the tasks of water quality management and construction of sewage plants are delegated to the

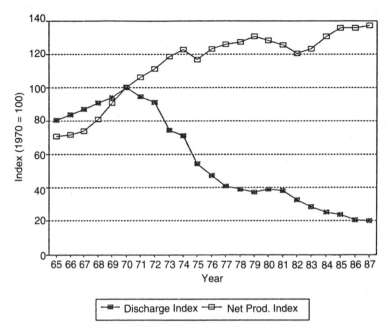

Figure 7.1 Industrial discharges of organic pollutants before treatment and net production index

water boards by the provinces. Three provinces have decided to carry out the task themselves, because local water boards have been too small, and because the provincial councils have been dominated by the Dutch Social Democratic Party, the PvdA, which originally viewed the water boards as being too dominated by farmers. Also, the city of Amsterdam has held on to sewage control. The result has been a complicated, not to say confused, structure of water quality management, such that a water quality map of the Netherlands looks like a veritable patchwork (see Figure 7.2). In the western part of the country, principal water boards (responsible only for sewage) have been established, whereas southern Holland still has many small boards, though in some cases having a joint technical service. At present, thirty-one different authorities are responsible for the administration of water pollution: twenty water boards, seven sewage boards, three provinces and the Rijkswaterstaat for state waters.[11]

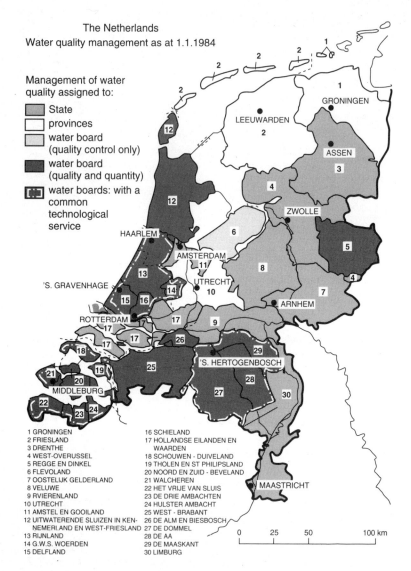

Figure 7.2 Dutch authorities in water quality management

The Rijkswaterstaat and the Ministry of Transport and Public Works have maintained their position that water management should be integrated and delegated to the water authorities, and it is now expected that water boards will take over in the three remaining provinces. The complicated organisational framework reflects, however, that water management is adapted to hydrological as well as to local political circumstances. The SWPA was passed at the end of a period in Dutch politics characterised as 'politics of accommodation', and the framework was sufficiently flexible to ensure accommodation between the most important interests in water management.[12]

The fact that the water boards are dominated by farmers and a professional staff of engineers has not, however, promoted 'accommodation' between the boards and polluters. Rather, the approach of the water boards to water pollution control was from the very beginning quite straightforward. Their task was to ensure pollution control, and for that purpose they constructed sewage plants and passed the costs on to households and manufacturing industries. As a result, the bill for water quality management has been steadily increasing since 1970. In contrast with Denmark, France and Germany, there were practically no options for subsidising public sewage treatment.

Did this system then make water boards more conscious of the costs that they imposed on their members, since, after all, their administration is made up of those contributing to their activities? Apparently, the water boards were quite insensitive to that question, and it should be recalled that water quantity interests have maintained their majority on the boards. In the Rijnland water board, for instance, water quantity interests control two-thirds of the thirty seats, and only two seats are occupied by polluting manufacturers.[13] Pollution problems have been quite severe, with foam and detergents entering the canals, and farmers have not hesitated to pass the costs of sewage treatment on to the polluters.

The question of phosphorus emissions provides an example of opposition to pollution control from the water boards.[14] The boards felt that industry and households accounted for only a small part of phosphorus pollution, while the greater part stemmed from the international rivers. In the late 1970s they were not prepared to increase pollution levies to finance these measures. Neither the Rijkswaterstaat nor the provinces succeeded in inducing the water boards to establish dephosphorisation on any larger scale, and in the meantime the government reached an agreement with the detergent industry to phase out the use of phosphorus. In 1987, however, the Rhine countries agreed to reduce phosphorus discharges by 50 percent, and the water boards were then obliged to take part in this concerted and to them also more acceptable effort.

With the steady extension of sewage plants, the water boards increased the costs and effluent charges for discharges, thus providing an indirect incentive for the reduction of emissions. For all those companies located along provincial waters, the costs of water management rapidly increased, and they began to search for methods to reduce their emissions.

The permit procedure and RIZA

As a consequence of SWPA, Dutch firms were required for the first time to apply for a discharge permit from the authorities. Under pressure from the levies, firms became quite interested in reducing their emissions, and firms from the most polluting sectors – sugar, pulp and paper and starch – were put under severe strain. The starch industry was also in a difficult economic position, and they all complained about their added expenses.

RIZA played a key role in transmitting control technologies to firms, since RIZA had to review all permits. In practice, RIZA started with the largest polluters, and with funds from the state water levy could offer subsidies to companies that controlled pollution. The Netherlands had more than thirty-five pulp and paper mills, but, after having reviewed the first two of them, the RIZA staff had gained sufficient insight into the production technology to suggest solutions for the whole sector. Under pressure from the levies, firms were eager to undertake pollution control, so bargaining was limited between RIZA and the companies.

For some companies, especially in the starch industry, pollution was so severe that payment of the levy would have closed them immediately if they had not been protected by the special 'hardheidsclausule' – a clause in Dutch law that offers protection against taxes that one cannot afford. These companies were offered exemption from the levy for a number of years, provided that they reduced pollution. To give firms the maximum incentive to control pollution, the levy was to be paid for the exemption period with an amount equivalent to the pollution level attained at the end of the period.

It is interesting that RIZA had not undertaken any large-scale research programmes in industrial water pollution control prior to 1970. The technologies used for pollution control derived mostly from foreign sources, such as guidelines from the American Environmental Protection Agency or international journals. This know-how was then applied to Dutch conditions by the RIZA staff. In the early 1970s, the challenge to the RIZA staff was no smaller than the challenge to industries:

There was nothing, we didn't know anything, there was a gap. I went to the industries with empty hands. I could only ask them: tell me what you are doing and why you are doing that. The way we got in was by asking them to give us the information and to look what EPA had written and what was sensible . . . For instance the paper and pulp industry. There was a big problem there. Every factory was discharging about 2 million inhabitant equivalents. It was impossible to build a sewage plant for that, so they talked with the economic department of the government and they said 'we give you more time'. There was a period of transition . . . The factories then said, 'we don't want to build that biological sewage plant, we want to take other measures'. For instance the use of straw was finished because it was too expensive to use that . . . At the same time they changed the process in the factory and built a buffer capacity to reuse the waste water. For that they got 25 percent.[15]

Using funds obtained from the state water levy, RIZA offered a subsidy of approximately 60 percent for biological treatment plants and 90 percent for physical–chemical plants. Subsidies were offered only when possible in-plant measures had also been applied. Such measures were eligible for a 25 percent subsidy from a scheme financed by a general government programme for cleaner technologies. In many cases, environmental investment was profitable for the firms. In the mid-seventies, abatement costs were on average 300 guilder per inhabitant equivalent. Since the levy was around 10–20 guilder, there remained a gap up to the annual 60 guilder, which would be the abatement costs in the case of a five-year depreciation period. This gap was then filled with the subsidy, which was what explained the 60 percent and 90 percent subsidy. The abatement costs were calculated on the basis of public sewage plants' investments. Industries were often able to install sewage plants at lower costs, so for companies ready to take measures it was in fact possible to 'earn' money on pollution control in more than one sense, owing to the levy. Since 1971, the funds accumulated by the state water levy have accounted for approximately two-thirds of total industrial investment in water pollution control, so this tax–bounty scheme has certainly been quite important for the measures undertaken.

RIZA was not the only research institute able to provide companies with advice. Following the implementation of the SWPA, other research institutes began to work on waste water problems:

When the levies were raised you saw the factories were taking measures. For instance the milk processing industry. There was an institute here in Holland, they were specialised in milk factories. You saw that they had studied the measures, they knew what was possible, and they were waiting until the levies were high enough to take those measures.[16]

Today, companies receive advice from a number of research institutes and consulting firms, but in the early 1970s RIZA played an essential role. As a result, pollution control with regard to organic pollutants made great strides in the 1970s, even before any official guidelines had been issued. As in Germany, it was a lengthy process to reach agreement about standards, and it was not until 1975 that the first guidelines were issued.[17] The major reductions in emissions took place prior to 1975.

National water quality planning
The approach to the planning of water quality has been more centralised in the Netherlands than in any of the other three countries. The Dutch have never really adopted the recipient quality planning of the European Community, and detailed and minute examination of each single surface water is not characteristic of the Dutch approach. This policy instrument was adopted only after two cases at the European Court, and with reluctance.[18]

Still, the Netherlands is quite renowned for its national planning systems, as set up under the Central Planning Bureau, and the environment too has been subject to comprehensive planning procedures.*[19] A cornerstone of environmental regulation has been the so-called indicative Multi-year planning (IMP). For the different sectors such as air pollution and water pollution, five-year

---

* In the 1950s, CPB was in fact a place of pilgrimage for planners from Eastern Europe.

plans were drawn up and used to set new priorities.*[20] National planning was important for the formulation of the general strategy, although it was not a tool for practical implementation, and the IMP-Water set out not only a 'stand-still principle', which banned an increase in discharges, but also a deliberate use of cleaner production technologies to reduce pollution.

The first IMP-Water, issued in 1975, was remarkable for its clear devotion to cleaner technologies: 'as a rule in-plant measures are the most effective and least expensive. Such arrangements would, by changing or adapting the industrial process, help to reduce the volume of the effluent and the quantity of waste matter it contains.'[21] The IMP-Water listed a number of initiatives taken by industry to curb pollution, and estimated that the pollution load of specific industrial sectors could be reduced from 25 million IE in 1969 to 8 million IE in 1980. The Dutch experience must astonish most implementation researchers, since this ambitious aim was in fact attained: in the second IMP, issued in 1980, it was established that the selected sectors of industry had decreased their pollution load to 7.9 million IE.[22] However, the second IMP-Water of 1980 also noted that only 65 percent of the public sewage plants foreseen in 1975 had actually been constructed in 1980. This could be explained partly by the problems of locating the plants, but also by the fact that the considerable industrial pollution reductions had diminished the need for public sewage capacity.

Summary
The lever of Dutch policy design has clearly been the effluent levy, which gave polluters an incentive to control discharges and provided the national authorities with funds that made subsidies possible. The role of the water boards has been primarily to impose charges so high that pollution control became profitable, and for that purpose these unique Dutch institutions were almost immune to political pressures. RIZA played an essential role in communicating know-how to firms through its review of permits,

---

* In the mid-1980s, the sectoral IMPs were integrated into a common IMP-E for all environmental problems. This procedure was enforced with the issue of the ambitious NEPP plan (National Environmental Policy Plan) in 1989, which was a detailed account of measures to be taken as part of the new integrated approach towards environmental protection.

but it is food for thought that the know-how that RIZA applied
was inspired by international sources, and that RIZA did not possess any specific knowledge compared with neighbouring countries.

Impact of the levy

The Dutch levy has been not a pure incentive levy, but an earmarked levy intended to finance public sewage plants and provide
funds for industrial control of discharges. It is actually the existence of the state water levy, and the fact that water boards also
charge levies for direct emissions into their surface waters, that
differentiates the levy system from the ordinary systems of user
fees.

It is occasionally claimed that policy-makers did not expect the
levy per se to provide an incentive for polluters to limit discharges,
but this is clearly an understatement. Dutch policy-makers had
read their economic textbooks and, in fact, praised the regulatory
effects of environmental charges. In complete disregard of the rather
modest levies to be introduced initially, they claimed that 'for
those affected [the levies] will be an incentive to reduce water
pollution as far as possible'.[23] Since the levy imposed costs on all
industries discharging organic pollutants, it primarily affected certain manufacturing industries, such as food processing and pulp
and paper, but in general the levy had an impact on most of Dutch
industry.

The Bressers study
Dutch environmental statistics are among the most detailed in the
world, and the data gathered by the Central Bureau of Statistics
(CBS) on waste water emissions have been employed by Bressers
to study the effect of the levies.[24] Bressers studied fourteen industrial sectors, which together accounted for 90 percent of organic discharges, and their responses to the increase in levies in the
period from 1969 to 1980. Bressers found a strong correlation
between the charges to be paid as a share of the production value
and the decrease in discharges ($r = .73$). In the potato starch industry, an exemption had been granted by the authorities, so the
charges paid were reduced, and in the stock-raising industry levies
were paid according to table-based values. When these two sectors

were excluded from the analysis, the correlation was even stronger ($r = .84$).

A further analysis was carried out of fifteen water board districts, and here Bressers found a high degree of consistency in his data. The regional distribution of industries varies considerably, which makes it difficult to compare the incentive of the levy of the individual water boards with the reductions undertaken in that particular district. However, the reductions to be expected according to the industrial structure of the water board district can be calculated and, when compared with the actual reductions, this generates the variable of relative abatement success. When correlating this variable with the increase in levies from 1975 to 1980, a strong positive correlation is found ($r = .86$).

The Schuurman study

Schuurman conducted a study of 150 firms discharging more than 3,000 IE and analysed the evolution of their discharges between 1975 and 1980, the same period covered by Bressers.[25] Interviews were carried out with managers responsible for pollution control according to a structured questionnaire.

The interviews reveal a certain inconsistency between the perception of the levy and its actual impacts among the firms: 50 percent considered the levy to be fiscal, and they did not even consider it a payment for a public service; 30 percent answered that they regarded the levy as a kind of informative price on the loss of products and raw materials, while only 15 percent regarded the levy as a regulatory instrument; 9 percent considered the levy to be a fine.

Schuurmann asked the firms to provide information about their own pollution control and to list the actual reasons behind the decision in each individual firm for undertaking this. Schuurman found that 88 percent of the companies had taken steps to control discharges. Although the firms were asked to list their most important motives, more than one motive was mentioned in a number of cases, thus producing a total of 147, although only 132 firms were questioned (see Figure 7.3). However, 82 percent listed public regulation as the most important factor, while the second most important factor causing pollution control, mentioned by 12 percent, was the regular monitoring of production processes. Six percent instituted pollution control because it was profitable from

Reason for pollution control	Highest rank	%
Pollution control is a company responsibility	6	4.5
Safety and considerations for workers' health	–	–
To avoid bad reputation	–	–
Influence from neighbours	3	2
Influence from environmentalists	2	1.5
Influence from consumers	1	1
Profitable investments because of the levy	2	1.5
Profitable investments for other reasons	9	6
As part of regular production monitoring	16	12
Public regulation	108	82
Total	147	110.5

N = 132

Figure 7.3 Reasons given by companies for instituting pollution control

an ordinary management point of view. The non-regulatory factors such as company responsibility or environmental pressure groups have had little impact.

The firms were then asked to list the influence of various policy instruments. Figure 7.4 indicates that the role of levies was 2.5 times more important than that of permits. Among the firms that undertook pollution control, 54 percent mentioned the levy as the single most important factor, whereas 20 percent pointed to the permit; 18 percent controlled pollution not because of public regulation but for the reasons listed in Figure 7.3.

The sectors differed concerning the role of policy instruments. In the food-processing and textile industries the levy was clearly the most important instrument, and was mentioned by 75–80 percent of the managers. In the chemical industry, levies figured in only 50 percent of the responses, and their importance declined in the leather and printing industries.

When considering the ranking of policy instruments, Schuurman concludes that, among those who controlled pollution, the levy was important for 67 percent, while the permit procedure was important for 25 percent of the respondents. When considering the amount of pollution eliminated by the different firms, Schuurman finds that 80 percent of the actual pollution reductions undertaken were caused by the levy, merely 11 percent by the permit procedure, and 10 percent for other reasons. Firms that

Policy instrument	N = 132 %	N = 150 %
Effluent permit	20	17
Effluent levy	54	47
Permit & levy	1	1
Permit & subsidy	2	2
Other reasons	5	5
Not public regulation	18	16
No pollution control	–	12
Total	100	100

Figure 7.4 Pollution control and impact of policy instruments

respond to the levy reduce their pollution more than those responding to a permit, a finding that clearly supports the traditional critique of lax permit procedures.

Among firms that had constructed biological sewage plants before 1975, 47 percent pointed to the permit procedure as decisive, while only 24 percent cited the levy. In 1980, merely 30 percent cited the permit procedure and 60 percent the levy. The biological treatment plant represents end-of-pipe response, and here the permit procedure is of greater importance than among all the firms that controlled pollution; 30 percent of those who build sewage plants pointed to the permit procedure as the most important factor influencing their decision, compared with only 20 percent of the whole sample.

Technological responses

The studies of Schuurman and Bressers provide clear evidence of the regulating impact of the Dutch system of levies. The question that remains is: 'How did they respond? – By end-of-pipe measures or by employing cleaner technologies?'

Unfortunately the CBS, unlike its German and French counterparts, does not calculate the distribution of industrial investment in sewage plants and cleaner technologies. As part of IMP, however, some data have been published on the capacity of industrial sewage plants. In 1980, organic pollution from industry had decreased by 17 million IE since 1970, but the total capacity of industrial sewage plants was only 5 million IE.[26] An amount of 12–13 million IE plus the additional pollution to be expected from

Response	Firms (N = 95)	Pollution reduction ('000 IE)	Levy-savings ('000 guilder)
Moving production to new location	5	8	256
Closure or reduction of production	7	63	2,082
Temporary closure or reduction	2	8	248
New production process	19	1,462	48,314
Change of production process	87	578	19,105
Abandonment of investments	19	–	–
Total	149	2,119	70,005

Figure 7.5 Consequences for investment decisions of firms responding to the levy

the increased industrial output had been eliminated by other means within the category of cleaner technologies.

The starch potato flour industry, as already mentioned, presented an extraordinary case. This sector consists of two or three plants with immense discharges. Initially these accounted for nearly 9 million IE in annual pollution. In 1980, discharges had been reduced to 3.5 million IE and were projected to come down to only 0.15 million IE in 1985. Although these reductions were not achieved through end-of-pipe solutions, one must take into consideration the special circumstances of this particular industry. Nevertheless, a reduction of 7.5 million IE between 1970 and 1980 still remains to be explained by factors other than end-of-pipe solutions.

Schuurman's study included the impacts of the levies on investments. Nearly 66 percent of the firms interviewed mentioned that levies had influenced their investment decisions. For these companies, Figure 7.5 shows how much pollution they reduced and the charges they saved. Eighty-seven companies adjusted their production processes, and nineteen companies undertook more extensive changes in their production processes.

Of the eighty-six companies that controlled pollution because of the levy, forty-nine responded by building an end-of-pipe treatment plant. Half of these were merely mechanical works providing only primary treatment, whereas the other half offered biological (eighteen companies) or advanced treatment. Thirty-two companies responded by taking 'other' measures, most of them in the category of cleaner technologies.[27]

What appears is a mixed response to the levy, where no one kind of solution prevails. The manufacturers have employed end-of-pipe solutions as well as cleaner technologies, but the levies have a strong influence on the investment decisions. This means that, in the long run, cleaner technologies will become more important.

The permit procedure encourages standardised end-of-pipe technology, but this is also a technology that can be prescribed on a standardised basis. In contrast, changes of process technologies require in-depth information about the particular plant in question.

Overcapacity in public sewage plants

An unintended consequence of industry's successful pollution control has been a surplus of public treatment capacity.[28] As firms have responded to the waste water levy by employing cleaner technologies, or simply establishing their own pre-treatment, the water authorities have correspondingly seen their revenues decrease. Since water authorities have undertaken investment in public treatment plants, to be depreciated over a certain period, they have reacted by increasing the rate of the levies. Between 1975 and 1989, industry's share of the levies paid to water boards decreased from 44 to 30 percent, while the share of households increased from 56 to 70 percent. Between 1980 and 1989, the deflated rate of the levies increased by 20 percent.[29] Part of this increase is due to improved methods of treatment, such as phosphorus removal at the public works, and part due to the investment trap spiral. Schuurman estimates that the savings achieved by industry could be offset by a 10 percent increase in the rate of the levy. At present, two Dutch water boards face the problem of overcapacity.[30]

The surplus is not directly an environmental problem, since the performance of treatment plants usually improves, but a surplus is still economically inefficient. The capital tied up in the surplus could have been used for other environmental purposes. The problem of the investment trap spiral is discussed in detail in Chapter 8.

Conclusions

The successes of Dutch water pollution control policy are a result not simply of effluent charges, but also of the specific institutional framework provided by the traditional water authorities and the historically important water management system.

The Dutch water boards did little that differed from what local authorities did elsewhere: they constructed sewage treatment plants and passed the costs on to households and affiliated industries. Unlike many municipal authorities, however, Dutch water boards are not occupied with matters of employment or general tax revenue. They merely ensure satisfactory water management, and they have no possibilities of subsidising the waste water service. The water boards are staffed with engineers, who have a professional attitude rather than a political view on the question of pollution control. The staff have been supported by water quantity interest groups, who may even have a direct interest in clean canals and streams for irrigation purposes, and who are able to use their majority on the boards to ensure clean water. There are no indications, however, that the three provinces, although headed by political bodies, have performed less successfully than the water boards. Yet, the provinces were operating within the same framework of self-financing water pollution control as the water boards and did not have much leeway in terms of subsidising industries from the SWPA.*

The tax–bounty scheme provided for firms to undertake pollution control may have encouraged a more co-operative style from industry. However, Dutch industry has certainly also complained about the levies, and without the supervision of national authorities, like RIZA, they might not have performed so well. The levies had a great deal of influence, but the transition was facilitated by general planning and by the agreements reached by RIZA with certain large polluters. No doubt the indicative multi-year planning had an impact in setting long-term goals and identifying major polluters. Furthermore, the existence of RIZA meant that considerable know-how could be directed to the major polluters. RIZA played an important role in aquiring an overview of the technological options in polluting industries. Hence, the SWPA

---

* The possible conflictual relationship between the 'red' provinces and the water boards might even have spurred a certain competition in performance.

and the ministry provided the lubrication that ensured that the pressure generated by the levies was transformed into action. Although the use of the water boards makes the Dutch policy design appear rather fragmented at first sight, it was in fact a concerted and centralised effort, which helped provide the impressive results.

The Dutch programme for water pollution control has been so effective that the tax–bounty scheme for state waters will be terminated in a few years. The bounties were intended to cover only investment for polluters having 'historical rights' to pollute, and their purpose has now been achieved. The levy will be maintained so as not to support factories linked to state waters as compared with factories on regional waters. Revenue, however, will be used to cover other aspects of water management.

Notes

1 WHO (1954).
2 Tellegen (1981).
3 For an account of the manure levy, see Brussaard and Grossman (1990).
4 Kroon (1990).
5 See Hoogheemraadschap van Rijnland (1989).
6 Scheltinga (1972).
7 de Goede et al. (1982), 6–7.
8 Environmental Resources Limited (1982); text of Pollution of Surface Waters Act as last published in *Staatsblad* 1981, 414; Cappon (1991).
9 Interview with H. Kraaij, Rijkswaterstaat head office, 6 June 1990, The Hague.
10 Central Bureau of Statistics (1987), 77.
11 Unie van Waterschappen (1988).
12 Lijphardt (1968).
13 Interview with M. A. Heinsdijk, Director, Rijnland Water Board, 12 November 1992, Leiden.
14 Ministry of Transport and Public Works (1980).
15 Interview with L. V. M. Teurlinckx, Head of Division of Communal and Company Waste Water, RIZA (Institute for Inland Water Management and Wastewater Treatment), 11 November 1992. Jan Schoot Uiterkamp and Jos van Dalen also participated in the interview.
16 Ibid.
17 Ministry of Transport and Public Works (1975); Wolters (1979).
18 Bennett (1986b).

19 See Tinbergen (1971).
20 Rottschäfer and Flaman (1979). See VROM (1989); Bennett (1991).
21 Ministry of Transport and Public Works (1975), 18.
22 Ministry of Transport and Public Works (1980), 31.
23 *Kammerstuken* II, 1964/65, 7 884, 3, blz. 12; quoted from Rijkswaterstaat (1990).
24 Bressers (1983a, 1983b, 1988).
25 Schuurman (1988).
26 Ministry of Transport and Public Works (1980), 30.
27 Schuurman (1988), 108.
28 Schuurmann, 1988; Bongaerts and Kraemer (1989).
29 Centraal Bureau voor de Statistick (1989).
30 According to interview with Mr Teurlinckx (1992).

8

The cost-effectiveness of policy designs

Introduction

It is remarkable that national policy designs exhibit such differences in spite of the common environmental policy pursued since the mid-1970s within the European Community. The differences, which undeniably reflect deeply rooted national traditions of public administration, have indeed caused considerable difficulties for international co-operation on water pollution control – both within the Community and in most international water pollution control commissions, ranging from the International Commission on the Rhine to the North Sea Commission. For many years, differences of policy design and the interests of certain polluting states have been an impediment to concerted action.[1]

The four cases presented here provide a more detailed picture of policy designs for pollution control than the idiomatic contrasts usually depicted in the pollution control literature. This chapter presents a comparison of the policy designs and their outcomes in terms of pollution control, costs and technological response. The ultimate goal of this comparison is to assess the cost-effectiveness of the various policy designs, a question not only of emission reductions compared with costs, but also of the choice of technological response.

Differences in policy design

Although these water pollution control policies have been at the core of environmental policy for twenty years, they only partly substantiate the standard distinction in the literature between command-and-control policy on the one hand, and a market approach on the other.

The Danish approach, prior to 1987, certainly belongs to the more adaptive versions, since few precise requirements were set for the technologies applied. The current bargaining on optional guidelines between peak interest organisations and the Environmental Agency, as well as the unique role of the Board of Appeal, ensured consensus among the most influential actors. And the delegation of permit procedures and inspection of local authorities ensured that local circumstances would be taken into consideration. The pronounced bargaining even during implementation and the importance attributed to the discretion of local authorities, following from the water quality principle, make it more reasonable to interpret the policy design as a 'consensus-and-delegation' approach.

Command-and-control has been practised only in Germany, where sector guidelines are based on specific technological solutions: a 'best available technology' approach for most pollutants and a 'generally accepted technological standard' for organic discharges. In Germany, however, command-and-control policies have been combined with an effluent charge as a supplementary policy instrument. From the existence of the charge, one might have expected to find a more market-like approach in Germany, but this proved not to be the case. The charge is really an implementation charge, because it is linked to compliance with the standard system.

The French policy design leans more towards the market approach, owing to the use of earmarked charges and special-purpose agencies. It is distinguished from the German design by the fact that the charge applies to all discharges, although under certain conditions premiums are offered. The absence of national guidelines means that the charge assumes an important position as a policy instrument for financing measures within industries or along rivers by the use of voluntary agreements or covenants.

The Dutch policy design comprises a more purely market approach than either the German or the French design. The pollution levy not just provides marginal funds for pollution control, as do the French and German levies, but constitutes a closed scheme that finances pollution control by industry as well. Dutch policy makers have imposed a tax-bounty scheme and arranged a proper

Policy instruments	DK	F	G	NL
Permit procedure	++	++	++	++
Mandatory guidelines			++	
Optional guidelines	+	+		+
Planning	++	+	+	+
Covenants		++		
Appeal procedure	+			
Effluent charge		+	+	++
User charge	+	+	+	
State subsidies	+	+	+	(+)
Local subsidies	++	+	++	
Local authorities	+	+	+	
Regional authorities	+	+	+	+
Special-purpose agencies		++	(+)	++
Private tenders		+		
Water quality principle	+	+		
Emission principle			+	+

Figure 8.1 Policy instruments for water pollution control

institutional framework in terms of special water authorities responsible for implementation.

The policy instruments applied

Figure 8.1 presents a matrix of the policy instruments applied, in each of the four policy designs. The policy instruments are divided into four sub-categories: (1) administrative instruments, (2) economic instruments, (3) agency instruments and (4) discharge principle instrument. The role of each policy instrument is indicated by the number of '+' signs assigned to it. Parentheses indicate that the policy instruments are available but have not had significant importance for implementation.

National differences in policy design are indicated by the matrix. The permit procedure has been significant in all four countries, but apart from that the significance of various policy instruments differs. The French policy design reveals the largest number of policy instruments available; France makes use of nearly twice as many policy instruments as the Dutch, who possess the simplest policy design. The Danish and German designs resemble each other in their complexity.

Administrative instruments

The Germans have been the only ones to pursue their aims on the basis of mandatory sector guidelines. In both France and Denmark, discretion with regard to water quality of the recipient in question has been preferred, and this means that the resources have been employed for planning and setting targets for the quality of surface waters. The German regulators have been more concerned about the choice of process technologies in specific industries. In Germany, a 'best available technology' standard has been applied to dischargers, rather than considerations about water quality. The German approach has not been less demanding in terms of personnel and resources, since the drawing up of sector guidelines is a complicated task, which is probably best undertaken by large countries with many firms within each sector.

The French have to some extent bargained over the choice of technology in firms through sector contracts, by offering an incentive in terms of revenue from the levy, but precise technological standards have not been set.

Denmark has been the only country with a formal complaints procedure, thus offering a better legal position for possible plaintiffs. The complaints procedure has had a significant negative effect on the functioning of the administrative system as a whole, however, since a large number of cases were repealed.

Economic instruments

The Dutch have emphasised the levies strongly, and have not subsidised water pollution control by means of a general tax revenue, except for a small programme for cleaner technology. In the three other countries, state and especially local subsidies have played a major role. Local subsidies have been offered for the construction of sewage plants in especially Germany and Denmark, and Germany also offered state subsidies. Such subsidies meant that user charges were not set on the basis of the full costs of discharging, and that industries discharging into public sewer networks were indirectly subsidised. This was also the case in France, but here it was rather on the basis of state subsidies.

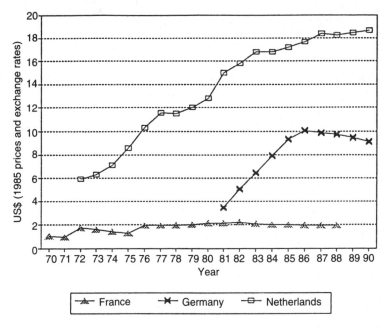

Figure 8.2 Annual effluent charge per inhabitant equivalent (US$ at 1985 prices and exchange rates)

In Denmark no effluent charge has been applied, and in Germany and France the effluent charge is a supplementary incentive combined with user charges. In the Netherlands, the effluent charge covers costs traditionally financed by user charges, but also applies to discharges that receive no treatment at sewage plants, hence the Dutch possess a system that is more uniform.

The Dutch effluent charges have been higher than both the German levy and the French levies (see Figure 8.2). For industries discharging directly into surface waters, Figure 8.2 establishes the considerable differences in the taxation burden. The French levy has remained at the same level in deflated prices since 1970, $1 or $2 per inhabitant equivalent (IE), while the German levy has increased to $9–10 and the Dutch to over $18 in 1989. The pure price incentive from the Dutch charge is thus the most significant, and, according to the theory, should also account for the largest effects.

Agents responsible for implementation
Similarities exist among the four countries concerning the use of local authorities. Regional authorities tend to play a key role in issuing permits to large, direct emitters, in supervision of surface waters and with regard to planning. French *départements*, Danish counties and German *Länder*, however, are staffed very differently for this purpose.

Similarities exist in Germany, Denmark and France with regard to the responsibility for public sewage plants, which rests with the communes or municipalities, although in France private tenders play a major role. The fact that France has not undertaken any reform of its local authorities means, however, that, in terms of personnel and finances, French communes are badly equipped for this task, compared with their German and Danish counterparts.

One reason for the complexity of the French design is the number of agents responsible for the implementation. The use of specific-purpose agencies is built on top of existing local authorities. In the Netherlands, water boards have replaced local authorities more, which leaves a role for provinces only in issuing licences.

Environmental benefits

From the case studies, it is obvious that since the early 1970s the Netherlands has achieved considerable reductions in industrial discharges, whereas Denmark has had little success. In Germany and France, reductions have also occurred, but their relative success is uncertain. Because pollution control programmes were not initiated in the same years, and since data are lacking for the first half of the 1970s, it is not possible to draw a complete picture of the development from 1970 to 1990. However, since the mid-1970s reliable data are available, and a closer look at developments from 1977 to 1987 will provide some hints as to the environmental effectiveness of different policy designs, although differences in national accounting principles and measurement methods must be taken into account. Still, the period from 1977 to 1987 may in fact offer a more reliable basis for evaluating effects, since some of the impressive emission reductions in the early years of the French and Dutch systems might represent 'paper' reductions due to improved measurement techniques. In 1977, all four countries had begun to regulate discharges, and the period provides a good

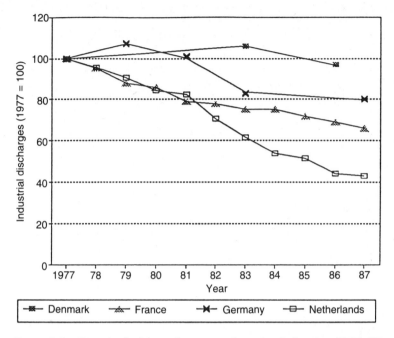

Figure 8.3 Organic discharges from manufacturing industries, 1977–87 (1977 = 100)

picture of the dynamics inherent in different policy designs. Figure 8.3 depicts the discharges from manufacturing industries between 1977 and 1987 in the four countries, and Figure 8.4 shows the economic significance of the water-intensive sectors and the differences in industrial structure.

In 1977, the Dutch and French programmes had already been operating for six or seven years, whereas the German charge was passed in 1976 and implemented in 1981. Still, even in the 1977–87 period, the Dutch programme turns out to be the most successful in terms of continuous reductions in discharges. Over this decade, emissions from manufacturing industries were reduced to 43 percent of the 1977 level. France also achieved considerable reductions, but only to 67 percent. In the case of Germany, it is remarkable that discharges continued to increase from 1977 to 1979, and that discharges did not begin to diminish until the implementation of the waste water levy in 1981. The fact that the German curve

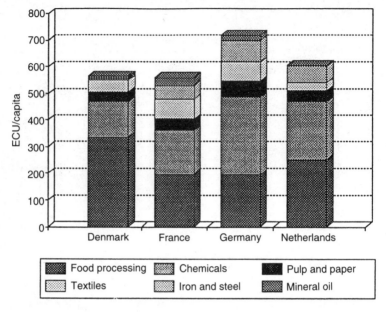

Figure 8.4 Industrial structure: gross value added per capita by water-intensive sectors, 1982

bends just after 1981 indicates the possible impact of introducing the waste water charge, but also of the introduction of sector guidelines. In Denmark, discharges increased until the mid-1980s and were only slightly reduced in 1986 compared with 1977. The absence of emission reductions is remarkable, since the larger share of food-processing industries in Denmark would lead one to expect to find the most significant reductions here.

To interpret these findings, figures for the most water-intensive sectors are presented in Figures 8.5 and 8.6. Figure 8.5 shows emission reductions distributed by sector. In Figure 8.6 a de-linkage index is constructed for each sector; this is the sum of changes in emissions and in the net production index. Since reliable time-series for the Danish sectors were not available, only France, Germany and the Netherlands are included in Figures 8.5 and 8.6.

From the figures it is obvious that some reductions have been achieved because of closures or production decreases in sunset

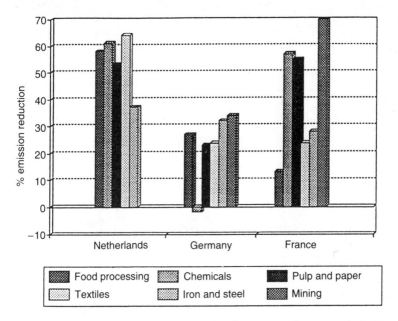

Figure 8.5 Emission reductions in manufacturing industries, 1977–87 (1977 = 100)

industries such as mining, textiles and steel, whereas others have been offset by increases in production in growth sectors. Although the German chemical industry has not reduced its emissions in actual values, it has in fact increased its output by approximately 60 percent without increasing emissions.

The general picture is still clear. The Netherlands has achieved the most considerable de-linkage in all sectors. France has a high de-linkage score in the pulp and paper industry and in chemicals, but mediocre results in textiles and food-processing industries as compared with Germany. This is somewhat of a paradox, since the German levy has been much higher than the French (see Figure 8.2).

The difference is most likely explained by the fact that the French aimed their sector contracts at the chemicals and pulp and paper industries. The sector contracts were implemented during the mid-1970s, and Figure 8.3 indicates that reductions in France between 1977 and 1981 were undertaken at almost the same speed as in the Netherlands. As the sector contracts were phased out, however,

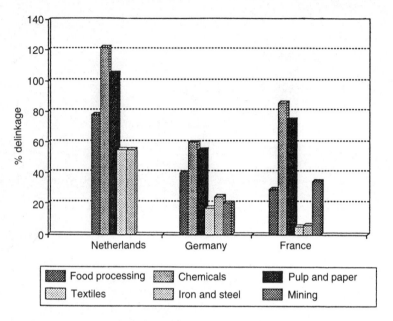

Figure 8.6 Percent de-linkage (change in emissions and net production index), 1977–87 (1977 = 100)

French pollution control slowed down. Most food-processing industries, except sugar, did not receive any aid under the sector contract scheme and have probably primarily responded to licence procedures and the moderate pressure from pollution levies. This explains why the food-processing industries performed less successfully than their German counterparts.

Costs

On the basis of data compiled by the four national census bureaus, it is possible to compare costs of water pollution control in the four countries. Differences in national accounting principles render a complete picture of the period 1970–90 impossible, but the following analysis draws on data available in statistical yearbooks, environmental statistics and data available on request from national census bureaus. In spite of lacunas in time-series, the data

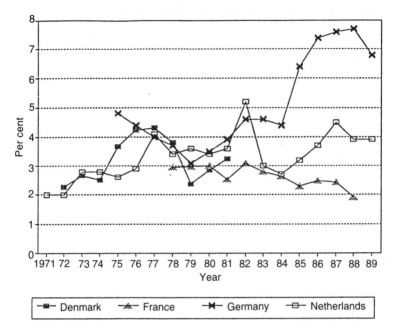

Figure 8.7 The share of environmental investment by industry in relation to total industrial investment

available make a comparative estimate of costs to industry and citizens possible.

Industry
Figure 8.7 shows the share of environmental investment by industry as a percentage of total investment.* It can be seen that environmental investment was at the same level and followed similar trends in Denmark, Germany and the Netherlands in the first decade studied. Figure 8.7 also reveals that German industry in particular gave high priority to the environment in the second part

---

* In Denmark, the accounting of environmental investment in industry was terminated in 1982. In the Netherlands, environmental investment that is profitable is not included in the figures, whereas profitable environmental investment is included in both Germany and France. Profitable environemental investment is typical within the domain of clean technology. In both Germany and France this category of investment accounts for less than 10 percent of total environmental investment, and, if this also applies to the Netherlands, it does not change the figures decisively.

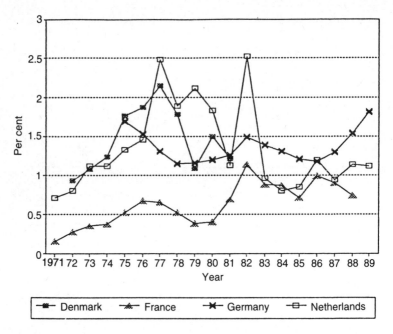

Figure 8.8 The share of investment in water pollution control by industry in relation to total industrial investment

of the 1980s and took the lead with nearly 8 percent of total industrial investment devoted to the environment.

Figure 8.8 shows the share of investment devoted only to water pollution control. For this purpose, German, Dutch and Danish industries undertook similar investments during the 1970s, the first decade of water pollution control. In the 1980s, Dutch and German industry followed similar trends as well. The general increase in environmental investment in Germany in the late 1980s did not apply to the sector of water pollution control, but concerned rather air pollution control and waste management. Through the 1970s, French industry appears to have devoted less than half the investment by the industries of the other three countries.

From Figure 8.8 it is obvious that, in terms of emission reductions at least in the first decade, the lax Danish policy design did not relieve Danish industry of water pollution control costs as compared with the costs that have burdened Dutch and German competitors. In fact, German industrial investment in water pollution control during the late 1970s was somewhat lower than Danish investment. In France, industry's investment has been low, reflecting problems of policy design (see Chapter 5). This is surprising in view of France's otherwise adequate performance with regard to emission reductions (see Figures 8.3, 8.5 and 8.6).

The public sector
We still need to compare the costs of public sewage treatment between the four countries. The case studies indicated that the Dutch policy design provided firms with an incentive to control water pollution using in-plant measures, rather than discharging to public treatment, because of the pollution levy. There is a difference, however, between the Dutch charge design, on the one hand, and the French and Danish, on the other. In Germany and France as well as in Denmark, firms connected to public treatment are subject not to a pollution levy but to regular user charges. Since public treatment has to some extent been subsidised, industry has obviously not paid the full price. Furthermore, while Dutch levies are paid on the basis of pollutants emitted, Danish, French and German user fees are primarily paid on the basis of the hydraulic load (the amount of water).

Figure 8.9 indicates gross public investment in water pollution control. By using a GNP deflator, prices have been converted into US$ at 1985 exchange rates.* Investment has clearly been highest in Germany. In Denmark, investment was high in the mid-1970s but decreased with the implementation of the ten-year programme, started in 1972. Investment increased again after the Plan for the Aquatic Environment was passed in 1987. The level of investment in France has been fairly low, reflecting the modest share of the population connected (less than 55 percent; see Figure 3.3, Chapter 3). Dutch investment in public sewage treatment has been extremely low, even lower than French investment. However, the marked difference in investment between the densely populated Netherlands and Germany and Denmark partly reflects the differences in costs of sewer networks. In the Netherlands, investment in sewer networks – carried out by the Dutch communes and not the water boards – is almost suspiciously low.

---

* In Germany and the Netherlands figures on public investment are available only from 1975 or later. The figures for France from 1970 to 1980 are derived from a graphic presentation.

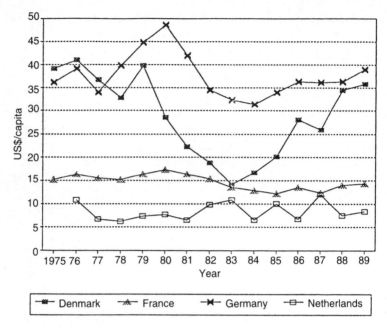

Figure 8.9 Public investment per capita in water pollution control (US$ at 1985 prices and exchange rates)

Thus, Figure 8.10 shows investment in sewage treatment only, excluding investment in sewer networks. The figure contains only three countries, as accounting principles make it impossible to identify sewage plant investment for Germany. Figure 8.10 reveals a remarkable difference in public investment between the Netherlands and Denmark. In the period 1976–87, the Dutch invested $71 per capita, while the Danes invested $114. In spite of the small investments, it should be recalled that the Dutch achievements are quite impressive. From 1976–1987, the share of the population connected to sewage plants rose from 35 percent to nearly 90 percent. In Denmark the share of the population connected increased from 75 percent to 95 percent. It appears that the Dutch achieved twice as much at only 60 percent of the Danish costs.

Generally, however, the Netherlands has centralised its sewage treatment, and advantages of large-scale operation begin for works serving 10,000 inhabitant equivalents (IE) or more. While more

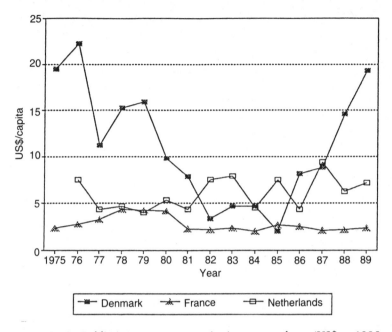

Figure 8.10 Public investment per capita in sewage plants (US$ at 1985 prices and exchange rates)

than 80 percent of the Danish and German plants were smaller than 10,000 IE, only 39 percent belonged to that category in the Netherlands (see Figure 8.11). Despite the presence of many small plants, the bulk of discharges were treated by larger plants in all three countries. Like so many other countries, Denmark sought to centralise its waste water treatment in order to benefit from large-scale operation. In the period 1976–87, the number of small plants in Denmark decreased, while the only increase occurred among plants larger than 10,000 IE. Hence, it was the large plants that became the target for public investment between 1976 and 1987.

Therefore, the larger number of sewage plants, caused by a more dispersed population, cannot explain why Danish investment was so much higher than Dutch investment. The explanation, rather, is that the Danish market for sewage technologies in the late 1970s was overheated, with high profits, and, more importantly, Denmark's capacity for sewage treatment has become overextended, as will be explained in detail below.

Capacity (IE)	Denmark		Germany		Netherlands	
	No.	%	No.	%	No.	%
201–1,000	510	42	1,325	24	24	5
1,001–10,000	545	44	3,318	60	167	34
10,001–25,000	84	7	464	8	101	21
25,001–100,000	65	5	398	7	136	28
100,000+	23	2	64	1	62	13
Total	1,227	100	5,569	100	490	100

Figure 8.11 Numbers and capacities of sewage treatment plants, 1987
Note: Figures are not available for France

Summarising, it appears that costs are not very clearly related to emission reductions. Industry's investment in water pollution control has been remarkably low in France compared with the effects achieved, whereas similar investments in the three other countries have generated quite different results. Public investment has been low in both France and the Netherlands, whereas Denmark and Germany account for considerably higher investment.

Technological responses

Clearly, end-of-pipe measures have been the most important element of public water pollution control. Municipalities, communities and water boards constructed public sewage plants so as to be able to treat effluents from households and from connected industries. A wide range of technological solutions to sewage treatment exist, but it is not the intention here to evaluate the costs and benefits of such technologies. In spite of probable engineering and technological differences, all these solutions clearly fall within the category of end-of-pipe technologies. Public authorities have generally provided biological treatment, and from the late 1980s dephosphoration and denitrification began to be applied.

The essential question concerns the technological response of manufacturing industries. Have manufacturing industries responded to water control policies by the innovation of production processes and by employing cleaner technologies, or have they – like public authorities – installed end-of-pipe technologies? Since end-of-pipe solutions can be applied both by discharging to public sewage treatment and by constructing separate treatment works on location, it is quite difficult to estimate the extent of technological change. The fact that industrial discharges to public works have declined may simply reflect the fact that end-of-pipe technologies have been employed at the level of the individual plant.

In both cases of end-of-pipe applications, the long-term cost-effectiveness of emission reductions is questionable. End-of-pipe technologies are costly in terms of investment and operating costs, and they do not increase productivity. The employment of cleaner technologies, on the other hand, may be innovative, may increase production efficiency by improving utilisation of raw materials, and may provide the firm with competitive advantages, especially if environmental standards are tightened. As cleaner technologies are integrated into production facilities, their potential productivity is preferable to improvised end-of-pipe technologies.

Furthermore, end-of-pipe technologies are more likely to represent a technique of problem displacement. The costs of treating sludge are increasing, and the disposal of sludge causes conflicts. Farmers are reluctant to spread sewage sludge on arable land, as the sludge may be contaminated and damage future crops. Sewage treatment is energy intensive, and the treatment of waste water is thus replaced by increased emissions of CO_2 and other airborne pollutants. Calculations have shown that the energy necessary for denitrification may cause greater emissions of NO_x (if energy is produced at coal-based power plants) than the quantity of nitrogen removed from waste water discharges. Sewage treatment certainly has the potential of problem-shifting, and its cost-effectiveness, especially in the long term, is questionable compared with cleaner technologies. Because of inadequate investment figures, data on public sewage plant capacities and on gross discharges have to be used as the basis of the following estimates of technological responses.

We can obtain a measure of the importance of public end-of-pipe measures by comparing the capacities of public treatment works. Figure 8.12 shows the capacity of public sewage plants measured in inhabitant equivalents per capita. On this measure, Denmark has the greatest capacity, a reflection of the fact that a large public capacity is reserved for the treatment of industrial effluent in Denmark. In France, the capacity is quite small, primarily a reflection of the modest extent of public plants (see Chapter 5). The figures confirm that in Denmark the use of public end-of-pipe

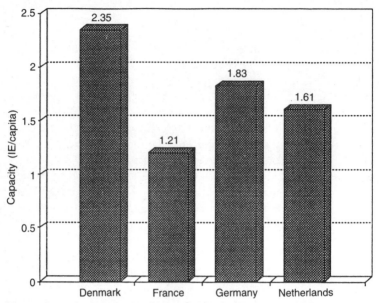

Figure 8.12 Capacity of sewage plants (inhabitant equivalents per capita), late 1980s

solutions has been more popular than measures at the individual plant, as compared with the other countries. When cooling water is excluded, more than 50 percent of Danish industrial discharges are treated by public works, compared with approximately 15 percent in Germany and 20 percent in France.

Figure 8.13 shows the quantity of organic discharges produced by manufacturing industries at source. The figure depicts the gross amount of pollution that is emitted either to sewer networks or into surface waters, and the intention is to portray industrial pollution before the effects of public sewage plants.

Even when measured per capita (rather than in relation to industrial output), it is evident that Danish industry has been less effective at reducing discharges at source. Danish industry produced 1.1 IE per capita, against only 0.4 in the Netherlands. This remarkable difference reflects Denmark's lack of pollution control at the source. Figure 8.13 also gives an estimate of the discharges by various industrial sectors. Here the environmental efficiency of Danish manufacturing industry is not very impressive, although these figures are more uncertain than the total figure for each country. For instance, the contribution from the Danish pulp and

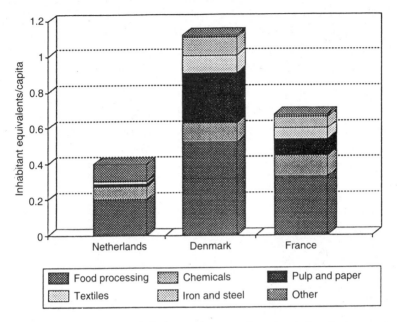

Figure 8.13 Estimate of discharges by manufacturing industries per capita, 1987

Note: Data for the Netherlands and France are derived from CBS and INSEE, respectively. Data for Denmark are calculated on the basis of Danmarks Statistik/Miljøstyrelsen (1990) and DK-Teknik (1992). Data on direct discharges are complete, whereas data on indirect discharges are assumed to account for 90% of the 4.6 million IE discharged from non-households into public sewers. The data on indirect discharges from individual branches in Denmark are estimated on the basis of DK-Teknik (1992). National accounting principles are not exactly similar, and the figures represent a rough comparison.

A few major Danish pulp and paper manufacturers have hardly reduced emissions since 1970. In France and the Netherlands, the pulp and paper industry was a major target for environmental investment and subsequent emission reductions. Even if we consider the larger share of food-processing industries in Denmark, the pollution level is found to be significantly higher than in the Netherlands. In the food-processing industry itself, the pollution level is more than twice as high in relation to gross value added compared with the Netherlands, and at the same level as in the French food-processing industry, which as a matter of fact has not been subject to pollution control measures of any significance.

It is difficult to ascertain whether the emission reductions achieved in the Netherlands, France and Germany have been achieved by means of cleaner technologies or by means of end-of-pipe measures. The Dutch case is best known, and it will be recalled from the case study that clean technology played an important role.

In Germany, reductions in emissions are less impressive than in the Netherlands, but production-specific waste water has in fact declined since 1979. In Germany, 60 percent of industrial discharges are processed in private sewage plants, and approximately 5,000 firms have their own unit (this figure was higher in the late 1970s and decreased during the 1980s); 15 percent are discharged to public sewers and 25 percent discharged untreated. Obviously, the decline also reflects closures, but, since production-specific waste water is measured on the basis of the hydraulic load, reductions in discharges reflect the introduction of less water-intensive production technologies. Regarding Germany, a careful conclusion would be that cleaner technologies have been the response to a limited extent, but that the primary response has been end-of-pipe treatment.

Regarding France, figures show that 60 percent of organic pollutants are controlled at source, while 20 percent are discharged to public sewer networks and 20 percent directly to surface waters. How pollution is controlled at source is uncertain. Harrison and Sewell claim that in France the sector contracts primarily promoted the application of end-of-pipe technologies, and figures show that approximately 5,000 firms have their own sewage plants.[2] The case study points to a modest application of cleaner technologies.

Finally it can be concluded that none of the countries studied has experienced a substantial application of cleaner technologies in manufacturing industries in the course of water pollution control policies. In all four countries, both end-of-pipe solutions and cleaner technologies have been applied, but there are significant differences. In Denmark, public end-of-pipe solutions have dominated, whereas Germany and France have seen more widespread application of private end-of-pipe solutions. This may reflect the small size of Danish companies and the achievements of economies of scale when connected to public works. In the Netherlands, the innovation of cleaner technologies has been the most significant, and as a result the Dutch have been relieved of investment in a large public capacity for sewage treatment. We may conclude that the Dutch response has been mixed, consisting of equal shares of end-of-pipe solutions and production facility changes.

Policy cost-effectiveness

Earlier in this chapter it was stated that policy approaches adopted in the four countries were quite different and highly individual. From the analysis of effects, costs and technological responses, it is clear that the cost-effectiveness of water pollution control programmes has also been quite different.

The Dutch programme has clearly been the most successful in terms of both emission reductions, costs and technological responses. The Dutch emission reductions are the most significant even in the period from 1977 to 1987, and, in spite of a policy design that has imposed an internalisation of environmental costs on industry, industrial investment has not substantially exceeded that in the other countries. The main reason may have been the application of cleaner technologies rather than expensive end-of-pipe measures. The major advantage of internalising pollution costs in industries has been reduced public responsibilities and costs. Consequently, public sewage capacities are significantly smaller, and considerable savings have been achieved.

The French cost-effectiveness is two-fold. As regards industrial emissions, pollution control has been quite successful: emission reductions have been substantial and costs have been below average. The nature of the technological response is uncertain, however. With regard to household discharges, the programme has been an outright failure: there have been limited effects and comparatively high costs, and it is quite surprising that an affluent country like France has shown such poor performance in public water pollution control. In spite of high environmental awareness among the population and good economic preconditions, France is lagging far behind and is now being superseded even by certain southern European countries in public water pollution control.[3]

The German programme seems to have been quite expensive for the public sector, although only a small fraction of industrial discharges receives public treatment. As separate figures on sewage plant investment are not available, it is difficult to give precise estimates. The emission reductions obtained by industry, however, are less significant than those in France and the Netherlands. Industrial investment was modest in the 1970s, but since the 1980s German industry has devoted slightly greater investment to water pollution control than the Netherlands and France. It is most likely that expensive end-of-pipe measures take a larger share in Germany than they do in France and the Netherlands.

Like the German and Dutch programmes, the Danish programme has been successful with regard to the extension of public treatment, but also quite expensive. Danish costs for sewage plants have been 60 percent higher than in the Netherlands, which primarily reflects the considerable capacity. In Denmark, the approach up to 1987 seems to have been to accept public responsibility for industrial discharges and to subject them to public treatment. This approach has not relieved industry of costs, however, since industry has had to pay contributions to public sewage plants, despite their being partly subsidised. Denmark thus has a low performance score on both emission reductions, costs and technological response. Denmark is certainly a world leader in public sewage treatment, but perhaps in another way than originally anticipated.

The long-term outcome of policy design

While it can be established that Denmark has been less successful than the Netherlands in the period studied, what are the long-range consequences of Denmark's unsuccessful water pollution control policy? Public expenditure, especially in the late 1970s, was too high, but what are the implications for taxpayers – or for the environment?

The Danish Environmental Protection Act has recently been amended to accord application and innovation of clean technology the highest possible priority, and the Danish government is running a subsidy programme for the development of clean technology pilot projects. Taking this point of departure, it is most likely that Danish industries should be able to pass through the same conversion to clean technology as their Dutch counterparts. Consequently, it should be possible for Danish industries to reduce their emissions by as much as two-thirds in the coming years, to reach the Dutch emission level. However, since more than 80 percent of discharges go to public sewage plants, these plants would not only receive less waste water but also lose a substantial basis of income.

During the Danish Plan for the Aquatic Environment, user fees for treatment of waste water have already been increased in order to cover the costs of the removal of phosphorus and nitrates. Because local subsidies for operating costs are phased out, Danish firms thus have a clearer economic incentive to reduce discharges than previously. However, this potential threatens to leave the Danish municipalities, the operators of local sewage plants, with an overcapacity in sewage plants. Because the emphasis in Denmark has been so strongly on taking public responsibility for pollution control, capacity is already too great, and, if Danish firms are able to convert their production facilities to the same degree as in the Netherlands, overcapacity problems might become severe.

If, for instance, one supposes that company discharges to public sewers are reduced by two-thirds, which would decrease Danish emissions to the Dutch level (see Figure 8.13), the resulting overcapacity in public sewage plants could become as high as 30–35 percent, as a national average.* The exact overcapacity would, of course, depend on the nature of local firms served by the works, and would therefore vary considerably from one municipality to another. The overcapacity would initially not do any further harm to the environment, but the municipalities would have to raise user fees in order to cover their costs. First, this would most likely cause embarrassment among local politicians, since the population is sensitive to increases in taxes and public user fees. Second, where firms anticipated that reductions in discharges would be offset by increased user fees, this could serve to slow their conversion to clean technology. By constructing large public sewage plants, Denmark has thus created a pollution control infrastructure whose profitability depends on the continuous 'presence' of waste water, and the mere existence of end-of-pipe-solutions in effect serves to maintain the present level of pollution. To avoid the predicted scenario of overcapacity, municipalities may even seek to put a brake on the conversion to clean technology; for instance, by offering discounts on user fees to local firms. By over-investing in

* To allow for natural fluctuations in waste water discharges, there is usually an overcapacity of 20 percent in sewage works. The grosss overcapacity may therefore become 42 percent.

public sewage plants, Denmark has evidently been placed in an investment trap that also has political and environmental ramifications.*[4]

Regulations for user fees have recently been changed, so that local authorities now have the option of not collecting the surplus user fee for industrial waste water. As a result, several municipalities have abandoned the surplus user fee, which in fact constituted the strongest part of the incentive to control pollution at source. From the point of view of local authorities, it is economically most sensible to maintain pollution levels. From a social and environmental point of view, however, the approach is certainly questionable. The approach is especially harmful to companies that have managed to control pollution at source. For instance, a food-processing factory invested DKr 18 million to reduce its discharges by 90 percent. In the meantime, the user fee scheme changed and, despite pollution control, the factory's annual payment of user fees was increased from DKr 3.3 million to 4.3 million.†[5]

Danish policy design has had not only a primary result, in terms of ineffectiveness, but also a secondary result in terms of the institutionalisation of interests that have maintained ineffectiveness, the eco-industrial complex. By oversupplying public sewage plants, the municipalities have become part of an eco-industrial complex in water pollution control that thrives on the provision of expensive end-of-pipe solutions, and that in Denmark has become particularly powerful.‡

* The results of the Dutch–Danish comparison of surface water policies were presented at the Consensus Conference on the Aquatic Environment, organised by the Danish government, in Copenhagen in January 1991. In response to the results, the Director of Miljøstyrelsen stated that the essential problem was to forecast the impact of clean technology and thus the future quantities of discharges, and that extra capacity might facilitate the establishment of new industries (Erik Lindegård, 'Kommunerne har rent vand i posen', *Dagbladet Børsen*, 8 August 1991).

† In another case, municipal authorities in a medium-sized town agreed to pay one of its largest companies, Nordic Candy, DKr 1.5 million annually to continue discharging its 25,000 IE, rather than reducing effluents. The payments were even introduced two years before the sewage plants had been completed, and were a result of threats by the firm that it would have to lay off eight employees. In the latter case, the practice probably does not fall within the legal framework of the setting of user fees.

‡ In Denmark, the modern 'purveyors to the court' (to paraphrase Jänicke) are dominated by one large company, Krüger, which, apart from providing municipalities with sewage plants, also plays an important role in consulting and advising the Danish Environmental Protection Agency. When the Plan for the Aquatic Environment was approved in 1987, Krüger played a key role, not only providing the main

Do policy designs matter?

To a die-hard, free-market economist, it will probably come as no surprise that policies relying on economic instruments have been more successful than the Danish consensus approach to water pollution control. To other scholars, perhaps a few words still need to be added to the apparently clear cause and effect relationship in order to be fully convincing.

The four countries selected for the case studies were similar in terms of economic development, as well as of general popular support for pollution control. The technological options available to them have been quite similar in the international scientific community. It is mainly with regard to the environmental background that there are significant differences: Denmark has had easy access to the sea, whereas the other three countries depend more on their rivers, and for this reason problems have perhaps been less visible in Denmark. If, however, the environmental context variable is that significant, why has Germany, with the most limited access to the sea, not been the most successful country? In fact, the Netherlands' access to the sea is nearly as good as the Danish. The Dutch industrial heartlands are located around Rotterdam, and the large factories discharge into the Rhine just a few kilometres before it reaches the North Sea. Hence, the differences in environmental background conditions are, after all, not so significant.

Even were we to accept environmental background or concentration of industries as independent variables, this cannot explain the differences in performance. The environmental background variable does not independently lead to more pollution control. It could perhaps have caused greater environmental awareness, which then led to a stricter policy or affected the way in which certain policy instruments were implemented. When it comes to public opinion, concern about pollution has, paradoxically, been higher in Denmark, and the population also more prepared to pay the costs than in the other countries. In 1982, 75 percent of Danes stated that they would give priority to the environment even if it meant restricting economic growth, while the corresponding figure

elements of the report on which the plan was based, the NPO report (Miljøstyrelsen, 1984), but also lobbying for specific guidelines. The present chairman of Krüger's board is Jens Kampmann, former Danish Environment Minister in 1971–73 and Director of the Environmental Protection Agency in 1978–90.

for the Dutch population was 56 percent – the lowest in all of the four countries.[6] The Dutch have been the least willing to sacrifice economic growth for pollution control, but this has not impeded their success in anti-pollution policies.*

What might surprise some observers is that policy designs do in fact matter, and that there are immense differences in what may be attained under policy designs, depending on the policy instruments and strategies applied. The Dutch preconditions in terms of the special-purpose water authorities helped the country overcome the entrenched resistance of local authority bureaucracies faced by other countries, but the available administrative framework does not by itself explain the success. In neighbouring Belgium, special-purpose authorities in water quantity management have existed for centuries, but Belgium has not yet developed a plan for water pollution control that matches the Dutch success. Denmark also had older, though weaker, institutions of water management, which could have evolved into more effective organs than the scheme practised. National policy styles are not simply a reflection of deeply rooted traditions of public regulation; policy styles develop continuously as a result of political choices, and such deliberate choices, e.g. about policy instruments and administrative questions, are as important for the outcome of environmental policies as are the basic policy styles.

Notes

1 Sætevik (1988).
2 Harrison and Sewell (1980).
3 See Eurostat (1992).
4 See Andersen (1991a, 1991b).

* Another difference pertains to the size of companies in the four countries. Denmark is generally perceived to have many small and middle-sized firms, and few of the large research and development intensive firms. The share of small enterprises is, at 39 percent, fairly high in Denmark, but the highest share is found in Germany – 42 percent. In the Netherlands, the share is 35 percent and in France 28 percent. When it comes to the number of large firms, Denmark has even more large firms in relation to its population than has the Netherlands. Of manufacturing industries with more than 500 employees, Denmark has 18 for each million inhabitants, whereas the Netherlands has only 13 (see Eurostat, 1981, and national statistical yearbooks for 1988).

5 Birgitte Erhardtsen, 'Industrien får intet for miljøinvesteringerne', *Dagbladet Børsen*, 28 April 1992; Michael Bjerre, 'På slamstøtte', *Weekendavisen*, 12–18 December 1992.

6 Eurobarometer (1983), 38.

9

Conclusions: Environmental policy – A case for earmarked taxes

Introduction

The present study concerns four of the most affluent countries in Europe. Because of this bias, one should be careful when suggesting implications or in trying to apply the conclusions too schematically to the Eastern or Mediterranean countries, which are in the process of designing environmental policies under quite different political and economic circumstances. One obvious conclusion is that each country needs to consider its own preconditions and policy style when designing an environmental policy.

On the other hand, because the study has focused on four affluent countries with high public support for pollution control, it may serve to demonstrate what may be attained by the use of particular policy instruments under some of the most favourable circumstances available for environmental policy. Since we can learn more about the potentials of policy instruments when they are employed in an advantageous context, rather than under more pressing conditions, these countries' experiences in water management are indeed important for the general account of such instruments.

As the analysis in the preceding chapter shows, Danish water pollution control policy with regard to organic emissions has been both expensive and ineffective. On the other hand, Dutch water pollution control policy has been quite effective, in terms of both reducing organic emissions at low costs, and the use of cleaner technologies. The German and French experiences are less clear-cut; although effluent charges have been applied, German and French water pollution control policies have been less successful than in the Netherlands. The French achievements with regard to industry are nearly at the Dutch level, while the results with regard to public works are poor. The German results are closer to the Danish: high costs and apparently less control at source.

The Danish case does not support the assumptions of ecological modernisation capacity theory about the general benefits of a consensus-seeking policy style for environmental policy. The fact that consensus-seeking was extended into the implementation phase as well, through the institutionalisation of the Environmental Board of Appeal and the bargaining on guidelines and individual cases, did not, compared with the other three countries, promote more effective pollution control. In fact, consensus–seeking tended to reinforce problem-shifting, because it was more convenient to solve the disagreements by extending and subsidising public sewage plants.

Theories about ecological modernisation capacity would be better served by differentiating more among various policy styles, and indicating more precisely the general relationship between the national policy style and specific regulatory programmes of pollution control. The Danish experience makes it quite clear that the application of a consensus-seeking policy style was highly unsuitable to water pollution control.*[1]

The Danish policy response to the market failures of water pollution caused, relatively speaking, a stronger state failure in this sector than in any of the other three countries. By accepting great public responsibility for control of industrial pollution, in terms of a marked emphasis on public sewage plants and public planning, Denmark found itself unable to achieve the benefits that would have accrued from using economic incentives to internalise pollution costs. The high level of public expense on water pollution control in Denmark seems to reflect a powerlessness with regard to the eco-industrial complex, rather than effective pollution control.

According to economic theory on effluent charges, and following the replication logic of the case study methodology, it was initially expected to find three cases of success and one of failure, reflecting the three countries having economic instruments and the

* On the other hand, Denmark has achieved remarkable energy savings during the last two decades (e.g. 45 percent for heating purposes). The receptiveness to the energy movement is only part of a complex explanation in which high energy taxes and subsidies for insulation also have an essential role.

one without. The case studies indeed confirmed the case of failure in Denmark, but on the other hand failed to support our initial hypothesis that the use of the effluent charge policy instruments ensured similar degrees of successful pollution control in all three of the remaining cases. In fact, only the Dutch programme proved to be successful, in terms of both emissions, costs and technological responses.

For analytical reasons, this result is not as discouraging as it would seem. The fact that some charging programmes have proved more successful than others makes it possible to specify the particular conditions under which this policy instrument may prove effective to deal with pollution.

The conditions that will be suggested in the discussion below are the following:

- institutional constraints deriving from the policy design will affect economic instruments;
- because policy designs to some extent reflect national policy styles, including well-established interests, charging programmes will frequently be distorted or biased to fit these;
- a combined tax-bounty scheme, however, may help overcome institutional constraints, and is perhaps more suitable than proper green taxes in a situation with both market and regulatory failures.

Policy design and institutional constraints

Surface waters are no longer 'free goods' in any of the four countries studied here. Pollution control policies are not new, and discharges have required a formal permit from the authorities for nearly a century in some of the countries. Although enforcement has perhaps been mediocre, it has not changed the legal position of property rights, which have been assigned to the state. Nevertheless, the state ceased to require damage compensation for pollution, but has simply issued permits to the extent that it was thought to be justifiable. In three countries, however, the government added an additional restraint on discharges by imposing moderate levies, but the level of the levies has not been set on the basis of the estimated cost of the harm to the environment. The levies have been set pragmatically, in order to generate sufficient revenue to run closed tax-bounty schemes.

It is obvious that effluent charges have different positions in the clean water policies of Germany, France and the Netherlands. In Germany, the charge is intended to be only a supplementary instrument to a command-and-control policy. In the Netherlands, a more coherent system, which combines the financing of all pollution control in the levies, is imposed by the water authorities. The French charge is, like the German, only a supplement but, because of the closed tax-bounty scheme, proceeds are also used for pollution control measures in industry. In all three cases, the taxes help to correct the failures following from the historical rights to pollute – not by withdrawing these rights, but by presenting an incentive to perform better. One major reason for Denmark's poor performance was that very favourable permits had been granted under the 1949 Water Course Act, and the only tool to limit these rights was the tedious process of recipient quality planning.

The major distortions to the economic incentives stem from the choice of policy agents, i.e. the administrative authorities responsible for water pollution control. One of the most influential policy design choices has been the choice between employing specialised water agencies or using the infrastructure of local authorities. The general problem with the use of municipalities is that they are multiple-purpose bodies, which are also responsible for local employment and to a certain extent for taxation as well, and they are naturally concerned about the terms of competition in their district. Being politically governed, they are very sensitive to local preferences, which becomes a problem when the political choice is between losing jobs 'here' or accepting pollution somewhere 'downstream'. Because local authorities do not seek simply to ignore pollution problems, they frequently try to escape the difficult choice by offering direct or indirect subsidies for pollution control. In Germany and to some extent France, this solution has been very popular, although the limited financial autonomy of French communes frequently impedes this third option. Pollution 'downstream' is then preferred.

The Dutch municipalities were too small and too weak to be entrusted with water pollution control, and the reorganised water authorities in the Netherlands did not have any other goals except achieving efficient water management, an approach that, from the point of view of the environment, has been quite superior to that of the other three countries.

The major cause behind the poor French performance in public water pollution control is that the communes are responsible for implementation. There is reason to believe that if France had allowed its river basin agencies to take over water management fully, thereby gaining full autonomy from both communes and the central ministries, the present situation with regard to water pollution control would have improved significantly. The limited cost-effectiveness of the German policy seems also to be caused by the municipalities having been made responsible. Although sewage plants are widespread, subsidies have apparently distorted effectiveness.

Independent pollution control authorities with a high degree of autonomy and flexibility will most likely be able to pursue the targets on a more professional and cost-effective basis than will general-purpose local authorities. It is remarkable that Dutch industries have not been burdened with higher costs than firms in countries where local authorities sought to 'protect' local companies, jobs and taxes by avoiding or subsidising water pollution control. In the long run, the Dutch solution may even have been more beneficial to industry, since there has been less problem displacement. Hence, this study indicates that the local municipalities' perception of a trade-off between pollution and jobs does not apply to the same extent when more professional authorities, covering a larger hydrological area, manage pollution control. Rather, it is the preference for the 'third' option, following from municipal ambiguity, that may cause a long-term outcome, imposing future losses on the local economy.

The impact of standard operating procedures

Policy designs for water pollution control have been strongly influenced by the existing patterns and types of national policy styles. It was no coincidence that Denmark refused to introduce pollution levies and relied on a complex scheme of bargaining and consensus-seeking. Nor was it a coincidence that levies were introduced the way they were in the Netherlands. The choices were a result of well-established, standard operating procedures for public intervention, and of the existence of powerful public bureaucracies capable of maintaining these procedures. What made the Netherlands so successful in water pollution control was that the standard operating procedures helped support the establishment of a policy design that was in fact rather impositionary. The existence of specialised water authorities with a tradition of user payment provided an unusual but effective infrastructure for water pollution control.

The fact that the Dutch chose not to provide general subsidies for local pollution control, financed out of general taxation, was perhaps one of the most vital decisions in helping to maintain the 'polluter pays' principle. In both Germany and France the traditions of providing subsidies to local authorities were well institutionalized; in Germany this was even through the fiscal equalisation principle in the constitution. This institutionalisation made the granting of federal and *Länder* subsidies to local sewage works a 'standard operating procedure'.

It is curious that in Denmark no formal justification for the granting of local subsidies appeared until 1987. The present provisions in the Environmental Protection Act were transferred from the 1949 Water Course Act, the wording of which had been copied directly from the 1907 Sewerage Act. Neither in the formal comments on the legislation nor in the numerous preparatory reports is it possible to find any formal reasoning for the granting of subsidies.[2] In fact, the present wording simply stems directly from the first proposal for a Sewerage Act, which was put forward in 1901 in unusual circumstances by two members of the parliament. The originators of the wording indicated no other reason than the 'general interest', a concept sufficiently vague as to institutionalise the practice for nearly a century.

Local authorities represent a factor of considerable political importance, because of their vertical integration via political parties and because local authorities, like most other organisations, tend to prefer more responsibility, larger staffs and bigger budgets. For that reason, the establishment of specific-purpose agencies will encounter difficulties. Both in France and in Germany there were countervailing interests that succeeded in influencing and eroding the initially proposed, and more ideal, policy designs.

Even in France the central technocracy, despite its strong position during de Gaulle's presidency, was unable to establish river basin agencies fully responsible for water management. Perhaps because of the low priority assigned to pollution control by the political system, the Senate and the National Assembly, where the mayors' association has strong representation, were able to influence the assignment of tasks in the Loi de l'Eau. In Germany, the federal structure and the concurrent bargaining between the *Länder* and Bonn on administrative responsibilities made it necessary to abandon the high waste water levy initially proposed, since it could have been blocked by the Bundesrat.

A major finding of this study, therefore, is that, in spite of the advantages of effluent charges, political constraints tend to prevent charging policies from receiving the support they deserve. In cases where charging programmes are less successful than anticipated, the explanation often lies in the distortions caused by general policy styles, and in the interest coalitions established as part of the standard operating procedures for regulation.

Charging policies and combined tax–bounty incentives

The category of charging policies embraces a broad array of regulatory measures, and, as the analysis of Coase and Pigou revealed, such charging policies, rather than being a free-market approach to environmental policy, in fact represent a neglected welfare economics remedy. Using the economic theory on externalities, we are occasionally persuaded that such taxes should reflect the exact damage to the environment, and if we include the intertemporal costs of pollution, as Weizsäcker suggests, this would lead to quite significant green taxes as the most logical solution.

From an economic point of view, the 'standard' explanation for the Dutch success in water pollution control would certainly be that the Dutch effluent charges have been higher than French and German charges. Yet, we are left with the problem of why French effluent charges have had more significant effects than the German charge, despite being substantially smaller.

Since all the levies in question are equal to or even less than the costs of public sewage treatment, they are certainly too insignificant to reflect even the current damage they impose on the environment, not to speak of the potential intertemporal costs. At this point the die-hard economist might argue that, although too small to reflect the true social costs, the levies have been sufficiently high to provide an incentive to reduce pollution. This explanation may apply to the Netherlands, but hardly accounts for the French experience.

In most industries, the costs of water pollution control account for a very small proportion of the total costs, below 2 percent in most cases. Hence, the possible gain from controlling pollution has in most cases not been very significant and can hardly explain the immense changes reflected in the figures for most industries. The transaction costs at the level of the individual firm will frequently be too high to make it worthwhile to undertake control, except in specific industries such as sugar, pulp and paper and perhaps a few others. Why did companies after all undertake pollution control? And why was the policy design substantially more successful in only two countries with levy schemes?*

The level of levies, as will be recalled, was set not on the basis of the estimated cost of the damage to the environment, but pragmatically, with the goal of generating sufficient revenue to run closed tax-bounty schemes. The bounty part of the scheme has most probably played a far more important role than is usually assumed.

We obtain a hint about the importance of the bounty schemes from the French case, where transition took place in those sectors that received subsidies (pulp and paper, chemicals), while almost no changes occurred in food-processing industries, where subsidies played a minor role. Since French observers of the charge system regret that the charges are too low to provide an incentive, and taking into account the poor record of the permit scheme as well, the significant decrease in pollutants in French industry can best be explained by the subsidies offered to industries to control pollution on the basis of the revenue from the charge.

It appears that the bounty system also played a substantial role in the Netherlands, where RIZA was able to redistribute the state water levy revenue to industries. In fact, the reduction in pollution from industries discharging into those state waters administered by RIZA has been greater than the reduction from industries that discharge into waters managed by the water boards, and that did not have the option of subsidies.

In Germany, bounties have not been offered to control pollution by private companies, and emission reductions have also been less impressive. The German levy appears to have had much less influence despite being higher than the French levy. We may assume the explanation to be that the German authorities do not operate

---

* Altruism as an explanation can be ruled out if we examine the Danish case. Even though willingness to pay for pollution control was higher among Danes than in any other country, direct dischargers made very little voluntary effort to control pollution.

a subsidy scheme for firms on the basis of the waste water levy revenue.

Industrial investment has varied, but Danish industry, in spite of the lack of levies, did not escape with lower costs. French industry, with only half the investment volume in pollution control, achieved considerably more in terms of emission reductions, and it appears that the tax-bounty schemes have served to 'seize' a substantial share of the potential funds earmarked for pollution control, and to redistribute them in order to ensure control of the most important emitters. In France, the funds redistributed by the river basin agencies accounted for more than 50 percent of industrial water pollution control investment, and in the Netherlands the share exceeded 70 percent. Clearly, this reallocation of funds has been the result not of ideal considerations of lowest marginal abatement costs, but of pragmatic considerations to ensure control over large emitters.

If transaction costs are too high and levies too low to provoke control measures, a tax–bounty scheme may present a very preferable alternative, since policymakers would otherwise have to impose even higher taxes on industry in order to supersede transaction costs and to achieve pollution control targets.

A tax–bounty scheme consists, in fact, of two incentives, but its theoretical merits have never really been explored – despite the fact that it presents perhaps the 'true' Pigouvian solution (see Chapter 2). The bounty part of the tax–bounty scheme is usually treated as a random subsidy scheme, equivalent to the granting of across-the-board subsidies from general tax revenues. The standard argument against subsidies is that they will lead to over-investments (in whatever is subsidised), and that subsidies for pollution control may even help keep alive companies that would otherwise have gone out of business.[3]

Yet, as the case studies have demonstrated, the authorities may in fact choose to set priorities and bargain with companies on the measures to be subsidised. In the Netherlands, the authorities simply bargained with companies and required them to take measures at the source of pollution, i.e. in the production process (at a 25 percent bounty), before they could be granted a subsidy for sewage plant (at 60 or 90 percent). It is probably also more productive to focus on what and how subsidies are granted than to maintain a dogmatic resistance against the use of subsidies. In

Germany, public sewage works have been granted even larger subsidies than in Denmark, and the total costs of water pollution control indicate that Germany's experience has been just as costly as Denmark's. In spite of considerable indirect subsidies to firms serviced by public sewage plants, the two countries maintained a critical view on the direct support of pollution control at source in polluting industries. In Denmark, for instance, local municipalities have been allowed to spend as much as they liked on building advanced sewage plants, and even to compile fortunes in their sewer funds, but not to pass on a single crown to a local factory, even if it would have been cheaper to undertake control of pollution at the source. In France and the Netherlands the authorities appropriated a small share of companies' turnover, and redistributed the funds for pollution control, thereby making viable a concerted effort at the source of pollution. Clearly, the tax-subsidy schemes employed did not violate the 'polluter pays' principle, as did subsidies based on general tax revenue.

The fact that, according to an OECD report,[4] earmarked environmental taxes have in practice been applied more frequently than proper green taxes is best explained by the political difficulties associated with the introduction of new, higher taxes, sufficiently high to lead to a reduction in pollution. However, the widespread use of earmarked taxes must also be explained by the need to raise funds for environmentally urgent purposes in a period of restricted public spending. What the clean water experience suggests, however, is that the use of earmarked taxes is considerably underestimated in economic theory.

In general, earmarked taxes represent a second-best solution to user payment and must be regarded as especially appropriate for the production of public goods, such as environmental protection.*[5] Earmarked taxes are imposed where it is not technologically possible or feasible to implement user fees. The tax is levied on a good B, which has a turnover that co-varies with the good A, for which it is not possible or feasible to raise payment, and the revenue is reserved for the production of good A.[6] A perfect example is provided by Coase's description of the financing of lighthouses – the tax imposed on ships that called at British ports was

---

* As externality taxation, earmarked taxes descend from welfare economics; however, the line of descent is from a largely neglected tradition connected with the Stockholm School.

an earmarked tax. The turnover of ships in port was expected to
co-vary with the ships that benefited from the lighthouse.

Earmarked taxes often cause annoyance in financial ministries
because they link the size of the budget with the composition of
the budget, two elements traditionally decided separately. Earmarked taxes are criticised for rendering effective budget control
impossible, for creating inflexibility, for causing misallocations and
for limiting the autonomy of politicians. The criticism of earmarked taxation, however, is often raised on the assumption that
the public budget process is rational and carried out by social
planners, who seek to maximize a well-defined social utility function. Quite contrary to this view, most modern budget theories in
fact assume that budgeting processes proceed incrementally, as a
result of conflicts between the interests accepted in the budget of
the preceding year.

The risk associated with such earmarked taxes is clearly that
they survive their original purpose, and that funding is spent on
purposes that are less important from a general point of view.
Earmarked taxes may degenerate, the classic example being the
American tax earmarked for Confederate soldiers' pensions, which
survived in two American states until the 1960s, outliving those
for whom it was intended.[7] The fact that the Dutch state water
levy is no longer reserved for pollution control in factories, but is
used for general water management purposes, could reflect such a
tendency. However, in order to treat polluters in the same way,
regardless of whether they discharge into provincial or state
waters, the levy is maintained. Furthermore, there seem to be
relevant foundations for environmental funding for a very long
time to come.

Another risk associated with earmarked taxes is the funding
bureaucracies that tend to follow in their wake. Both the French
river basin agencies and the Dutch water boards give the impression of being very wealthy financial organisations, and one cannot
rule out the possibility that these bodies may have appropriated a
larger share of the levy revenue than necessary for administration.
Still, if the overall scheme is more cost-effective than other alternatives, the problem of funding bureaucracies is not too big
to find a solution. In Germany an upper limit has been set on
the proportion of the waste water levy that can be spent on
administration.

The deficiencies of earmarked taxes must be compared with the possible deficiencies of proper green taxes, which are fiscal in the sense that the revenue is assigned to the general treasury. Since 1988 Denmark has begun to employ green taxes on a larger scale, but these are mainly fiscal and support the budget of the Ministry of the Environment. They are not earmarked for the budget of the ministry, but, because of Budget Office procedures, the ministry has to propose either savings or new sources of income in order to expand its disbursements. As a consequence, the ministry has been able to make substantial expansions of its budget, and its disbursements are now nearly 100 percent 'covered' by various green taxes.[8] None of these is earmarked for direct pollution control measures, and the most significant of these taxes is a general waste tax, which, in spite of the revenue it generates (approximately DKr 500 million), has been found to be too insignificant to reduce waste, except of building materials.[9]

As Weizsäcker's simple model indicates (see Chapter 2), proper green taxes will have to be quite onerous in order to have any impact on pollution. This is not only because of the immense intertemporal costs generated by most pollution sources, but also because of the frequently inelastic behaviour by polluters in response to such taxes. In cases where the demand for pollution-intensive services is rather inelastic, the explanation may lie with the transaction cost problem and the institutional constraints on the 'markets' in question.*[10]

* A good example is provided by Danish water prices. Copenhagen's water consumption is estimated to be almost twice as high as the island of Zealand can supply on a sustainable level. However, an analysis of responses to previous increases in water prices shows that household demand (which accounts for more than half of water consumption) is very inelastic (Hansen and Westergaard, 1991). To achieve the desired halving of water demand, one would have to impose a tax of approximately 300 percent on the present water bill, which is already DKr 20–25 per cubic metre. Only such a price increase would make households invest in the technologies – which are in fact already available – to reduce water demand. The fact that a large proportion of households are rented apartments, and that tenants do not have an interest in undertaking investment in dwellings that they do not own, presents an institutional constraint on the 'water market' and tends to put a further brake on the price signal from such a fiscal green tax. As an alternative, an earmarked water tax of only a few kroners per cubic metre would generate more than DKr 1 billion annually to be earmarked for subsidies on investment in water-saving taps, WCs and washing machines, and would most likely speed up the transition to lower water demand. The earmarked tax would not, however, create revenue for the state treasury.

Economic theory does not provide much guidance in the choice between fiscal and earmarked green taxes. Although economists frequently mention the possibility of returning the proceeds of environmental charges to the polluters, the theories generally work on the assumption that the proceeds are collected by the state and can be spent for other purposes. Green tax reforms that shift taxation from income to pollution may be desirable from a general point of view, but their implementation might not promote the transition to more sustainable development as fast as some economists would have us believe. The aim of this study has not been to compare fiscal and earmarked taxes, but a closer examination of the differences between these two instruments ought to be high on the research agenda of the environmental research community. On the basis of the Dutch and French experiences, we can conclude that even modest earmarked taxes are in practice significantly more effective than the conventional view would lead us to assume.

Finding patterns in the mosaic

For the future analysis of environmental policies, our study of the clean water experience makes it reasonable to carry out a more refined classification of environmental policies. The standard dichotomy used by most economists between command-and-control policies and effluent charge policies is too simple. The dichotomy proposed by political science, between adaptive and structured policies, is hardly more precise. The classification proposed in Figure 9.1 combines these two dimensions, thereby creating four

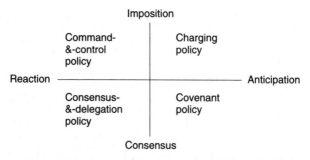

Figure 9.1   Environmental policy strategies

types of environmental policy, which in fact ought to be familiar to most observers.

Figure 9.1 indicates that, on the first dimension, environmental policies may be either imposed or consensus-seeking, a classification that refers to the entire decision-making and implementation process. On the other dimension, policies may be either predominantly reactive – which for environmental policies refers to removal strategies of either diffusion or end-of-pipe solutions – or they can be more anticipatory, in the sense of clean technology or structural change policies. From this classification one can differentiate among four types of environmental programme: command-and-control policy, consensus-and-delegation policy, charging policy and covenant policy.

By command-and-control policies is meant policies that prescribe technology-based 'best-available technology' guidelines, as practised in Germany and the United States.

Consensus-and-delegation policies, on the other hand, prescribe no specific *standards* but instead define a *process* by which bureaucracy and polluters will agree on measures to be taken, either on a case-by-case basis or on the basis of certain agreed-upon performance standards. In its extreme version, bargaining is delegated to local bureaucracies and authorities. Consensus-and-delegation policies have been practised, in varying degrees, in Denmark, Sweden and Great Britain.

Charging policies prescribe no mandatory measures, but establish a system of economic *incentives* by which to charge polluters for their emissions, for their input of raw materials or for their products. Charging policies always leave flexibility for polluters to choose how and to what extent they will reduce pollution. The charging principles may vary, however, from closed tax-bounty schemes and green taxes proper to tradable pollution rights, and charging policies often have very different institutional arrangements. Charging policies have been practised in the Dutch and French water policies and in Japanese air pollution policy.

This study of water pollution control policies supports the hypothesis that charging policies promote the development of clean technologies to a higher degree, and thus are more anticipatory than both command-and-control policies and consensus-and-delegation policies. However, their influence on the innovation of non-waste technologies should not be overestimated. Traditional end-of-pipe solutions also account for a considerable portion of the pollution reduction that follows from charging policies.

A fourth possible version of environmental policy is the covenant policy, where the emphasis is on reaching a *voluntary agreement* with the polluters on targets for pollution control. This method also allows for a degree of flexibility with regard to the technological response, and the consensus that is reached between the authorities and the polluters through such an agreement is often more acceptable to the polluters, who may resent having specific measures imposed. The use of voluntary agreements is currently advocated by industries and is implemented for specific products, such as detergents, batteries and packaging, in a number of countries, including the Netherlands and Denmark.*[11]

The experience of the Danish consensus policy, however, is not very promising, even when compared with the German command-and-control policy. Hence, it is difficult to accept the postulate put forward in much of the literature that consensus-seeking policies should be preferable to imposed policies when it comes to environmental policy. Since environmental policy, by imposing high costs on often well-defined groups of actors, differs fundamentally from many of the distributional welfare policies, it is necessary to maintain a high degree of pressure during implementation. On the results of this study we can surmise that, if a government does not establish regulations for imposing measures on polluters with the kind of speed that effluent charges ensure, it will most likely not be able to progress in the control of pollution. For this reason, and corroborated by the previous results of covenant policies, this revised version of consensus-seeking should be regarded cautiously.

By being subject to charges rather than to mandatory guidelines, polluters will be allowed a flexibility in deciding how to implement pollution control, and there is a constant incentive to take action. The imposition approach does not preclude talks and negotiations between governments, bureaucracies and polluters on the measures to be imposed. Yet, once a decision has been reached, few other policy instruments are as effective as levies and charges in securing self-interest among polluters in implementing the agreed-upon measures.

---

* The Dutch experience has been mixed, however, as an initial evaluation of eight 'covenants' shows. Compliance with the covenants is most suitable where measures can be justified by other than purely environmental aims.

It should not be overlooked that the Dutch policy was to some extent consensus seeking in that it took the most important interests into consideration during the decision-making process. However, the national water authority, Rijkswaterstaat, was a strong, independent actor, which took control over the area during implementation, and although water policy was both flexible and impositionary, it left few opportunities for the polluters to put a brake on its implementation. The system of levies and the insufficiency clause created a rigid framework for the responsible authorities at the local level, rather than the lax consensus-and-bargaining scheme established in Denmark. We may perceive the closed tax-bounty schemes as a less impositionary version of the charging policies than proper green taxes, and hence situated closer to the X axis in Figure 9.1. The findings of this study suggest that the most likely 'candidates' for relatively successful environmental policies are to be found among the various charging policies.

The national bias

The particular version of the charging strategy that proved so favourable in the Netherlands and France should in principle encounter less political resistance than fiscal green taxes. To environmental ministries, such charges create important incentives and raise revenues for particular pollution control programmes. And to industries they represent a smaller financial burden than proper green taxes. However, it is not environmental ministries that impose taxes or levies, but financial ministries and they have a need of the revenues themselves. Therefore earmarked taxes are likely to encounter considerable resistance from decision-makers within this sphere.

The fact that economic incentives provide a powerful policy instrument does not imply that policy-makers will necessarily choose to implement them. They may be more interested in the fiscal properties of green taxes, or they may simply abstain from using economic instruments for political reasons. There certainly also exist cases of pollution control where command-and-control or covenants would ensure more favourable outcomes than would economic incentives, not least in the case of toxic substances. Furthermore, polluters often prefer to comply with much more complicated and costly regulations if they can avoid paying environmental levies.[12]

The intriguing question is whether there are specific national policy styles that tend to impede the use of economic incentives. The increased use of economic incentives in Denmark and in the other Nordic countries recently seems to deny that this is the case. However, the strong tradition of consensus-seeking in Denmark has made the use of covenants a much more viable alternative to the traditional regulatory strategy. The strong position of the local authorities is gradually being undermined through voluntary agreements between the Ministry of the Environment and sectors of industry on the measures to be taken. In these negotiations the possible use of economic instruments often serves as a powerful incentive to enter into a voluntary scheme, but it is very seldom that they are actually applied.

National policy styles affect the choice of environmental policy strategies, but there is in general no incompatibility between certain national policy styles and certain strategies. Thus, Japan adopted economic policy instruments upon the pronounced failures of its standard operating procedures for policy-making in the late 1960s. And the USA did the same when the failures of the Clean Air Act became evident. However, national policy styles do tend to affect the institutionalisation and operationalisation of economic policy instruments. Whereas the US response, was to impose tradable pollution quotas, the Japanese set up a system of compensation payments to pollution victims in a concerted effort between industry and government. So there is no policy style that is able to block any of the four available policy strategies, particularly not in a period of crisis or environmental catastrophe. There are, however, national policy styles that may cause a bias in the implementation of such strategies.

Notes

1 See Krawinkel (1991).

2 *Rigsdagstidende*, 1901, A, 3531: 'Forslag til Lov om Anlæg og Vedligeholdelse af lukkede Spildevandsledninger'; *Rigsdagstidende*, 1946–47, A, 3625: 'Forslag til Vandløbslov'; *Betænkning afgivet af Kommissionen angaaende Revision af Vandløbslovgivningen* (Copenhagen: Schultz, 1947); *Folketingstidende*, 1972–73, 'Forslag til lov om Miljøbeskyttelse', A, 7707.

3 Baumol and Oates (1988).

4 OECD (1989a).

5   See Lindahl (1919).

6   Teja and Bracewell–Milnes (1991).

7   Ibid., 19.

8   Andersen (1990), A similar trend is reported for the Netherlands, see Vos (1989).

9   Christoffersen et al. (1992).

10   See Bente Andersen et al. (1992).

11   See Klok (1989).

12   For an account of the entrepreneurial conception of social science evaluations and the evasion of policy-makers, see Albæk (1989).

Bibliography

Agence Financière de Bassin Seine–Normandie (1986), *Agence Financière de Bassin Seine–Normandie* (Paris: AFBSN).

Agence Financière de Bassin Seine–Normandie (1987), *V'ème Programme d'Intervention 1987–1991* (Paris: AFBSN).

Agence de l'Eau Seine–Normandie (1991), *Le VI'ème Programme d'Intervention de l'Agence de l'Eau Seine Normandie 1992–1996* (Paris).

Akademiet for de Tekniske Videnskaber (1990), *Vandmiljøplanens tilblivelse og iværksættelse* (Vedbæk: ATV).

Albæk, Erik (1989), *Fra sandhed til information* (Copenhagen: Akademisk Forlag).

Andersen, Bente, Jens Andersen, Mikael Skou Andersen, Dorthe Bechmann, Arne Villumsen, Susanne Kaarøe, Ragnar Heldt Nielsen (1992), *Danmarks grundvandsressource*, Teknologinævnets rapport 1 (Copenhagen: Teknologinævnet).

Andersen, Mikael Skou (1989a), 'Miljøbeskyttelse – et implementeringsproblem', *Politica*, 21: 3, 312–28.

Andersen, Mikael Skou (1989b), 'Omsættelige forureningskvoter, *Nordisk Administrativt Tidsskift*, 2, 124–32.

Andersen, Mikael Skou (1990), 'Pollution Charges in Denmark: Budget Deficits and the Environmental Asset', 119–34 in Hans–Christoph Binswanger and Martin Jänicke, eds, *Environmental Charges – An International Exchange of Experiences*, Contributions held on a Symposium in Berlin (West), 3–5 November 1989 (Berlin: Forschungsstelle für Umweltpolitik, Freie Universität).

Andersen, Mikael Skou (1991a), 'Green Taxes and Regulatory Reform. Dutch and Danish Experiences in Curbing Surface Water Pollution', FS-II-401 (Wissenschaftszentrum Berlin).

Andersen, Mikael Skou (1991b), 'Hvordan er effektiviteten af den danske regulering af vandmiljøet sammenlignet med reguleringen i andre lande?', *Rapport fra konsensuskonference 31.1.–4.2.1991*, 18.1–18.15 (Copenhagen: Undervisningsministeriets Forskningsafdeling).

Andersen, Mikael Skou (1991c), 'Styring med miljøafgifter', *Samfundsøkonomen*, 2, 5–13.

Andersen, Mikael Skou (1992a), 'Er vandmiljøplanen pengene værd?', *Jord og Viden*, 137: 9, 20–1.

Andersen, Mikael Skou (1992b), 'Institutions, Markets and the Environment: The Coase–Pigou Controversy Revisited', Paper presented to the European Consortium for Political Research, Joint Sessions of Workshops, 'New Institutionalism', Limerick, Ireland, 30 March to 4 April (Århus: Institut for Statskundskab).

Andersen, Mikael Skou (1993), 'Governance by Green Taxes: Implementing Clean Water Policies in Denmark, France, Germany and the Netherlands 1970–1990', PhD dissertation (Århus: Department of Political Science).

Andersen, Mikael Skou (1994 forthcoming), 'Environmental Policy Performance: Finding Patterns in the Mosaic of Case Studies', in Jan van der Straaten and Stephen Young, *Green Politics* (London: Routledge).

Andersen, Mikael Skou and Michael W. Hansen (1991), *Vandmiljøplanen: Fra forhandling til symbol* (Århus: Niche).

Andersen, Peder (1984), 'Miljøpolitik og markedskræfterne, *Politica*, 16:2, 131–46.

Annales des Mines (1988), 'La Gestion de l'Eau', 7–8.

Århus Amtskommone (1986), 'Grenå Kommune & Miljøstyrelsen', *Spildevandsudledning og forureningspåvirkning ved Fornøs* (Århus).

Aslanbeigui, N. (1990), 'On The Demise of Pigovian Economics', *Southern Economic Journal*, 56:3, 616–27.

ATV (Abwassertechnische Vereinigung) (1982), 'Planspiele zum Vollzug des Abwasserabgabengesetzes', *Umweltbundesamt Berichte 5/82* (Berlin: Schmidt).

ATV (Abwassertechnische Vereinigung) (1988), 'Wirksamkeit des Abwasserabgabengesetzes für die Reinhaltung der Gewässer', *Dokumentation und Schriftenreihe der ATV aus Wissenschaft und Praxis*, 18 (St. Augustin: ATV).

Basse, Ellen Margrethe (1987), *Miljøankenœvnet* (Copenhagen: GAD).

Baumol, W. J. (1972), 'On Taxation and the Control of Externalities', *American Economic Review*, 62:3, 307–21.

Baumol, William J. and Wallace E. Oates (1971), 'The Use of Standards and Prices for Protection of the Environment', *Swedish Journal of Economics*, 73:1, 42–54.

Baumol, William J. and Wallace E. Oates (1979), *Economics, Environmental Policy and the Quality of Life* (New Jersey: Prentice–Hall).

Baumol, William J. and Wallace E. Oates (1988), *The Theory of Environmental Policy* (Cambridge: Cambridge University Press).

Bayreuther, U. (1990), 'Steuern – Instrument der Umweltpolitik?', *IPW–Berichte*, 19:5, 52–4.

Becker, J. W. (1979), 'Public Opinion and the Environment 1970–1975', *Planning and Development in the Netherlands*, 11:2, 179–85.

Benkert, Wolfgang et al. (1990), *Umweltpolitik mit Ökosteuern?* (Marburg: Metropolis).

Bennett, Graham (1986a), *European Community Environmental Policy in Practice*, 2, Netherlands: Water and Waste (London: Graham & Trotman).

Bennett, Graham (1986b), *Netherlands: Water and Waste* (London: Graham & Trotman).

Bennett, Graham (1988), 'A Common Environmental Policy for a Common Market?', in F. J. Dietz and W. Heijman, eds, *Environmental Policy in a Market Economy* (Wageningen: Pudoc).

Bennett, Graham (1991), 'The History of the Dutch National Environmental Policy Plan', *Environment*, 33:7, 7–33.

Bennett, Graham (1992), 'Rhine Brine', 54–91 in *Dilemmas: Coping with Environmental Problems* (London: Earthscan).

Berendes, K. (1981), 'Die Mindestanforderungen nach art. 7a aus der Sicht des Bundes', 9–16 in Bayerischen Landesanstalt für Wasserforschung, *Allgemein anerkannte Regeln der Technik – Mindestanforderungen Gewässerschutz* (Munich: R. Oldenbourg Verlag).

Berman, Paul (1980), 'Thinking about Programmed and Adaptive Implementation', Helen M. Ingram and Dean E. Mann, eds, *Why Policies Succeed or Fail* (California: Sage).

Binswanger, Hans–Christoph and Martin Jänicke, eds (1990),

Environmental Charges, Forschungsstelle für Umweltpolitik FFU-rep. 90–1 (Berlin: Freie Universität).

Bochniarz, Zbigniew (1990), 'Economic Incentives to Protect Water Quality in Market and Planned Economies', *Natural Resources Forum*, 14:4, 302–11.

Bongaerts, Jan and Andreas Kraemer (1989), 'Permits and Effluent Charges in the Water Pollution Control Policies of France, West Germany and the Netherlands', *Environmental Monitoring and Assessment*, 12, 127–47.

Bower, Blair T. et al. (1981), *Incentives in Water Quality Management* (Washington DC: Johns Hopkins University Press).

Bressers, Hans Th. A. (1983a), *Beleidseffektiviteit en waterkwaliteitsbeleid. Een bestuurskundig onderzoek* (Enschede: T. H. Twente).

Bressers, Hans (1983b), 'The Role of Effluent Charges in Dutch Water Quality Policy', 143–68 in P. B. Downing and K. Hanf, eds, *International Comparisons in Implementing Pollution Laws* (Boston: Kluwer-Nijhoff).

Bressers, Hans (1988), 'A Comparison of the Effectiveness of Incentives and Directives: The Case of the Dutch Water Quality Policy', *Policy Studies Review*, 7:3, 500–18.

Bromley, Daniel W. (1991), *Environment and Economy: Property Rights and Public Policy* (Oxford: Basil Blackwell).

Brunowsky, Ralf–Dieter and Lutz Wicke (1984), *Der Öko-Plan. Durch Umweltschutz zum neuen Wirtschaftswunder* (Munich: Piper).

Brussaard, Wim and Margaret R. Grossman (1990), 'Legislation to Abate Pollution from Manure: The Dutch Approach', *North Carolina Journal of International Law and Commercial Regulation*, 15:1, 86–110.

Buchot, Ténière (1991), 'Agence de l'eau, mode d'emploi', *La voirie et l'environnement*, 1496, 26–7.

Bucksteeg, Klaus (1991), 'Water Resources Management and Water Pollution Control: National Case Studies from the Federal Republic of Germany', *European Water Pollution Control*, 1:4, 34–44.

Bundeshaushaltsplan (1976–88) (Bonn: Bundestagdrs.).

Bundesminister des Innern (1977), *Auswirkungen des Abwasserabgabengesetzes auf Investitionsplanung und-abwicklung in Unternehmen, Gemeinden und Abwasserverbänden* (Bonn).

Bundesminister des Innern (1983), *Erfahrungsbericht zum Abwasserabgabengesetz* (Bonn).

Bundestag Drucksachen (1990), *Bericht der Bundesregierung an den Deutschen Bundestag über die Auswirkungen der 5. Novelle zum Wasserhaushaltsgesetz auf die Gewässer*, Drs. 11/ 7327.

Cairncross, Frances (1991), *Costing the Earth* (London: Business Books).

Cappon, J. J. (1991), 'Water Resource Management and Water Pollution Control in the Netherlands', *European Water Pollution Control*, 1:5, 28–44.

Centraal Bureau voor de Statistiek (1974–88), *Waterkwaliteitsbeheer. Deel A: Lozing van Afvalwater. Deel B: Zuivering van Afvalwater* (The Hague).

Centraal Bureau voor de Statistiek (1979–89), *Milieukosten van bedrijven* (The Hague).

Centraal Bureau voor de Statistiek (1980–88), *Kosten en financiering van het milieubeheer* (The Hague).

Centraal Bureau voor de Statistiek (1989), 'De druk van de waterschapslasten 1989', *CBS Monthly*, 9, 31–9.

Central Bureau of Statistics (1975–92), *Statistical Yearbook of the Netherlands* (The Hague: Staatsuitgeverij).

Central Bureau of Statistics (1990), Correspondence with J. van Marseven, Head of Department for Financial Statistics.

Central Bureau of Statistics (1987), *Environmental Statistics of the Netherlands* (The Hague: Staatsuitgeverij).

Christoffersen, Henrik et al. (1992), *Affaldsafgiftens effekter* (Copenhagen: AKF-Forlaget).

Coase, R. H. (1988), *The Firm, the Market and the Law* (Chicago: University of Chicago Press).

Coase, R. H. (1974), 'The Lighthouse in Economics', *Journal of Law and Economics*, 17:2, 357–76.

Coase, R. H. (1960), 'The Problem of Social Cost', *Journal of Law and Economics*, 3, 1–44.

Collard, David (1981), 'A. C. Pigou, 1877–1959', 105–39, in D. P. O'Brien and J. R. Presley, eds, *Pioneers of Modern Economics in Britain* (London: Macmillan).

Commission of the European Communities, DG XI (1987), *The State of the Environment in the European Community* (Luxembourg).

Crampes, Claude, Ahmed Mir and Michel Moreaux (1984), 'The Experience of the River Basin Agencies in France', 343–88 in Gunter Schneider and Rolf–Ulrich Sprenger, eds, *Mehr Umweltschutz für weniger Geld* (Munich: Ifo-Institut für Wirtschaftsforschung).

Crandall, Robert W. (1983), *Controlling Industrial Pollution* (Washington DC: Brookings).

Dales, J. H. (1968), *Pollution, Property and Prices* (Toronto: University of Toronto Press).

Danmarks Statistik (1972–90), *Statistisk Årbog* (Copenhagen).

Danmarks Statistik, Miljøstyrelsen og Skov-og Naturstyrelsen (1990), *Tal om natur og miljø* (København: Danmarks Statistik).

de Goede, B. et al. (1982), *Het Waterschap* (Deventer: Kluwer).

Despax, M. and W. Coulet (1982), *The Law and Practice Relating to Pollution Control in France* (London: Graham & Trotman).

DIOS (1987), *Tilsynsundersøgelse 1986* (Copenhagen: Dansk Institut for Organisationsstudier).

Direction de l'eau et de la prévention des pollutions et des risques (1989), *Enquête nationale sur le prix de l'eau et de l'assainissement – Synthèse* (Paris).

DK–Teknik (1992), *Vandforbrug i fremstillingsindustrien* (Copenhagen).

Downing, Paul B. (1979), 'Implementing Pollution Laws', *Zeitschrift für Umweltpolitik*, 4, 357–92.

Downing, Paul B. and K. Hanf, eds (1983), *International Comparisons in Implementing Pollution Laws* (Boston: Kluwer Nijhoff).

Drouet, Dominique (1987), *L'Industrie de l'eau dans le monde* (Paris: Presses de l'école nationale des ponts et chaussées).

Drouet, Dominique (1987), *L'Innovation dans les industries de l'environnement* (Paris: RD International).

Dubgaard, Alex (1991), *The Danish Nitrate Policy in the 1980s*, Rapport nr. 59 (Copenhagen: Statens Jordbrugsøkonomiske Institut).

Environmental Resources Limited (1982), *The Law and Practice Relating to Pollution Control in the Netherlands*, 2nd edition (Brussels: Graham & Trotman).

Enyedi, Gyorgi et al., eds (1987), *Environmental Policies in East and West* (London: Taylor Graham).

Eurobarometer (1974–90), *Public Opinion in the European Community* (Brussels).
Eurobarometer (1983), *Europæerne og deres miljø* (Brussels).
Eurostat (1992), *Environment Statistics 1991* (Brussels).
Eurostat (1981), *Structure and Activity of Industry* (Brussels).
Ewringmann, D. and F. Schafhausen (1985), *Umweltbundesamt Berichte 8/85: Abgaben als ökonomischer Hebel in der Umweltpolitik* (Berlin: Erich Schmidt Verlag).
Ewringmann, D. et al. (1981), *Umweltbundesamt Berichte 2/81, Auswirkungen des Abwasserabgabengesetzes auf industrielle Indirekteinleiter* (Berlin: Erich Schmidt Verlag).
Ewringmann, D., K. Kibat and F. Schafhausen (1980), *Umweltbundesamt Berichte 8/80: Die Abwasserabgabe als Investitionsanreiz* (Berlin: Erich Schmidt Verlag).
Fenger, Bent and Christian Jensen (1977), 'Spildevandsplanlægningen – hvordan er det gået hidtil?', *Stads-og havneingeniøren*, 3, 57–64.
Fichtner/Ecoplan (1989), *Einfluss der Wirtschafts-und Technologieentwicklung auf die Emissions- und Immissionsentwicklung*, Auftrags-Nr 01-VQ-8708 (Bonn: Bundesministerium für Forschung und Technologie).
Foljanty-Jost, Gesine (1988), *Emissionsabgabe in Japan – Rückblick auf ein umweltpolitisches Modell* (Berlin: Forschungsstelle für Umweltpolitik).
Forureningsrådet (1971), *Vand: En redegørelse fra målsætningsudvalget og hovedvandudvalget* (Copenhagen: Statens Trykningskontor).
Friege, Henning (1984), 'Das Abwasserabgabengesetz – erweitern, konkretisieren, vereinfachen', *Zeitschrift für Umweltpolitik*, 2.
Gamby, Rune et al. (1988), *Miljøproblemer og miljøregulering i Grenå*, Rapportserien nr. 4, Institut for Miljø, Teknologi og Samfund (Roskilde Universitetscenter: Tek-Sam forlaget).
Gemeindefinanzbericht (1989), *Der Städtetag*, no. 2.
Gerau, Jürgen (1978), 'Zur politischen Ökologie der Industrialisierung des Umweltschutzes', 114–49 in Martin Jänicke, ed., *Umweltpolitik* (Opladen: Leske & Budrich).
Giwer, Alfred (1984), 'Erfahrungen mit dem Abwasserabgabengesetz aus der Sicht der *Länder*', FGU-seminar Novellierung des Abwasserabgabengesetzes, 24–25 September, Berlin (Berlin: Umweltbundesamt).

Gregersen, Birgitte (1984), *Det miljøindustrielle kompleks* (Ålborg: Ålborg Universitetsforlag).

Gresser, J., K. Fujikura and A. Mrishima (1981), *Environmental Law in Japan* (Cambridge, Mass.: MIT Press).

Gunlicks, Arthur B. (1986), *Local Government in the German Federal System* (Durham, NC: Duke University Press).

Haagen–Jensen, Claus (1982), *The Law and Practice Relating to Pollution Control in Denmark* (London: Graham & Trotman).

Hahn, Robert W. (1989), 'Economic Prescriptions for Environmental Problems: How the Patient Followed the Doctor's Orders', *Journal of Economic Perspectives*, 3:2, 95–114.

Hanf, Kenneth (1989), 'Deregulation as Regulatory Reform: The Case of Environmental Policy in the Netherlands', *European Journal of Political Research*, 17, 193–207.

Hanley, N., S. Hallett and I. Moffatt (1990), 'Why Is More Notice not Taken of Economists' Prescriptions for the Control of Pollution?', *Environment and Planning A*, 22, 1421–39.

Hansen, Charlotte (1991), *Environmental Administration in France*, Student's report (Ålborg: AUC).

Hansen, Jens Muff and Nanna Rask (1986), 'Vurdering af den marine recipientkvalitetsplanlægning', *Vand og Miljø*, 3:2, 50–2.

Hansen, Lars Gårn and Mona M. Westergaard (1991), *En undersøgelse of vandforbrugets prisfølsomhed for husholdninger i København* (Copenhagen: Amternes og Kommunernes Forskningsinstitut).

Hardin, Garrett (1968), 'The Tragedy of the Commons', *Science*, 162:1, 1243–8.

Harremoës, Poul (1970), 'Vandkvalitet', *Vand – Tidsskrift for vandkvalitet*, 1:1, 2–11.

Harremoës, Poul (1986), 'Recipientkvalitet og rensningskrav for spildevand', *Vand og Miljø*, 6, 233.

Harrison, Peter and W. R. Derrick Sewell (1980), 'Water Pollution Control by Agreement: The French System of Contracts', *Natural Resources Journal*, 20:4, 765–86.

Hartog, H. (1973), 'The Quality Control of Surface Waters in the Netherlands: The Economic Consequences', *Planning and Development in the Netherlands*, 7:2, 130–9.

Hayward, Jack (1982), 'Mobilising Private Interests in the Service of Public Ambitions: The Salient Element in the Dual French

Policy Style', 111–40, in Jeremy Richardson, ed. *Policy Styles in Western Europe* (London: Allen & Unwin).

Helm, Dieter and David Pearce (1990), 'Assessment: Economic Policy Towards the Environment', *Oxford Review of Economic Policy*, 6:1, 1–15.

Hidefumi Imura (1990), 'Economic Incentives as a Means of Environmental Policy: Interactive Effects of Standards and Economic Incentives in Air Pollution Control in Japan', 57–91 in H. C. Binswanger and M. Jänicke, *Environmental Charges* Berlin Forschungsstelle für Umweltpolitik).

Hill, Michael (1983), 'The Role of the British Alkali and Clean Air Inspectorate in Air Pollution Control', 87–106, in Paul B. Downing and Kenneth Hanf, eds, *International Comparisons in Implementing Pollution Laws* (Boston: Kluwer-Nijhoff).

Hjorth–Andersen, Chr. (1978), 'Kommunale Spildevandsvedtægter: En undersøgelse af finansieringen af offentlige rensningsanlæg', *Juristen og Økonomen*, 455.

Holm, Karin (1988), 'Wasserverbände im internationalen Vergleich: Eine ökonomische Analyse der französischen Agences Financières de Bassin und der deutschen Wasserverbände im Ruhrgebiet', *IFO Studien zur Umweltökonomie*, 3 (Munich: IFO-Institut für Wirtschaftsforschung e.V.).

Honert, Siegfried (1973), 'Erhebung und Verwendung von Abwasserabgaben in ausländischen Staaten', *Wasserrecht und Wasserwirtschaft*, Band 15 (Berlin: Erich Schmidt Verlag).

Hood, Christopher C. (1983), *The Tools of Government* (London: Macmillan).

Hoogheemraadschap van Rijnland (1989), *We and Water* (Leiden: HvR).

Hudson, James F., E. Lake and D. Grossman (1981), *Pollution-Pricing. Industrial Responses to Wastewater Charges* (Massachusetts: Lexington Books).

Husingh, Donald et al. (1985), *Proven Profits from Pollution Prevention* (Washington DC).

Hydro+ (*International Water Review*), 'Water Industry: The British Revival', 15 (Paris: Hyecom).

INSEE (1974–91), *Annuaire Statistique de la France* (Paris: Institut National de la Statistique et des Études Économiques).

International Water Supply Association (1988), *International Water Statistics* (Zürich: IWSA).

Jänicke, Martin (1978a), 'Blauer Himmel über den Industriestädten – eine optische Täuschung', 150–65 in Martin Jänicke, ed., *Umweltpolitik* (Opladen: Leske & Budrich).

Jänicke, Martin, ed. (1978b), *Umweltpolitik: Beiträge zur Politologie des Umweltschutzes* (Opladen: Leske & Budrich).

Jänicke, Martin (1986), *Staatsversagen – Die Ohnmacht der Politik in der Industriegeselfschaft* (Munich: Piper).

Jänicke, Martin (1988), 'Ökologische Modernisierung. Optionen und Restriktionen präventiver Umweltpolitik', 13–26 in Udo Simonis, ed., *Präventive Umweltpolitik* (Frankfurt: Campus).

Jänicke, Martin (1989), 'Environmental Charges and Change in Political Paradigms', Paper presented to Symposium on Environmental Charges, West Berlin, 3 November (Berlin: Freie Universität).

Jänicke, Martin (1990a), 'Erfolgsbedingungen von Umweltpolitik im internationalen Vergleich', *Zeitschrift für Umweltpolitik*, 3, 213–31 (English version: 'Conditions for Environmental Policy Success: An International Comparison', 71–95 in Markus Jachtenfuchs and Michael Strübel, eds, 1992, *Environmental Policy in Europe* (Baden-Baden: Nomos Verlagsgesellschaft).

Jänicke, Martin (1990b), *State Failure – The Impotence of Politics in Industrial Society* (Cambridge: Polity Press).

Jänicke, Martin and Harald Mönch (1988), 'Ökologischer und wirtschaftlicher Wandel im Industrieländervergleich', in Manfred Schmidt, ed., *Staatstätigkeit* (Opladen: Westdeutscher Verlag).

Jänicke, Martin and Harald Mönch (1990), *Ökologische Dimensionen Wirtschaftlichen Strukturwandels*. FFU rep. 90–10 (Berlin: Forschungsstelle für Umweltpolitik).

Jänicke, Martin, Harald Mönch and Thomas Ranneberg (1989), 'Strukturwandel und ökologische Gratiseffekte', *Zeitschrift für angewandte Umweltforschung*, 2:1, 55–68.

Jänicke, Martin, Harald Mönch, Thomas Ranneberg and Udo E. Simonis (1988), *Structural Change and Environmental Impact*, WZB Paper FSII-88–402 (Berlin: Wissenschaftszentrum Berlin).

Johnson, Ralph W. and Gardner M. Brown (1976a), *Cleaning up Europe's Waters* (New York: Praeger).

Johnson, Ralph W. and Gardner M. Brown (1976b), 'Water Quality Management in France', 32–72 in *Cleaning up Europe's Waters* (New York: Praeger).

Johnson, Ralph W. and Gardner M. Brown (1976c), 'Water Quality Management in West Germany', 102–37 in *Cleaning up Europe's Waters* (New York: Praeger).

Johnson, Ralph W. and Gardner M. Brown (1984), 'Pollution Control by Effluent Charges: It Works in the Federal Republic of Germany, Why Not in the United States?', *Natural Resources Journal*, 24:4, 929–66.

Journal Officiel de la République Française, (1981), 'Régime et répartition des eaux et lutte contre leur pollution', 1320 (Paris).

Journal Officiel de la République Française, (1982), 'Pollution des eaux – Redevances', 1456 (Paris).

Kamieniecki, Sheldon and Eliz Sanasarian (1990), 'Conducting Comparative Research on Environmental Policy', *Natural Resources Journal*, 30:2, 321–40.

Katzenstein, Peter (1985), *Small States in World Markets* (Ithaca: Cornell University Press).

Kelman, Steven (1981), *What Price Incentive?* (Boston: Auburn House).

Keune, Heinz (1984), 'Erfahrungen mit dem Abwasserabgabengesetz aus der Sicht der Industrie, FGU-Seminar, 24–25 September, Berlin (Berlin: Umweltbundesamt).

Klasema, M. (1970), 'Water Management', *Planning and Development in the Netherlands*, 4:1, 8–27.

Klok, P. J. (1989), *Convenanten als instrument van milieubeleid* (Enschede: Twente Universiteit).

Kneese, A. and B. Bower (1968), *Managing Water Quality; Economics, Technology, Institutions* (Baltimore: Resources for the Future).

Kneese, Allan V. and Charles L. Schultze (1975), *Pollution, Prices and Public Policy* (Washington DC: Brookings Institution).

Knoepfel, Peter and Helmut Weidner (1985), *Luftreinhaltepolitik im internationalen Vergleich*, Band 1–6 (Berlin: Edition Sigma).

Knoepfel, Peter et al. (1987), 'Comparing Environmental Policies: Different Styles, Similar Content', 171–87 in Meinolf Dierkes et al., eds, *Comparative Policy Research* (Aldershot: Gower).

Kool, A. de (1971), 'The Threatening Reality', *Planning and Development*, 5:1.

Koppen, Ida Johanne (1988), *The European Community's Environment Policy*, EUI Working Paper No. 88/328 (Florence: European University Institute).

Kramer, R. Andreas (1990), *The Privatisation of Water Services in Germany*, FFU rep. 90–9 (Berlin: Forschungsstelle für Umweltpolitik).

Krawinkel, Holger (1991), *Für eine neue Energiepolitik: Was die Bundesrepublik Deutschland von Dänemark lernen kann* (Frankfurt a.M.: Fischer).

Kristensen, Erik Basse et al. (1987), 'Nye perspektiver i miljøplanlægningen', *Vand og Miljø*, 4:6, 275–7.

Kromarek, Pascale (1986), *European Community Environmental Policy in Practice: Federal Republic of Germany; Water and Waste* (London: Graham & Trotman).

Kroon, John (1990), 'Waterschappen worden gedemocratiseerd', *NRC-Handelsblad*, 13 November.

Lalonde, Brice (1990), 'Plan national pour l'environnement', *Environnement actualité, Supplément spécial*, 122 (Paris: Ministère de l'environnement).

Lalonde, B. (1991), 'Projet de loi sur la répartition, la police et la protection des eaux', *Seconde session ordinaire de 1990–1991*, 346 (Paris: Sénat).

Lamm, Jochen and Markus Schneller (1988), *Umweltberichterstattung in Statistischen Jahrbüchern. Ein Internationaler Vergleich*, FFU rep. 88-III (Berlin: Forschungsstelle für Umweltpolitik).

Langeweg, F. (1989), *Concern for Tomorrow* (Bilthoven: RIVM).

Larrue, Corinne (1992), 'The Implementation of Environmental Policies by the French Administration', Paper delivered at the Workshop on Comparative Research on Environmental Administration and Policy-making, Drøbak, 11–14 June (Tours: Centre d'Etudes Supérieures d'Aménagement).

Lavoux, Thierry (1986), *European Community Environment Policy in Practice: France; Water and Waste* (London: Graham & Trotman).

Le Grand, Julian (1991), 'The Theory of Government Failure', *British Journal of Political Science*, 21, 423–42.

Les Cahiers Français (1991), *Environnement et gestion de la planète* (Paris: Documentation Française).

Liefferink, J. Duncan (1990), 'Dutch Environmental Policy and International Environmental Cooperation', Paper presented at the Institute of Political Science, Århus University, 3 May (Wageningen).

228 Governance by green taxes

Lijphardt, Arend (1968), *The Politics of Accommodation: Pluralism and Democracy in the Netherlands* (Berkeley: University of California Press).

Lijphardt, A. (1984), 'Time Politics of Accommodation: Reflections Fifteen Years Later', *Acta Politica*, 1, 9–18.

Lindahl, Erik (1919), *Die Gerechtigkeit der Besteuerung* (Lund: Gleerupska Universitetsbokhandeln).

Lindahl, Erik (1967), 'Just Taxation – A Positive Solution', 168–76 in R. A. Musgrave and A. T. Peacock, *Classics in the Theory of Public Finance* (London: Macmillan).

Liroff, Richard (1980), *Air Pollution Offsets: Trading, Selling and Banking* (Washington DC: The Conservation Foundation).

Liroff, Richard A. (1986), *Reforming Air Pollution Regulation: The Toil and Trouble of EPA's Bubble* (Washington DC: The Conservation Foundation).

Lorrain, Dominique (1991), 'Public Goods and Private Operators in France', 89–109 in Richard Batley and Gerry Stoker, eds, *Local Government in Europe* (London: Macmillan).

Lühr, H. P. (1984), 'Erfahrungen mit dem Abwasserabgabengesetz aus der Sicht des Bundes', 110, Seminar des Fortbildungszentrums Gesunheits- und Umweltschutz. Berlin, 24–25 September (Berlin: Umweltbundesamt).

Lundgren, Lars (1992), 'Swedish Environmental Policy during the 20th Century', Paper delivered to workshop on environmental policy, Drøbak, 11–14 June.

Lundqvist, Lennart J. (1980), *The Hare and the Tortoise: Clean Air Policies in the United States and Sweden* (Ann Arbor: University of Michigan Press).

Maas, Christof (1987), 'Einfluss des Abwasserabgabengesetzes auf Emissionen und Innovationen', *Zeitschrift für Umweltpolitik*, 1, 65–85.

McIntyre, R. J. and J. R. Thornton (1978), 'On the Environmental Efficiency of Economic Systems', *Soviet Studies*, 30:2, 173–92.

Maclean, Mairi (1991), *French Enterprise and the Challenge of the British Water Industry* (Aldershot: Avebury).

Maier–Rigaud, Gerhard (1988), *Umweltpolitik in der Offenen Gesellschaft* (Opladen: Westdeutscher Verlag).

Majone, Giandomenico (1976), 'Choice among Policy Instruments for Pollution Control', *Policy Analysis*, 2, 589–613.

Majone, Giandomenico (1989), *Evidence, Argument and Persuasion in the Policy Process. Changing Institutional Constraints* (London: Yale).

Mann, Dean E. ed. (1982), *Environmental Policy Implementation* (Lexington: D.C. Heath).

Marcus, A. A. (1980), *Promise and Performance: Choosing and Implementing an Environmental Policy* (Connecticut: Greenwood Press).

Marcus, Alfred A. (1982), 'Converting Thought to Action: The Use of Economic Incentives to Reduce Pollution', in Dean E. Mann, ed., *Environmental Policy Implementation* (Lexington: D.C. Heath).

Mayntz, Renate et al. (1978), *Vollzugsprobleme der Umweltpolitik* (Wiesbaden: Kohlhammer).

Metals miljøudvalg (Kampmann-udvalget) (1988), *Betænkning om miljøregulering og økonomisk vækst* (Copenhagen: Dansk Metalarbejderforbund).

Meyer–Renschhausen, M. (1990), 'Ökonomische Effizienz und politische Akzeplanz der Abwasserabgabe', *Zeitschrift für Umweltpolitik*, 1, 43–66.

Miljøministeriet & Miljøstyrelsen (1974), *Spildevandsrensning 1972/1982* (Copenhagen).

Miljøministeriet (1984), *Miljøet: En grundbog om miljøpåvirkninger og miljøets tilstand i Danmark* (Copenhagen: Miljøministeriet).

Miljøministeriet (1988), *Enkelt og Effektivt* (Copenhagen).

Miljøstyrelsen (1974a), *Vejledning*, 2, 'Miljøhensyn ved planlægning' (Copenhagen).

Miljøstyrelsen (1974b), *Vejledning*, 6, 'Spildevand' (Copenhagen).

Miljøstyrelsen (1976), *Spildevandsanlæg: Vejledning vedrørende bedre udnyttelse af investeringer inden for den kommunale spildevandssektor* (Copenhagen).

Miljøstyrelsen (1977), *Nyt fra Miljøstyrelsen 10*, Revision af spildevandsvejledningen (Hvorfor Miljøstyrelsen vil udskyde revisionen?) (Copenhagen).

Miljøstyrelsen (1979), *Miljøreformen: En foreløbig redegørelse om miljøreformens virkninger* (Copenhagen).

Miljøstyrelsen (1980), *Miljøprojekt*, 24, Analyse af spildevandsplaner (Copenhagen).

Miljøstyrelsen (1981a), *Miljøbeskyttelse: Indsats, resultater, perspektiver* (Copenhagen).

Miljøstyrelsen (1981b), *Spildevandsplanlægningen: Sektorrrede-gørelse for status og udviklingstendenser i den kommunale spildevandsplanlægning* (Copenhagen).
Miljøstyrelsen (1984), *NPO-redegørelsen* (Copenhagen).
Miljøstyrelsen (1985a), *Miljøafgifter* (Copenhagen).
Miljøstyrelsen (1985b), *Miljøtilsyn* (Copenhagen).
Miljøstyrelsen (1986), *Betalingsvedtægter* (Copenhagen).
Miljøstyrelsen (1990), *Vandmiljø 90* (Copenhagen).
Minister für Umwelt, Raumordnung und Landwirtschaft des Landes Nordrhein-Westfalen (1989), *Entwicklung und Stand der Abwasserbeseitigung in Nordrhein-Westfalen* (Düsseldorf).
Ministère de l'Environnement (1978), *Water Management in France* (Paris).
Ministère de l'Environnement (1980–90), *Données Economiques sur l'Environnement* (Paris: Documentation Française).
Ministère de l'Environnement (1985–90), *L'État de l'environne-ment* (Paris: Documentation Française).
Ministère de l'Environnement (1987), *State of the Environment* (Paris: Documentation Française).
Ministère de l'Environnement (1991), *Environnement actualité*, 12B, supplément (Paris).
Ministère de l'Intérieur (1991), *Les Collectivités locales en chiffres* Paris: Documentation Française).
Ministry of Transport and Public Works (1975), *The Combat Against Surface Water Pollution in the Netherlands, Prospec-tive Multi-Annual Program 1975–1979* (The Hague: SDU).
Ministry of Transport and Public Works (1980), *Water Action Programme 1980–1984* (The Hague: Rijkswaterstaat).
Ministry of Transport and Public Works (1989), *Water in the Netherlands: A Time for Action; National Policy Document on Water Management* (The Hague: MTPW).
Ministry of Transport and Public Works & Ministry of Public Housing, Physical Planning and Environment (1986), *The Water Quality in the Netherlands: Water Action Programme (IMP) 1985–1989* (The Hague: Government Printing Office).
Mitnick, Barry (1980), *The Political Economy of Regulation* (New York: Columbia University Press).
Miyamoto, K. (1990), 'Environmental Problems and Environmen-tal Policy in Japan after the Second World War', in *European Environmental Yearbook* (London: Docter International).

Mørch, Søren (1982), *Den ny Danmarkshistorie 1880–1960* (Copenhagen: Gyldendalt).

Mortensen, Jørgen Birk and Peder Andersen (1990), 'Økonomisk regulering', 127–42, Ellen Margrethe Basse, ed., *Regulering og Styring II* (Copenhagen: GAD).

Müller, Edda (1989), 'Sozial-liberale Umweltpolitik: Von der Karriere eines neuen Politikbereichs', 3–15 in *Beilage zur Wochenzeitung Das Parlament*, 47–8.

Musgrave, R. A. and A. T. Peacock (1967), *Classics in the Theory of Public Finance* (London: Macmillan).

Nannestad, Peter (1991), 'Danish Design or British Disease', *Acta Jutlandica*, 67:2 (Århus: Århus University Press).

Nicolazo, Jean–Loïc (1989), *Les Agences de l'Eau* (Paris: Pierre Johanet & Fils Ed.).

Nielsen, Klaus (1988), 'Institutionel Økonomi', 107–35 in Torben M. Andersen et al., *Nyere udviklingslinier i økonomisk teori*, (Copenhagen: DJØF-forlaget).

Nielsen, Wittus (1985), *Cheminova* (Copenhagen: Gyldendal).

Niskanen, W. A. (1971), *Bureaucracy and Representative Government* (Chicago: Atherton).

Noël, Jean–Claude (1991), 'French Water Policy: The Water Agencies', *Journal of European Water Pollution Control*, 1:4, 30–3.

Nue, Claes (1980), 'Den danske miljøbeskyttelseslovs tilblivelse', *Retfærd*, 15 (Århus: Modtryk).

Nutzinger, Hans G. and Angelika Zahrnt (1990), *Für eine Ökologische Steuerreform* (Frankfurt a.M.: Fischer).

Observa (1971), *Pollution of the Danish Marine Environment in the Future* (Copenhagen: Observa).

OECD (1975), *The Polluter Pays Principle* (Paris).

OECD (1977), *Water Management Policies and Instruments* (Paris).

OECD (1979, 1985, 1987, 1989, 1991), *OECD Environmental Data* (Paris).

OECD (1985), *Environment and Economics* (Paris).

OECD (1986), *OECD and the Environment* (Paris).

OECD (1987), *Pricing of Water Services* (Paris).

OECD (1989a), *Economic Instruments for Environmental Protection* (Paris).

OECD (1989b), *Environmental Policy Benefits: Monetary Valuation* (Paris).

OECD (1989c), *Water Resource Management – Integrated Policies* (Paris).

OECD (1991a), *Environmental Indicators* (Paris).

OECD (1991b), *Environmental Policy: How to Apply Economic Instruments* (Paris).

OECD (1992), *Historical Statistics 1960–1990* (Paris).

O'Riordan, Timothy (1988), 'Anticipatory Environmental Policy: Impediments and Opportunities', 65–78 in Udo Simonis, *Präventive Umweltpolitik* (Frankfurt: Campus).

Pearce, David, ed. (1991), *Blueprint 2: Greening the World Economy* (London: Earthscan).

Pearce, David, et al. (1989), *Blueprint for a Green Economy* (London: Earthscan).

Pedersen, Carl Th. (1987), *Den kemiske industris miljøforhold* (Odense: Universitetsforlaget).

Pehle, Heinrich (1990), 'Umweltschutz vor Ort – Die Umweltpolitische Verantwortung der Gemeinden', *Das Parlament*, B 6/90, 24–34.

Petschow, Ulrich et al. (1990), *Umweltrapport DDR* (Frankfurt a.M.: Fischer Verlag).

Pigou, A. C. (1932), *The Economics of Welfare* (London: Macmillan; first published 1920).

Pigou, A. C. (1947), *A Study in Public Finance* (London: Macmillan; first published 1928).

Pressman, Jeffrey and Aaron Wildawsky (1973), *Implementation* (Berkeley: University of California Press).

Prittwitz, Volker von (1990), *Das Katastrophenparadox: Elemente einer Theorie der Umweltpolitik* (Opladen: Leske & Budrich).

Rat von Sachverständigen für Umweltfragen (1974), *Gutachten*, Bundestagdrs. 7/2802.

Richardson, Jeremy, ed. (1982), *Policy Styles in Western Europe* (London: Allen & Unwin).

Richardson, Katherine and Gunni Ærtebjerg (1991), 'Effekter af kvælstof og fosfor i Kattegat og Bælthavet', Chapter 16 in *Rapport fra konsensuskonference* (Copenhagen: Undervisningsministeriets Forskningsafdeling).

Rijkswaterstaat (1990), *De verontreinigingsheffing Rijkswateren in de toekomst* (The Hague: Rijkswaterstaat).

Romi, Raphaël (1991), 'Droit de l'eau: émergence d'une réforme', *La voirie et l'environnement*, 1496, 20–4.

Roth, Horst (1977), *Wasserhaushaltsgesetz. Abwasserab-gabengesetz. Wasserrecht und Wasserwirtschaft*, Band 17 (Berlin: Erich Schmidt Verlag).

Roth, Horst (1991), *Abwasserabgabengesetz, Wasserrecht und Wasserwirtschaft*, Band 22 (Berlin: Erich Schmidt Verlag).

Rottschäfer, K. F. and D. J. Flaman (1979), 'Indicative Multiyear Programmes', *Planning and Development in the Netherlands*, 11:2, 109–27.

Royston, Michael G. (1979), *Pollution Prevention Pays* (Oxford: Pergamon Press).

Rudolph, K. U. (1989), 'Zur Kostenstruktur der kommunalen Abwasserentsorgung im Hinblick auf die Bedeutung der Abwasserabgabe', 1412–15 in *Korrespondenz Abwasser*, 12.

Sabatier, Paul A. and D. A. Mazmanian (1981), *Effective Policy Implementation* (Masschusetts: Lexington Books).

Sætevik, Sunneva (1988), *Environmental Cooperation between the North Sea States* (London: Belhaven Press).

Salzwedel, J. and W. Preusker (1982), *The Law and Practice Relating to Pollution Control in the Federal Republic of Germany* (London: Graham & Trotman).

Samuelson, Paul A. (1983), *Economics* (Massachusetts: McGraw-Hill).

Scheltinga, H. M. J. (1972), 'The Surface Waters Pollution Act in the Netherlands', *Environmental Pollution Management*, 2:6, 223–5.

Schmidt, Manfred (1986), 'Politische Bedingungen erfolgreicher Wirtschaftspolitik', *Journal für Sozialforschung*, 26:3, 251–73.

Schneider, Günter and Rolf–Ulrich Sprenger, eds. (1984), *Mehr Umweltschutz für weniger Geld* (Munich: Ifo–Institut für Wirtschaftsforschung).

Schroll, Henning (1985), 'Miljøgodkendelser af danske virksom-heder', *Vand og Miljø*, 4.

Schuurman, Jacob (1988), *De Prijs van Water* (Arnhem: Gouda Quint BV).

Simonis, Udo E. (1987), 'Federal Republic of Germany', 168–87 in G. Enyedi, A. Gijswit and Barbara Rhode, eds, *Environmental Policies in East and West* (London: Taylor Graham).

Simonis, Udo F. (1988), *Präventive Umweltpolitik* (Frankfurt: Campus).

Snijdelaar, M. (1970), 'The Water Management of the Netherlands', *Planning and Development in the Netherlands*, 4:2, 168–89.

Soest, J. J. (1973), 'Water Management in the Netherlands', *Planning and Development in the Netherlands*, 7:2, 88–97.

Springmann, F. (1986), *Steuerreform zum Abbau von Arbeitslosigkeit und Umweltbelastung – ein Szenario*, IIUG dp 86–11 (Berlin: WZB (Wissenschaftszentrum Berlin)).

Staaten–General (Dutch Second Chamber) (1964), *Wet verontreiniging oppervlaktewateren (The Surface Waters' Pollution Act)*, Bijlage Handelingen II 64/65, blz. 7884.

Staaten–General (Dutch Second Chamber) (1968), *Wet verontreiniging oppervlaktewateren (The Surface Waters' Pollution Act)*, Handelingen II 67/68, blz. 2422–2472, 2537–2540, 2583–2584.

Statistisches Bundesamt (1976–88), *Rechnungsergebnisse der kommunalen Haushalte* (Wiesbaden).

Statistisches Bundesamt (1976–91), *Statistisches Jahresbuch* (Wiesbaden).

Statistisches Bundesamt (1977–87), *Fachserie 19, Reihe 2.1., Öffentliche Wasserversorgung und Abwasserbeseitigung* (Wiesbaden).

Statistisches Bundesamt (1977–87), *Fachserie 19, Reihe 2.2., Wasserversorgung und Abwasserbeseitigung im Bergbau und Verarbeitenden Gewerbe* (Wiesbaden).

Statistisches Bundesamt (1977–89), *Fachserie 19, Reihe 3., Investitionen für Umweltschutz in Produzierenden Gewerbe* (Wiesbaden).

Statistisches Bundesamt (1988), *Umweltinformationen der Statistik* (Wiesbaden).

Statistisches Bundesamt (1990), *Ergänzung der Fachserie 19 'Umweltschutz' Reihe 2.2 Tabelle 7.1 um Produktionsspezifisches Abwasser* (Wiesbaden).

Stavins, Robert N. and Bradley W. Whitehead (1992), 'Dealing with Pollution', *Environment*, 34:7, 7–41.

Straaten van der, Jan (1992), 'The Dutch National Environmental Policy Plan: To Choose or to Lose', *Environmental Politics*, 1:1, 45–71.

Tavernier, M. Yves (1990), *Rapport d'information sur le financement à long terme de la politique de l'eau*, 1358 (Paris: Assemblée Nationale).

Teja, R. and B. Bracewell–Milnes (1991), *The Case for Earmarked Taxes: Government Spending and Public Choice*, Research Monograph 46, Institute of Economic Affairs (London: IEA).

Tellegen, Egbert (1981), 'The Environmental Movement in the Netherlands', 1–32 in T. O'Riordan and R. Kerry Turner, eds, *Progress in Resource and Environmental Planning*, 3 (London: Wiley).

Teufel, D. (1988), *Ökosteuern als marktwirtschaftliches Instrument im Umweltschutz*, Umwelt- und Prognoseinstitut, Bericht Nr. 9 (Heidelberg: UPI).

Thierbach, Dieter (1991), 'Selbst Experten sprechen von einem kleinen Wunder', *Die Welt*, 9 October.

Thijsse, Jac. P. (1971), 'A Survey of the Dangers Threatening the Living Environment in the World, with the Accent on the Dutch Situation', *Planning and Development in the Netherlands*, 5:1.

Thijsse, Jac. P. (1973), 'The Environmental Problems of the Netherlands against the World Background', *Planning and Development in the Netherlands*, 7:2, 83–7.

Thoms, Eva–Maria and Cornelia Uebel (1992), 'Gesetzesflut und Wassernot', *Die Zeit*, 41, Dossier, 2 October.

Tietenberg, T. H. (1985), *Emissions Trading* (Washington DC: Resources for the Future).

Tietenberg, T. H. (1990), 'Economic Instruments for Environmental Regulation', *Oxford Review of Economic Policy*, 6:1, 17–33.

Tinbergen, J. (1971), 'The Development of the Planning Idea', *Planning and Development in the Netherlands*, 5:2, 103–10.

Truchot, Claude (1989), 'Water Control in France' (Paris: Ministry of the Environment).

Tsuru, Shigeto and Helmut Weidner (1985), *Ein Modell für uns: Die Erfolge der japanischen Umweltpolitik* (Cologne: Kiepenheuer & Witsch).

Umwelt (1986), 'Novellierung der Wassergesetze des Bundes', 6, 14 November, 26–7.

Umweltbundesamt, *Act Pertaining to Charges Levied for Discharging Waste Water into Waters* (Waste Water Charges Act).

Umweltbundesamt (1980), *Berichte 8/80: Die Abwasserabgabe als Investititonsanreiz* (Berlin: Erich Schmidt).

Umweltbundesamt (1981), *Berichte 6/81; Umweltpolitik und Umweltschutzindustrie in der Bundesrepublik Deutschland* (Berlin: Erich Schmidt Verlag).

Umweltbundesamt (1982), *Berichte 2/82: Technische Alternativen zur Unterverteilung der Abwasserabgabe* (Berlin: Erich Schmidt Verlag).

Umweltbundesamt (1985a), *Berichte 6/85: Instrumente zur Handhabung des Abwasserabgabengesetzes* (Berlin: Erich Schmidt Verlag).

Umweltbundesamt (1985b), *Berichte 8/85: Abgaben als ökonomischer Hebel in der Umweltpolitik* (Berlin: Erich Schmidt Verlag).

Umweltbundesamt (1989), *Berichte 5/89: Der Wasserpfennig* (Berlin: Erich Schmidt Verlag).

Umweltbundesamt (1990a), 3. Novelle; *Gesetz über Abgaben für das Einleiten von Abwässer in Gewässer (Abwasserabgabengesetz – AbwAG)* (Berlin).

Umweltbundesamt (1990b), *Jahresbericht 1989* (Berlin).

Unie van Waterschappen (1988), *The Dutch Waterboards* (The Hague: Unie van Waterschappen).

Valgreen–Voigt, Steen (1986), 'De kommunale forvaltninger er lysår efter forvaltningen', *Dagbladet Information* (31 December).

Verdenskommissionen (1988), *Vores fælles fremtid* (Copenhagen: FN–forbundet og Mellemfolkeligt Samvirke).

Vogel, David (1986), *National Styles of Regulation: Environmental Policy in Great Britain and the United States* (Ithaca: Cornell University Press).

Vogel, David (1991), 'Environmental Policy in Europe and Japan', 257–78, in Norman J. Vig and Michael Kraft, *Environmental Policy in the 1990s* (Washington DC: CQ Press).

Vogel, David and Veronica Kun (1987), 'The Comparative Study of Environmental Policy: A Review of the Literature', 99–170, in Meinholf Dierkes et al., eds., *Comparative Policy Research* (Aldershot: Gower).

Von Eyben, W. E. (1989), *Miljørettens grundbog* (Copenhagen: Akademisk forlag).

Vos, Hans (1989), 'De rol van marktconforme instrumenten in het milieubeleid', *Openbare Bestedingen*, 5, 195–9.

Vos, Hans (1990), '*Water Effluent Charges in West Germany*', European Community, Directorate General XI.

VROM (Ministerie van Volkshuisvesting, Ruimtelijke Ordening en Milieubeheer) (1989), *To Choose or to Lose: National*

Environmental Policy Plan (NEPP) (The Hague: SDU Uitgeverij).

VROM (Ministry of Housing, Physical Planning and Environment) (1983), *Environmental Protection in the Netherlands* (The Hague: Central Department for Information and International Relations).

VROM (Ministry of Housing, Physical Planning and Environment) (1990), *National Environmental Policy Plan Plus* (The Hague).

VROM (Ministry of Housing, Physical Planning and Environment & Ministry of Agriculture and Fisheries & Ministry of Transport and Water) (1985), *Environmental Program of the Netherlands 1986–1990* (The Hague: Central Department for Information and International Relations).

Waage, Per (1984), 'Use of Economic Instruments in Pollution Control Policy in Norway', 401–18 in G. Schneider and Rolf–Ulrich Sprenger, *Mehr Umweltschutz für weniger Geld*, IFO Studien zur Umweltökonomie (Munich: IFO-Institut für Wirtschafts forschung).

Weale, Albert (1992), *The New Politics of Pollution* (Manchester: Manchester University Press).

Weidner, Helmut (1986), *Air Pollution Control: Strategies and Policies in the Federal Republic of Germany* (Berlin: Ed. Sigma).

Weidner, Helmut (1987), *Clean Air Policy in Great Britain* (Berlin: Ed. Sigma).

Weidner, Helmut (1989), 'Die Umweltpolitik der konservativ-liberalen Regierung', 16–28 in *Beilage zur Wochenzeitung Das Parlament*, 47–8.

Weidner, Helmut and Shigeto Tsuru, eds (1988), *Environmental Policy in Japan* (Berlin: Sigma).

Weizsäcker, Ernst Ulrich von (1989/1992), *Erdpolitik – Ökologische Realpolitik an der Schwelle zum Jahrhundert der Umwelt* (Darmstadt).

Weizsäcker, Ernst Ulrich von (1990), 'Regulatory Reform and the Environment: The Cause for Environmental Taxes', 198–210 in Giandomenico Majone, ed., *Deregulation or Re-regulation* (London: Pinter).

Weizsäcker, Ernst U. von and Jochen Jesinghaus (1992), *Ecological Tax Reform* (London: Zed Books).

Wey, Klaus-Georg (1982), *Umweltpolitik in Deutschland* (Opladen: Westdeutscher Verlag).

WHO (1954), *Water Pollution in Europe* (Geneva: WHO).

Wicke, Lutz (1986), *Die ökologischen Milliarden* (Munich: Piper).

Wilson, James Q. (1980), *The Politics of Regulation* (New York: Basic Books).

Wirtschaftswoche (1986), 'Schlag ins Abwasser', 26, 20 June, 20–2.

Wolters, G. J. R. (1979), 'Standards for Environmental Protection', *Planning and Development in the Netherlands*, 11:2, 89–108.

Wright, Vincent (1989), *The Government and Politics of France* (London: Unwin Hyman).

Wulff, Helge (1988), *Miljøret: Landbrug og vand i Sydfrankrig*, Skrifter fra Økonomisk Institut, Den kgl. Veterinær- og Landbohøjskole, 21 (Copenhagen: DSR-Forlag).

Yin, Robert K. (1989), *Case Study Research* (London: Sage Publications).

Ziegler, Charles E. (1980), 'Soviet Environmental Policy and Soviet Central Planning: A Reply to McIntyre and Thornton', *Soviet Studies*, 30:1, 124–34.

Zimmermann, Klaus (1988), 'Technologische Modernisierung der Produktion', 205–26 in Udo Simonis, ed., *Präventive Umweltpolitik* (Frankfurt: Campus).

Index